Yan-kit's
CLASSIC CHINESE
COOKBOOK

YAN-KIT'S CLASSIC CHINESE COOKBOOK

Yan-kit So

DK

DK PUBLISHING, INC.
www.dk.com

A DK PUBLISHING BOOK
www.dk.com

To my son, Hugo E. Martin

Editor Fiona MacIntyre
Art Editor Sue Story
Managing Editor Amy Carroll

Second American paperback edition, 1998

8 10 9 7

Published in the United States by
DK Publishing, Inc.
95 Madison Avenue,
New York, NY 10016

ISBN 0-7894-3300-1

Printed and bound in Singapore
by Star Standard Industries (Pte.) Ltd.

CONTENTS

Note Monosodium glutamate (MSG) is a white crystalline substance which adds a meaty
sweetness to food. It is used widely in Chinese restaurants, but as some
people react badly to it I do not use it in home cooking, nor have I used it in this book.

INTRODUCTION

My interest in food is inherited from my father. Although he did not cook himself, he always asked Mother to see to it that what was on the table was correct, right down to the last detail: for him, stir-fried dishes had to have "wok fragrance"; sugar was to be used very sparingly in marinades; chicken was not to be overcooked lest the flesh became tough; fish for steaming was to be bought live from the market and abalone was to be well seasoned with oyster sauce. Like children in other Chinese families, my brothers, sisters and I joined the grown-ups for dinner from the age of four or five, picking with chopsticks from the dishes served in the center of the table. So it isn't surprising that what has stayed in my mind is delicious well-prepared dishes, seasoned to Father's liking, rather than the bland food given young children in the West.

From those early childhood days in Hong Kong I also remember Father taking us to restaurants where we had delicate hot tidbits, *dim sum*, or to the boat restaurants in Aberdeen for special seafood. Every year, during the month following Chinese New Year, his *Hong* or import-export trading company, would give a banquet to which our whole family as well as those who worked for him would go. At these banquets the menu would follow a prescribed procedure: two small, hot seasonal dishes followed by shark's fin, either as a soup or braised in a sauce, next a chicken with crispy red skin to augur another prosperous year, then a duck or perhaps succulent pigeons, followed by another soup – turtle or something else equally exotic – then one or two more stir-fried dishes and lastly a whole steamed fish, the pronunciation of which is the same as the word "surplus," which can signify abundant wealth.

Having taken good food for granted, like so many other Chinese, I did not think seriously about it until I became a frugal postgraduate student at the University of London. Short of cash but nonetheless hungry, haunted by the tastes of both home-cooked and restaurant dishes, I began to try my own hand at cooking Chinese food. To my delight, I found I was adept at it. One dish led to another, and soon I found that I had become an enthusiast, cooking with zest and satisfying not only my own palate but also many others'.

This amateurish approach took a marked turn some ten years ago when I spent a long summer with my young son in Waterford, Connecticut. There I used to entertain my American family and friends with Chinese dishes, and I remember their surprise that the tiny Niantic scallops could be so succulently tender when simply stir-fried; that the Cherrystone clams, delicious served on the half-shell New England style, could make one's mouth water equally, if not more, when cooked in black bean sauce with garlic, and that sea bass and bluefish could be so refreshing steamed with slices of ginger and seasoned with a little soy sauce. They were equally enthusiastic about the strips of pork I roasted, then brushed with a little honey, and with ox tongue braised slowly in soy sauce and sherry. For my part, I found cooking remedial, relaxing and rewarding. The seed of this book was sown then.

Since that time, I have worked with different Chinese chefs in Hong Kong and London, been to China and Taiwan to sample different regional cuisines, entertained at home and taught and demonstrated Chinese cookery both privately and publicly. The invaluable reactions of friends and students led to much pondering over food and cookery in general, and Chinese food and cookery in particular. I discovered that many people who are very enthusiastic about Chinese food are, unfortunately, in awe of Chinese cookery. They claim it is time-consuming, fiddly and generally incomprehensible. But since every form of cooking takes a certain amount of time and involves some technique, however trivial, the first two points are irrelevant. On the third point, I strongly believe that Chinese cookery can be as comprehensible as any other, and this book is an expression of that belief. How? First, by taking each recipe and breaking down the method into clear steps, and by giving precise explanation (and in many cases an illustration) of how and why certain methods or techniques are used. Second, by illustrating every recipe to show what the dish should look like, and third, by describing and illustrating any special Chinese ingredients, so that they can be properly selected. Above all, by presenting a fair sample of classic dishes, my aim has been to enable every cook to achieve the desired authentic effect.

WHAT MAKES FOOD CHINESE

Whatever the arguments about the greatness of Chinese cuisine, it is undeniable that certain features make the food look Chinese, smell Chinese and taste Chinese.

One feature, unique to Chinese cooking, is the technique of stir-frying. A small amount of oil is poured into a heated wok and a few condiments are added to "arouse the wok" and lend fragrance to the main ingredients, which are rapidly stirred and cooked in a short time.

This technique requires specially prepared ingredients. In Chinese cooking these are cut into uniformly small pieces so that they will absorb the taste of the seasonings they are marinated in and retain their freshness, juiciness and crispness.

Another speciality of Chinese cuisine is its use of dried products. Before the invention of canning and deep-freezing, drying was the Chinese way of preserving food. But even though canning has become a Chinese industry and frozen food products are now exported abroad, dried products are still widely used and are very often more expensive than corresponding fresh ones. This is because the dried products, when reconstituted, add an extra dimension to the taste and richness of the finished dish. For instance, the flavor and fragrance that dried Chinese mushrooms so miraculously lend to other ingredients are beyond the capabilities of fresh mushrooms. The same can also be said of dried scallops, dried oysters, dried shrimp and dried abalone, one of the most exotic ingredients in Chinese cuisine.

Nowhere in other cuisines is there such a pronounced emphasis on texture. Exotic ingredients like shark's fin, bird's nest, edible jellyfish or duck's feet, and everyday ones such as cloud ears, bamboo shoots or cellophane noodles, often have little taste, yet the Chinese go to any amount of trouble preparing them, combining them with other ingredients to lend them taste. Why? Nutrition apart, it is the texture, whether crisp, elastic or slippery, that they provide that makes them invaluable. Emphasis on texture is also apparent at a more basic level: leaf vegetables, whether boiled or stir-fried, must retain their crispness; noodles must be served *al dente*.

REGIONAL CHINESE COOKING

China is a vast country and as such is exposed to extremes of both geography and climate. This naturally results in the growth of different agricultural products, so it is little wonder that cuisines vary from province to province. Even though there has never been agreement on the subject, many cookbooks divide Chinese cuisines into eight main streams: Peking, Shantung, Kiangsu, Anhwei, Kwangtung, Fukien, Szechwan and Hunan; others analyze the subregional cuisines within some of these provinces. However, I follow the practice of broadly carving the Chinese gastronomic map into four main regions: Peking or Northern, Shanghai or Eastern, Canton or Southern and Szechwan or Western.

One may well ask what constitutes regional

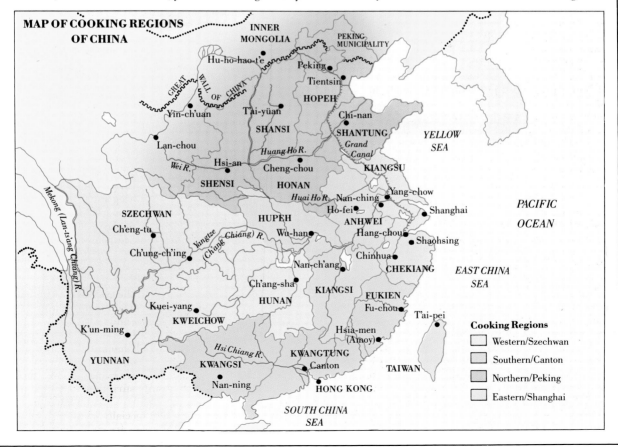

MAP OF COOKING REGIONS OF CHINA

differences, since there are basic national characteristics underlining all of the regional cuisines. The main cooking methods – boiling, steaming, braising, sautéing, deep-frying and stir-frying – are used by all Chinese, the wok is the national cooking utensil, and soy sauce is a ubiquitous and indispensable seasoning. The differences are subtle, and are related to climate, to local produce, to the mixing and use of different condiments, to the emphasis on a certain technique and to the manner of presentation.

PEKING OR NORTHERN CUISINE

This is the largest area, embracing Inner Mongolia, Hopei, Honan, Shantung, Shansi and Shensi provinces. Although Shantung has a more temperate climate, the overall climate of the area is very harsh; Peking itself suffers from extreme heat in the summer and extreme cold in the winter, and in the spring suffers from periodic sandstorms, blown in from the Gobi Desert.

Wheat, millet, sorghum, peanuts, corn and soybeans are the main crops and Tientsin cabbage, better known as Chinese leaf or Chinese celery cabbage, cucumber and celery are the main vegetables grown. Noodles, steamed breads and buns are a more popular staple than rice, and, unlike the Southern Chinese, who habitually eat their noodles in soup, Northern Chinese eat them on the dry side, seasoned with a sauce.

Food from Inner Mongolia and Shantung forms the backbone of Northern cuisine. The Mongolian influence is reflected in the many lamb dishes eaten, the most famous of which are Mongolian fire pot and lamb slices barbecued on a spit. In fact, mutton here is eaten and cooked in more ways than in any other region in China. Besides bringing refined dishes to the capital, Shantung chefs left their imprint on Peking cuisine with their liking for raw garlic and leeks.

Peking cuisine may be considered plain and robust, but since the 19th century it has exported one dish that has captivated the imagination of the whole world: Peking duck. The duck is fattened specially for the table, roasted in a special oven, then pancakes and a special sauce are made to accompany it. In Peking, the duck can be an all-in-one meal, in which the head, tongue and feet are served as separate courses alongside the more familiar crispy skin and meat.

SHANGHAI OR EASTERN CUISINE

This area, based around the Yangtze delta and covering Kiangsu, Chekiang and Anhwei provinces, is temperate in climate and its fertile land, traversed by many rivers and ponds, is a rich agricultural area growing both wheat and rice, and yielding much fish and seafood.

Taken as a whole, Eastern cuisine is rich, decorative and rather on the sweet side; unlike Peking food, garlic is used sparingly, if at all. Although Shanghai is the name used to identify the Eastern school, there are other culinary centers, represented by the main cities of the area – Hangchow, Yangchow, Suchow and Wuhsi, for example. The area as a whole is renowned for certain products and dishes: the specially cured Chinhua ham, with its pinkish red flesh and succulently savory-sweet taste, the rich dark Chinkiang vinegar and the amber-colored Shaohsing rice wine. Classic dishes include Crisp stir-fried shrimp, Eel cooked in oil, Yangchow fried rice, Lion's head and fish from the West Lake with a sweet and sour sauce.

One special cooking technique of the region has been adopted nationally. This is *hung-shao*, or the red-braising method of cooking, whereby the ingredients (mainly meat, poultry and fish) are cooked slowly in an aromatic mixture of thick dark soy sauce and rice wine. When, at the end of cooking, the sauce is reduced and spooned over the main ingredient, the resulting taste is both rich and fragrant.

Shanghai cuisine is the least known outside China. Its oiliness and sweetness are perhaps less appealing to the Western palate, and because it is decorative, it tends to be labor-intensive. Moreover, it depends largely on fresh local produce; the famous Shanghai crabs, studded with yellow roe in the autumn, have no counterpart elsewhere, and for the delicate taste of the famous West Lake fish one *has* to go to Hangchow.

SZECHWAN OR WESTERN CUISINE

Western cuisine is represented by the provinces of Szechwan, Hunan and Yunnan, and of these Szechwan is the most influential. A land of precipitous mountains and the Yangtze gorges, and home of the pandas, Szechwan is the most populous province in China. Fortunately it is also known as one of China's rice bowls. Very humid and rainy in the summer but mild in the winter, the temperate climate is suitable for agricultural growth almost all year round. With good irrigation, the Szechwan basin in the east of the province grows rice, wheat, rapeseed, corn and bamboo shoots; citrus fruits, especially tangerines, and mushrooms are also grown. A spice, Szechwan peppercorns, and a preserved vegetable are two special products.

Many people, when they first encounter Szechwan food, find it highly seasoned and spicily hot. Fresh and dried red chili are evident, providing the fiery result. But, in fact, the sophistication of Szechwan cooking goes far beyond this apparent overspiciness. Often in the same dish, the full spectrum of tastes can be experienced: salty, sweet, vinegary and hot. Rather than overpowering the taste buds, the Szechwanese claim that the chili pepper is only a harbinger awakening them, and that once stimulated, they will be able to appreciate the full range of tastes and aftertastes.

Special Szechwanese dishes are Hot and sour soup,

A street market where the Chinese go everyday to buy fresh vegetables. On display are some of their favorites: Chinese white cabbage, Tientsin cabbage, flowering cabbage and Chinese broccoli.

Fragrant and crispy duck, Twice-cooked pork and a range of fish fragrant dishes.

In terms of cookery techniques, Szechwan dishes often employ multiple processes; for example, its famous smoked duck, which is first marinated, then smoked, steamed and finally deep-fried.

CANTONESE OR SOUTHERN CUISINE

The climate of the area centered in the provinces of Kwantung and Fukien is subtropical, with heavy rainfalls between May and September; the coast is subject to typhoons. The Pearl River delta of Kwangtung and the coastal plains of Fukien are rich agricultural areas. Rice crops are harvested twice a year, and rice is the staple, eaten twice a day. Sweet potato, corn, taro and wheat are also cultivated. There are many pig and poultry farms, and fish ponds. Vegetables, especially green leafy vegetables, abound. Tropical fruits, oranges, bananas, peaches, pineapples and juicy lychees are plentiful. High-quality tea is a special product of Fukien, while all along the coast fish and seafood – crabs, crayfish, shrimps, prawns, scallops, clams – are plentiful. This wealth of ingredients has helped to make Cantonese cooking the most versatile and varied of Chinese cuisines.

Cantonese food is not highly seasoned. Instead, a harmonious blending of different flavors is sought in order to bring out the best of the ingredients. However, this does mean that it often relies upon fresh ingredients and when they are not available and substitutes have to be used the results can taste insipid.

Although they are adept at all Chinese culinary techniques, Cantonese cooks are at their most skillful when they stir-fry dishes. Red-braised dishes are an Eastern contribution to Chinese gastronomy, but Southern stir-fried dishes reign supreme nationwide. Their "wok-fragrance," a term used to describe the aroma so desirable in stir-fried dishes, is matchless.

Dim sum – hot hors d'oeuvre of pastry cases stuffed with a mixture of delicacies such as pork, beef or seafood, bamboo shoots or mushroom, steamed, sautéed or deep-fried – is another Cantonese specialty. There are, of course, *dim sum* in all the other regional cuisines, but none can beat the Cantonese for variety. Because of the time, labor and special skill called for to make *dim sum*, they are a treat to be enjoyed at restaurants more than at home.

WHAT IS A TYPICAL CHINESE MEAL?

To the Chinese, a meal comprises rice or another grain, with a few dishes. The number of dishes accompanying the rice depends on the number of people sharing the meal, but a family of six may have three or four dishes at dinner, and perhaps one less at lunch. Obviously the more dishes, the more festive and special the occasion.

Whatever the number of dishes, they should be well balanced, so that in one meal a variety of ingredients, including meat, seafood and vegetables, is eaten, and different cooking methods appreciated.

LAYING THE TABLE

Because a Chinese meal is a communal affair, a round table is usually used, being more conducive to sharing of the dishes. For each place setting you need one rice bowl, a matching saucer and a pair of chopsticks. As the name so aptly suggests, the rice bowl is for the rice, the saucer underneath is for food taken from the communal dishes before you eat it, or for the bones you gently spit out. The chopsticks are placed vertically to the right side of the bowl and saucer – the Chinese do not seem to have made concession to left-handers!

The basic table setting is a rice bowl, saucer and chopsticks. On occasion you may also need a soup spoon and small dish for sauces.

HOW TO SERVE A MEAL

On a day-to-day basis, all the dishes are served together in the center of the table (with extra rice kept warm for second or third helpings). There is no specific order for eating the dishes, so one may have a mouthful of chicken followed by another of bean curd, followed by yet another of fish. However, for more formal occasions, the dishes are served individually. The sequence of order varies from place to place, but generally one or two seasonal "delicacies" are served at the beginning, followed by substantial dishes of meat and poultry, with special soups in the middle and a fish to end the dishes.

("To have fish" is pronounced exactly the same as "surplus," in Mandarin and Cantonese, so the Chinese frequently use this pun and choose fish symbolically to end the main dishes.) Then, one fried rice and often one noodle dish will be served. This is the host saying, with traditional polite modesty, "Excuse my humble fare which may not have been sufficient, so please fill up with some grain food!"

HOW TO EAT RICE
The proper way is to raise the bowl with one hand and perch it on your lower lip and then, holding the chopsticks with the other hand, to shovel the rice into your mouth without dropping the grains on the table or floor. Rice symbolizes blessings in life for the Chinese and it is therefore vital for you to grab your blessings in rather than pick away at them.

In China it is considered good manners to hold the bowl on your lower lip and to shovel in the rice.

EATING OTHER DISHES
When you pick up a piece of food from one of the central dishes, it is quite all right to do so at the same time as another person so long as your chopsticks do not end up fighting in the dish. Having picked up a piece, remember to make a gesture of touching the rice in the bowl, however momentarily, before putting the food into your mouth.

When a piece is large in size, whether with or without bone, it is polite to eat it in bites rather than in one gulp. The bones can be sucked, quietly, before being gently spit out onto the side plate.

The main aim should be to enter into the spirit of the meal and to *enjoy* yourself. Don't forget, however, if you are host, always to put some choice pieces in the bowl or saucer of your guests.

WHAT TO DRINK WITH CHINESE FOOD
Like table manners, the Chinese are casual about what they drink with their meals. Traditionally, they drank warm rice wine with their food and tea after the meal, but some Chinese have now adopted a habit of drinking beer or cognac or whisky, sometimes straight and sometimes diluted, with the meal. In Chinese restaurants abroad a custom has developed of serving tea throughout the meal. Many Westernized Chinese have also found that some Western table wines, especially white or rosé, go well with Chinese food. Many Chinese never drink anything with their food; they are, on the other hand, more particular about the tea they drink after the meal. There is a wide choice of tea to serve after the meal – jasmin, keemun, Oolong, iron goddess of mercy or Tit-koon-yum, Pu-erh from Yunnan and chrysanthemum, to name but a few. Jasmin is a green tea scented with jasmin petals, originally beloved of the Shanghaiese but now popular throughout China and abroad. Tit-koon-yum from Fukien, gleaming with a dark luster, releases its subtle fragrance slowly after it has been infused in the pot for some minutes. Pu-erh tea is believed to have a slight medicinal property, and is excellent after a meal of rich dishes.

USING CHOPSTICKS

Perch the chopsticks on the first knuckles of the third and middle fingers so that they lie parallel to each other, resting in the crook of the thumb. Lay the thumb on top of the chopsticks to secure them – the lower chopstick should remain more or less stationary while the upper one is maneuvered by the first and middle fingers in a pincer movement.

INGREDIENTS

Beans and Bean Products

Beans and bean products play a prominent role in Chinese cooking, where they are used in much the same way as dairy products are in the West. The soybean, one of the most ancient staples grown in China, is richer in protein than an equivalent weight of any other food. However, because soybeans are hard to digest as beans, they are usually processed into sauces or, more important, into bean curd. Many imitation meat dishes, the backbone of Buddhist vegetarian food, are based on the numerous forms of bean curd. Fermented bean products are very important seasonings in savory cooking, while the red azuki bean, whole or in paste form, is used in many sweet dishes.

豆腐 **Bean curd, fresh**
Made from a mixture of finely ground soybeans and water, bean curd is used extensively in Chinese cookery.

豆腐泡 **Bean curd, puffed**
Deep-fried pieces of fresh bean curd, used to absorb tastes and juices.

三邊腐竹 **Bean curd sheet**
Thin, dried sheet of bean curd; has to be moistened before use.

豆豉 **Black beans, fermented**
Whole soybeans preserved in salt and ginger.

紅豆 **Red beans**
Highly proteinaceous azuki beans, most commonly used for puddings in Chinese cookery.

紅豆沙 **Red bean paste**
Thick paste made from puréed, sweetened red beans, frequently used as a sweet filling.

南乳 **Bean curd "cheese," red fermented**
Fresh bean curd, fermented with salt and rice wine.

辣椒腐乳 **Bean curd "cheese," white fermented**
Fresh bean curd, fermented with or without chili.

磨豉醬 **Crushed yellow bean sauce**
Purée of fermented yellow soybeans, wheat flour, salt and water

四川辣椒醬 **Szechwan chili paste**
Spicy hot paste of dried chili and crushed yellow bean sauce.

豆瓣醬 **Soybean paste**
Paste of crushed soybeans combined with chili, sugar and salt.

麵豉 **Yellow beans in salted sauce**
Whole yellow soybeans fermented with salt, wheat flour and sugar.

13

Cereals, Grains and Noodles

The most important staple for the Chinese, long-grain white rice, is usually eaten with every meal. Noodles are generally of secondary importance, except in the North, where wheat is the main crop and they are eaten just as much as rice. Symbolically rice is blessing in life and noodles are longevity. Not surprisingly, therefore, noodles are always served for a birthday celebration.

春卷皮 **Spring roll wrapper**
Paper-thin wrapper made from wheat flour and water.

雲吞皮 **Wonton wrappers**
Made from wheat flour, egg and water and used specifically for wontons.

糯米 **White glutinous rice**
Sticky when cooked, this rice is used for both savory and sweet dishes.

占末 **Long-grain rice**
The hulled, polished grains of this variety remain the ideal staple for the Chinese.

沙河粉 **River rice noodles**
Made from rice ground with water, which is then steamed into thin sheets before being cut.

米粉 **Dried rice noodles**
White, wiry noodles made from rice flour.

Dried egg noodles, flat

Dried egg noodles, round

Fresh egg noodles, flat

Yi noodles

Fresh egg noodles, round

Dried shrimp noodles

Egg noodles
Made from wheat flour, egg and water, these are the most commonly used and versatile of Chinese noodles, whether used in their fresh or dried form.

天津粉皮 **Tientsin fen pi**
Made from mung beans, these are eaten as an alternative between rice noodles and cellophane noodles.

Buckwheat noodles
Thin noodles made from buckwheat flour mixed with water.

日本麵 **U-dong noodles**
Common to Japan and Korea, these noodles are made from wheat flour and water.

Cellophane noodles
Eaten more as a vegetable than a pasta, these noodles are made from ground mung beans.

Dried Products

One cannot get very far with Chinese cooking without dried fungi. They are used, according to variety, to provide texture or taste, and very often make a simple dish outstanding. Black mushrooms, used whole or sliced into small pieces, provide their own taste but also absorb that of others. Both cloud ears and golden needles absorb tastes and are often used to give texture to stir-fried pork or beef dishes; wood ears, which need to be cooked longer, are best in soups.

Floral mushrooms

冬
菇 **Chinese mushrooms, dried and reconstituted**
These edible tree fungi vary in both quality and price, the most expensive being the floral mushroom. Medium-sized mushrooms are most frequently used in this book.

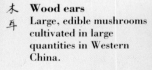

Straw mushrooms, canned

木
耳 **Wood ears**
Large, edible mushrooms cultivated in large quantities in Western China.

草
菇 **Straw mushrooms, dried**
Cultivated on rice straw in paddy fields, they are used more for their texture than their taste.

Straw mushrooms, dried

雲
耳 **Cloud ears**
Like wood ears, these mushrooms are grown in Western China, but they are more delicate in taste.

金
针

Golden needles
Dried buds of the tiger lily flower, generally used for their texture.

陳
皮

Tangerine peel
Dried peel, often used with star anise and Szechwan peppercorns.

紅
棗

Dried red dates
Sweet, prunelike fruit of the jujube tree.

椰
油

Creamed coconut
Concentrated coconut milk in solid form.

粟
米
粉

Cornstarch
Fine white starch extracted from corn, used as a thickener.

生
粉
淀
粉

Potato flour
Made from cooked potatoes, this flour produces a more gelatinous sauce than cornstarch.

馬
蹄
粉

Water chestnut flour
Made from ground water chestnuts, and used when a lighter sauce is required.

氷
糖

Rock sugar
Crystallized cane sugar.

大
菜

Agar
Gelatinous thickener derived from seaweed.

Dried Products

Chinese dried products, used as either the main ingredient or a seasoning for more bland ingredients, are regarded as second to none. Abalone, scallops, oysters and shrimp, although delicious fresh, are much richer in taste and more interesting in texture when dried. Bird's nest, shark's fin and edible jellyfish actually have no fresh counterpart in Chinese cooking and always have to be reconstituted before cooking.

燕窩 **Bird's nest**
Nests of the swallows of the genus Collocalia, who line their nests with a thick mixture of predigested seaweed, which then dries to a hard, transparent layer.

Pork and duck liver

Pork liver

臘腸 **Chinese sausages**
Wind-dried sausages made of pork or pork and duck liver. Both should be cooked before use.

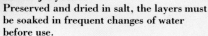

海蜇皮 **Edible jellyfish**
Preserved and dried in salt, the layers must
be soaked in frequent changes of water
before use.

魚翅 **Shark's fin**
The cured fin of one of several species of shark.
Processed fins *(right)* are more economical to use.

罐頭鮑魚 **Abalone**
Firm-fleshed mollusk that is often only available
canned. The juice is useful for soups and sauces.

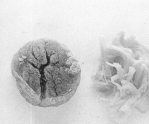

干貝 **Dried scallops**
Deriving their name from the
shell's shape, these mollusks have
a deliciously sweet taste.

蠔豉 **Dried oysters**
Dried and salted, these mollusks
add a "smoky" taste to other
ingredients.

蝦米 **Dried shrimp**
Dried shelled shrimp of various
sizes, frequently used as a
seasoning and in stuffing.

Herbs and Spices

Relatively few herbs and spices are used to produce the sophisticated simplicity of Chinese cuisine. The three indispensable ones are ginger, scallions and garlic, especially for stir-fried dishes. Next in line are star anise, Szechwan peppercorns and cinnamon, all of which enrich the taste of soy sauce-based, slow-cooked dishes. Chilies, especially the dried red ones, are part and parcel of Western Chinese regional cuisine, whereas coriander is the beloved of people in the North.

葱 **Scallions or spring onions**
An essential ingredient in Chinese cuisine. Both green and white parts are used.

蒜 **Garlic**
One of the three indispensable ingredients of Chinese cooking, along with ginger and spring onions.

乾葱頭 **Shallots**
Similar to, but less pungent than onions, they can, however, be used in the same way.

香菜 **Coriander**
Also known as Chinese parsley, it is used as both a garnish and a seasoning.

卤
水
料 **Mixed spices**
Used in flavor-potting. The ready-mixed packages usually contain star anise, Szechwan peppercorns, cinnamon, ginger, fennel, cloves, liquorice and cardamom.

五
香
粉 **Five-spice powder**
Liquorice-tasting powder used, sparingly, in marinades.

花
椒
粉 **Ground roasted Szechwan peppercorns**
Dry-roasted, then ground, and used to add aroma to other ingredients.

花
椒 **Szechwan peppercorns**
Not spicy hot like peppercorns, the roasted variety produces a slightly numbing effect.

辣
椒
乾
辣
椒 **Chili**
Indispensable hot ingredient of Szechwan cooking.

白
芝
麻 **Sesame seeds, white**
White seeds from the sesame plant.

八
角 **Star anise**
Pungent liquorice-tasting spice used to add flavor to meat and poultry.

Fresh ginger

Dried ginger

Ground ginger

生
薑 **Ginger**
The third essential ingredient in Chinese cooking, used to provide flavor and to counteract any rank odor of other ingredients.

桂
皮 **Cassia bark**
Dried bark of an evergreen tree, often confused with cinnamon (left), which can be used as an alternative.

Cinnamon stick

Vegetables

The Chinese love to eat vegetables, and the leafy green vegetables of the *Brassica* family are their special favorites. They boil or stir-fry them, but only for a short time, so that the vegetables retain both their crispness and their vitamins. They frequently use a little meat to enhance the taste of vegetable dishes, and, conversely, use some vegetables in meat dishes to provide an interesting texture.

菜
心
Chinese flowering cabbage
This vegetable is usually served stir-fried or simply blanched.

芥
菜
Mustard green
This variety of mustard green is less bitter than many others, and it is usually served blanched or stir-fried, or in soup.

芽菜 **Bean sprouts**
Tender sprouts of
mung beans, used to
provide a crunchy
texture.

雪豆 **Sugar peas**
Tender, flat green pea pods
with barely formed peas.
Usually served lightly
blanched or stir-fried.

紹菜 **Chinese celery cabbage**
Sweet, mild-flavored
cabbage, usually stir-fried
or braised.

白菜 **Chinese white cabbage**
Although similar in taste to Swiss
chard, it is sweeter and juicier.

芥菜 **Mustard green**
This more pungent
variety of mustard
green is served pickled
or in soup.

韭菜 **Chinese chives**
Used to provide
flavor, they are
stronger than chives,
although more fibrous
in texture.

23

Vegetables

As with many Chinese ingredients, texture is important in a vegetable: the spongy hair seaweed is both an absorber of sauce and a provider of texture; water chestnuts and bamboo shoots are pure texture foods. The flesh of winter melon is succulent and subtle, and the slippery taro goes especially well with duck. Ginkgo nuts and baby corn on the cob, often used in vegetarian dishes, add color and variety to a dish. The three preserved vegetables are popular seasonings for meat, soups and other vegetables.

冬瓜 **Winter melon**
Green gourd, the flesh of which becomes almost transparent when cooked. It is often used in soup with pork, chicken or duck.

馬蹄 **Chinese water chestnuts**
Crisp, sweet-tasting sedge bulbs, used to provide a crunchy texture. They are also ground into flour.

芋頭 **Taro**
Root vegetable, frequently cooked with duck or fatty pork.

髮菜 **Hair seaweed**
Product of Hopeh and Shensi provinces, this rather tasteless ingredient is used to absorb flavor and provide a slippery texture.

竹筍 **Bamboo shoots**
Young shoots of bamboo plants, used for their texture in many Chinese dishes.

白果 **Ginkgo nuts**
Tender, mild-tasting nuts from the ginkgo tree.

珍珠筍 **Young corn**
Miniature corn on the cob, used in both vegetable and meat dishes.

咸酸菜 **Pickled mustard green**
Mustard green preserved in brine.

雪菜 **Red-in-snow**
Red-rooted variety of mustard plant that sprouts up through the spring snows.

榨菜 **Szechwan preserved vegetable**
Mustard plant preserved in salt, then pickled with chili powder.

Sauces, Oils, Fats, Wines and Vinegars

Sauces of various types are used in marinades and to add flavor to cooked ingredients. Soy sauce is the most basic but also the most important seasoning. Used with salt, it helps to turn simple ingredients into Chinese cuisine. Because so many Chinese dishes are stir-fried or deep-fried, oil is obviously an important ingredient, but it is also important for the flavor it gives to marinades.

SAUCES

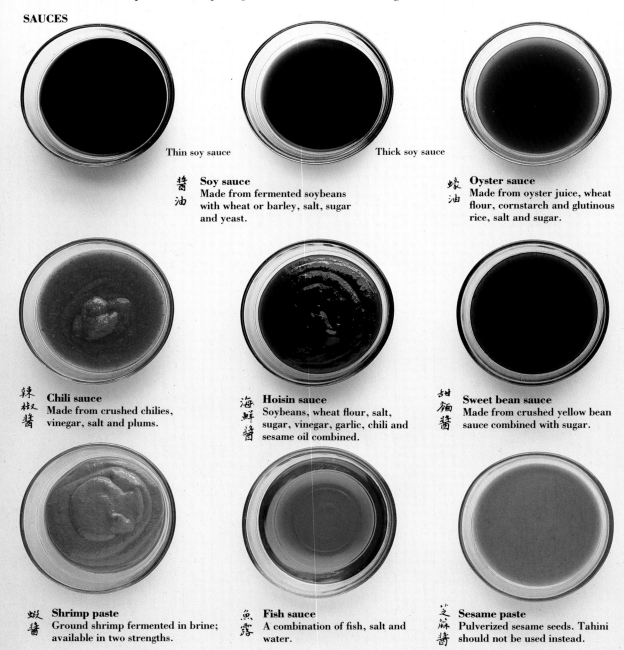

Thin soy sauce

Thick soy sauce

醬
油 **Soy sauce**
Made from fermented soybeans with wheat or barley, salt, sugar and yeast.

蠔
油 **Oyster sauce**
Made from oyster juice, wheat flour, cornstarch and glutinous rice, salt and sugar.

辣
椒
醬 **Chili sauce**
Made from crushed chilies, vinegar, salt and plums.

海
鮮
醬 **Hoisin sauce**
Soybeans, wheat flour, salt, sugar, vinegar, garlic, chili and sesame oil combined.

甜
麵
醬 **Sweet bean sauce**
Made from crushed yellow bean sauce combined with sugar.

蝦
醬 **Shrimp paste**
Ground shrimp fermented in brine; available in two strengths.

魚
露 **Fish sauce**
A combination of fish, salt and water.

芝
麻
醬 **Sesame paste**
Pulverized sesame seeds. Tahini should not be used instead.

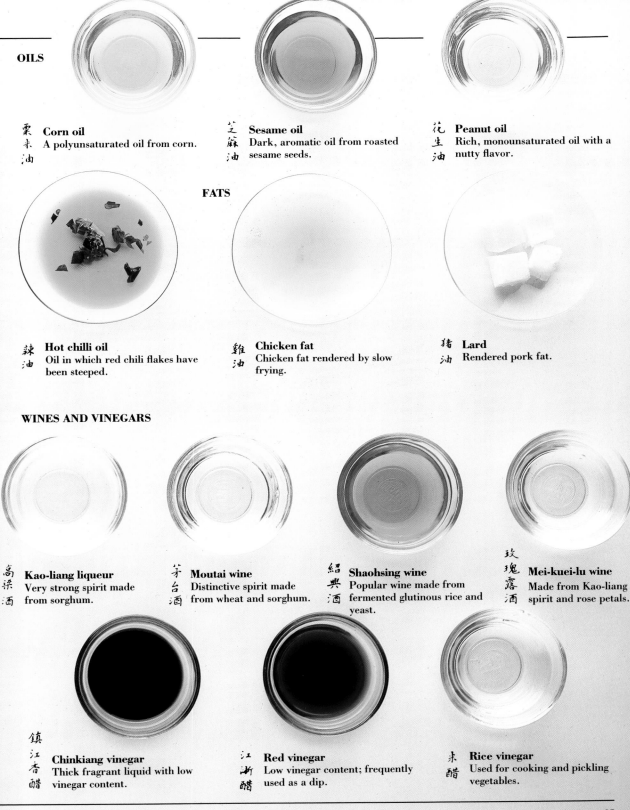

OILS

栗米油 **Corn oil**
A polyunsaturated oil from corn.

芝麻油 **Sesame oil**
Dark, aromatic oil from roasted sesame seeds.

花生油 **Peanut oil**
Rich, monounsaturated oil with a nutty flavor.

FATS

辣油 **Hot chilli oil**
Oil in which red chili flakes have been steeped.

雞油 **Chicken fat**
Chicken fat rendered by slow frying.

猪油 **Lard**
Rendered pork fat.

WINES AND VINEGARS

高梁酒 **Kao-liang liqueur**
Very strong spirit made from sorghum.

茅台酒 **Moutai wine**
Distinctive spirit made from wheat and sorghum.

紹興酒 **Shaohsing wine**
Popular wine made from fermented glutinous rice and yeast.

玫瑰露酒 **Mei-kuei-lu wine**
Made from Kao-liang spirit and rose petals.

鎮江香醋 **Chinkiang vinegar**
Thick fragrant liquid with low vinegar content.

江浙醋 **Red vinegar**
Low vinegar content; frequently used as a dip.

米醋 **Rice vinegar**
Used for cooking and pickling vegetables.

EQUIPMENT

The wok

A wok fitted with a lid is an essential cooking utensil, because it is suitable for all methods of Chinese cooking, especially stir-frying. Woks come in several different sizes, but for family use, a 14-inch one made of carbon steel is ideal.

竹
搽 **Wok brush**
Stiff wooden brush used for cleaning the wok after use.

鑊 **The wok**
Generally made of steel, these round-bottomed pans allow the heat to spread rapidly and evenly, which is essential in Chinese cooking. They are available with both wooden and steel handles – both styles should be used with a glove. Woks can be used for stir-frying, deep-frying, boiling and steaming.

蒸
籠 **Bamboo steamer**
Small steamer placed on wooden trivet; used with wok lid or its own bamboo lid.

hopsticks
he Chinese use long
ooden chopsticks in
ooking because they
on't conduct
eat.

Seasoning the wok
Before using your wok for the first time, heat it
over high heat, then brush it lightly with oil. Wipe
clean with paper towels and repeat the procedure
two more times. Rinse well and dry thoroughly.
The wok will rust if not in constant use. If it does,
scour the rust off, rinse and brush again with oil to
return it to good condition.

Bamboo strainer
Bamboo-handled
strainers are the best for
lifting ingredients from
steam or hot oil.

Wok stand
Used to provide a secure base for the
wok when it's used for steaming or
deep-frying. It can be dispensed with
when stir-frying as frying with a wok
stand takes longer.
Note Although wok cookery is more
suited to gas, it is possible to use
electricity successfully. However, the
food in the wok will take longer to reach
the desired temperature. Unless you use
a wok with a small, flattened bottom it is
usually necessary to use a wok stand on
an electric stove, especially for steaming
and deep-frying.

Wok scoop
Used to toss and turn
ingredients when
stir-frying.

Steamers and cleavers

There are two basic types of steamer: specially designed metal ones that act as both water boilers and food containers, and traditional-style bamboo steamers that fit on top of a wok, in which the water is boiled. These come in various sizes, from small (see page 28) for *dim sum* to those large enough to hold a whole fish (see below). The other method of steaming doesn't require a steamer but is just as effective, especially for everyday use (see page 45). Instead, the food (on a heatproof plate) is held above the water in the wok by a metal or bamboo trivet, and the steam is retained by a tightly fitting wok lid. For any cutting, fine or rough, all you need is a medium-weight cleaver and a solid wooden board.

蒸籠 **Steamer**
Made of stainless steel or aluminum, this specially designed steamer has a lower container for the water, on which sit one or two perforated containers for the food. The food is placed on a heatproof dish or muslin, and then covered with a tightly fitting lid.

Assembled metal steamer
Slotting snugly together so that all the steam is directed up through the holes to the food, this steamer can sit directly on the heat.

Bamboo steamer in wok
This traditional-style steamer can be used with one or more baskets to hold the food. The wok must rest on a wok rim for stability.

Cleaver
One of medium weight, about 3½ by 8 inches, made of carbon or stainless steel is ideal for general use.

If you find this too big, try a slender, lighter cleaver see below. In China, this type is frequently used to carve Peking duck.

竹
墊

Bamboo mat
To prevent meat from sticking during slow cooking, it should be placed on this latticed mat, which is placed inside the cooking pot.

砧
板

Chinese chopping board
A solid, wooden base is essential for chopping, and one 2 inches thick and 11 to 12 inches in diameter is ideal. When new, it should be soaked in water and oiled frequently to prevent splitting.

TECHNIQUES

Cutting Vegetables

In Chinese cooking, all vegetables are cut into uniformly small pieces, because this allows them to cook quickly without losing their crunchiness; it also means that they can absorb the taste of the oil and seasonings, despite the short cooking time. Some vegetables are cut according to their natural shape (for example, broccoli and cauliflower are cut into florets); others are sliced, shredded, diced or roll-cut depending on the dish. For stir-frying, Chinese celery cabbage is shredded, but for braising, it is cut into larger pieces. Bamboo shoots, if braised, are cut into wedges, but if put into a stir-fried dish they are sliced thin. Chinese mushrooms can be sliced thin or thick, quartered or cut into small cubes. Root vegetables such as carrots and white radishes are roll cut to expose as many surfaces to the heat as possible; celery is traditionally cut on the diagonal to make it look more attractive.

HOLDING THE CLEAVER

Method 1. *Curl your fingers tightly around the handle, which should rest in the palm of your hand. This way, the cleaver will cut downward with its own weight.*

Method 2. *Hold the handle in your palm as before, but slide your index finger down the side of the blade. Your thumb and forefinger then give you more control.*

GUARDING

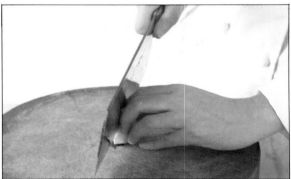

SLICING

Hold the food with your fingertips turned under, knuckles forward so that they act as a guide for the cutting blade. Never lift cleaver higher than knuckles.

Put the blade about ⅛ inch from one edge and slice downward. Regulate thickness by moving fingers farther away from, or nearer to, edge being cut.

SHREDDING

DIAGONAL CUTTING

Cut the food into uniform slices about ⅛ to ¼ inch wide, depending on preference. Cut across these slices to form shreds. With vegetables other than cabbage, stack the slices before slicing into strips.

Hold the top of the food firmly, with your fingers at a slant of 60°. Cut down at this angle and continue down to the end of the vegetable.

ROLL CUTTING

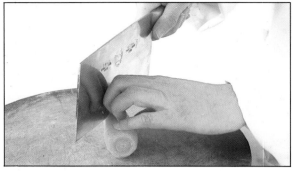 

1. *Hold one end of the vegetable firmly and make a diagonal cut.*

2. *Roll the vegetable a quarter turn toward you and make another diagonal cut. Continue rolling and cutting.*

CUTTING SCALLIONS

BRUSHES

1. *Trim the white ends of the scallions into 2½-inch lengths. Make repeated cuts through both ends, leaving the central section intact.*

2. *Place the scallions in iced water and refrigerate for several hours. This will make the ends curl up, forming the brushes.*

SILKEN THREADS

FIVE-WAY SCALLIONS

Cut off the roots and any withered tops. Chop into 2-to-3-inch lengths. Slice along the length of the scallions and then cut the two halves into strands.

Top: *trimmed;* **middle left:** *sliced;* **middle center:** *silken threads;* **middle right:** *brushes;* **bottom left:** *small rounds;* **bottom right:** *diagonal cut*

CUTTING GARLIC AND GINGER

SILKEN THREADS

1. *Slice thinly. Arrange the slices on top of each other.*

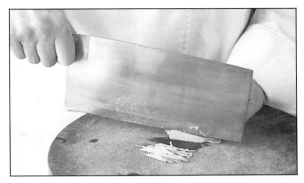

2. *Placing the cleaver carefully, cut the slices into narrow strips.*

CRUSHING GARLIC

1. *Lay the unpeeled cloves on a wooden board. Using the side of the cleaver, bang down on the garlic firmly.*

2. *Separate the flesh from the skin by peeling one from the other.*

FINELY CHOPPED

Place the garlic on a wooden board. Crush with the cleaver, remove the skin, then chop repeatedly until finely minced.

FIVE-WAY GARLIC AND GINGER

Top: *ginger root: sliced; silken threads; chopped fine*
Bottom: *garlic cloves: sliced; silken threads; chopped fine*

Cutting Meat

Because Chinese cooking methods rely on the rapid cooking of ingredients, any meat used has to be cut into small, uniform pieces. Invariably for stir-frying, and sometimes for steaming, the meat should be cut into thin slices, matchstick strips or cubes. This way it can be quickly stir-fried or steamed without losing any of its tenderness.

Beef should always be cut across the grain or it will be tough; pork and chicken can be cut either along or across the grain. Although the cutting of meat into small pieces is time-consuming, it is an integral part of Chinese cooking and is essential if you want the meat to taste good.

MATCHSTICK CUT

1. *Cut the meat into thin slices abut ⅛ inch thick.*

2. *Lay the slices on top of each other and cut them into narrow slivers like matchsticks.*

RECTANGULAR CUT

1. *Cut the meat into manageable pieces about 1½ inches wide.*

2. *Turn the chunks on their sides and cut across the grain into rectangular slices about ¼ inch thick.*

SLIVERED CUT

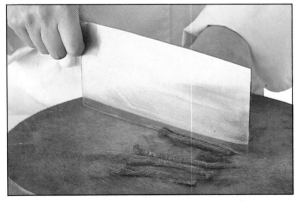

Cut ⅕-inch slices of beef. Lay them flat and cut into long slivers. Use especially for Dry-Fried Beef.

PAPER-THIN CUT

Slice the meat as thinly as possible. Freezing the meat for a couple of hours beforehand makes this easier.

MATCHSTICK HEADS

1. *Slice ham into uniform strips. Gather the strips together so that they're lying parallel to one another.*

2. *Hold the strips firmly with your free hand and cut across them to form small dice.*

CUBED CHICKEN

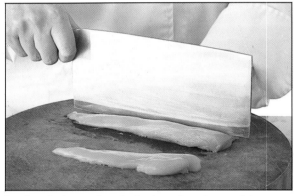 

1. *Cut the breast lengthwise into three long strips.*

2. *Gather the strips together and cut across them to form uniform cubes.*

MARCH-CHOPPING

1. *Cut the meat into small pieces. Using one or two cleavers, rhythmically chop the meat, moving from side to side.*

2. *As the meat spreads, slip a cleaver under one side and use it to flip the meat into the center. Then continue chopping.*

SPECIAL TECHNIQUES

RECONSTITUTING MUSHROOMS

1. *Rinse the mushrooms. Put them in a bowl and pour on enough boiling water to cover by about 1½ inches.*

2. *Set aside for about 20 to 30 minutes or until the mushrooms have become swollen and soft.*

DEVEINING PRAWNS

1. *Shell the prawns. Hold the tail end firmly and make a small cut along the center of the back.*

2. *Remove the black vein and discard it.*

MINCING PRAWNS

1. *Shell and devein the prawns and cut up roughly. Using the broad side of the cleaver, press down on the prawns to flatten them.*

2. *Repeatedly chop the prawns until they're minced.*

Stir-frying

Stir-frying is the unique contribution of the Chinese to world cooking. When cooked by this method, meat is tender, vegetables are crisp, and they both have a special fragrance. Because speed and instant control are essential, gas is preferable to electricity.

In Chinese cooking there are two types of deep-frying. In one, the ingredients are deep-fried until crisp and cooked through; in the other they are deep-fried just long enough to seal in their juices. This is known as "going through the oil," and is a preparatory step to the sophisticated stir-frying invariably used in Chinese restaurants. Although it produces a more refined result in certain dishes, it is not essential for everyday cooking.

STIR-FRYING

1. Stir-frying is a very quick cooking technique, so prepare all the ingredients before you start. Add the marinade to the main ingredient and stir well. If oil is to be added, blend it in last.

2. Heat the empty wok over high heat until smoke rises (you may also notice a slight blue/rainbow effect at the bottom). Heating the wok before adding the oil prevents the meat or fish from sticking.

3. Gently add the oil (usually about 3 to 4 tablespoons), and swirl it around to coat halfway up the side of the wok.

4. If you're using garlic, add this to the oil. Steady the wok with a gloved hand as you do so.

5. As soon as the garlic has started to sizzle and take on color, add the ginger. Stir.

6. As soon as the ginger starts to sizzle, add the white part only of the scallions (the green part needs less cooking and is added later). Stir well.

7. *Add the main ingredient (meat, fish or shellfish). Slide the scoop under the food to the bottom of the wok; turn and toss until the food is partially cooked.*

8. *Splash in the wine or sherry around the side of the wok and continue to stir until the sizzling subsides.*

9. *Add any other ingredients that need heating or reheating and stir and toss.*

10. *Make a well in the center of the wok and pour in the well-mixed sauce. Stir until the sauce has thickened and turned glossy.*

11. *Add the green parts of the scallions, which need the least cooking. Stir and toss briefly.*

12. *Scoop the stir-fried ingredients onto a warmed serving plate. Serve immediately.*

DEEP-FRYING

1. *Put the wok on a wok rim. Pour in enough oil to half fill it. Turn the heat on high.*

2. *If you're using a thermometer, put it in after you've poured in the oil. Heat until the thermometer registers the required temperature.*

3. *When you notice the oil moving put in a piece of stale bread. The oil will be at 350°F when the bread browns in about 60 seconds.*

4. *Using long wooden chopsticks, or tongs, carefully add the food to the oil.*

5. *With the chopsticks, move the food around. This prevents pieces from sticking together.*

6. *Using a large hand strainer (or a perforated spoon, carefully remove the food from the oil. Drain on paper towels before serving.*

Steaming

Steaming is a technique that evolved when a moist dish was required as an alternative to a roasted one. Compared with dishes cooked by other methods, steamed dishes are more subtle in taste and seem to bring out the freshness of the ingredients more. Thus, the fresher the ingredients, the better they are for steaming. In fact, steamed dishes cover the whole spectrum of ingredients: meat, poultry, vegetables (not leaf vegetables), breads, buns, hot hors d'oeuvre *(dim sum)*, seafood and, especially, fish. Preparation for steaming often entails cutting up ingredients, marinating them and then putting them on a heatproof plate so that the juices from the food and the seasonings can be served with the dish itself.

USING AN ALUMINUM STEAMER

1. *Pour boiling water into the lower container until it reaches halfway up the sides of the container.*

2. *Place the item to be steamed on a heatproof plate and put it in the upper container. Place this in the lower container and put the lid securely on top.*

USING A WOK

1. *Put the base of a small bamboo steamer or metal trivet in the wok. Fill with boiling water to within 1 inch of the container holding the food to be steamed.*

2. *Place whatever is to be steamed on a heatproof plate, and put it carefully on the stand. Place the wok lid on securely.*

ADDING THE CONDIMENTS TO STEAMED FISH

1. *When the fish is cooked, turn off the heat. Put in the scallions and ginger, then pour the prepared, heated oil over them.*

2. *If you're going to add ham, sprinkle it on top. Pour soy sauce over the fish and serve immediately.*

RECIPES

HORS D'OEUVRES

Pickled Vegetables Cantonese Style

INGREDIENTS

1 long cucumber, about 1 pound, halved
12 ounces young carrots, peeled
4 or 5 sticks celery, about 8 ounces, trimmed
2 level teaspoons salt
4 level tablespoons sugar
4 tablespoons rice or white wine vinegar

Serves 10

Illustrated opposite

True to form, Cantonese pickled vegetables are sweet and sour rather than spicy, and their unique taste is achieved by a harmonious and subtle blending of salt, sugar and vinegar.

1. Remove and discard the seeds in the cucumber. Slice it diagonally into thickish pieces at about ⅓ inch intervals.

2. Roll-cut the carrots (see page 34).

3. Slice the celery diagonally into pieces about the same size as the cucumber.

4. Put the vegetables into a large clean bowl. Sprinkle the salt over them, mix together and let stand at room temperature for 2½ to 3 hours, during which time excess water will be drawn out. Drain the excess water out but leave slightly damp.

5. Return to a clean bowl. Add the sugar and vinegar, mix thoroughly and let stand for about 3 hours at room temperature, or overnight in the refrigerator. Serve chilled.

Facing page, clockwise from the top: Crisp stir-fried shrimp (see page 48); Pickled vegetables Cantonese Style (see above); Edible jellyfish with cucumber (see page 49)

Crisp Stir-fried Shrimp

INGREDIENTS

1 pound 2 ounces fresh or frozen
    raw peeled shrimp or prawns,
    cut into ¾-inch pieces
peanut or corn oil for deep-frying
1 tablespoon Shaohsing wine or
    medium-dry sherry

FOR THE MARINADE

1 teaspoon salt
1 tablespoon cornstarch
1 egg white

FOR THE SAUCE

1 teaspoon cornstarch
4 tablespoons clear stock
¼ teaspoon sugar
salt to taste

Serves 6

Illustrated on page 47

Texture is the essence of this dish. The quickly cooked shrimp should be crisp yet tender, and the longer they are marinated in the refrigerator—up to 3 days—the better their texture becomes. The delicate color of the shrimp needs no garnish.

1. If frozen shrimp are used, defrost thoroughly. Wash the shrimp under cold running water. Pat dry with paper towels but leave damp. Put into a bowl (a).

2. *Prepare the marinade:* Sprinkle the salt over the shrimp and mix well. Stir in the cornstarch, then add the egg white and stir again to coat the shrimp evenly and thoroughly (b). Cover and let marinate for at least 5 hours.

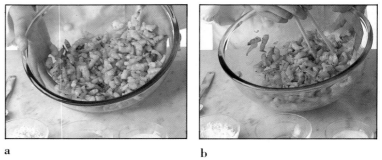

a   b

3. *For the sauce:* Mix the cornstarch, stock and sugar together in a small bow. Set aside.

4. Half fill a wok or deep fryer with oil. Heat until just hot, 300°F. Carefully add all the shrimp and fry for 30 to 45 seconds, separating them with a pair of long chopsticks or a long-handled wooden spoon. Remove the shrimp before they are quite cooked with a perforated spoon or strainer and drain on paper towels.

5. Pour most of the oil into a container, leaving only about 2 tablespoons in the wok. Reheat until smoke rises. Quickly add the shrimp to the wok and stir a few times with a wok scoop or metal spatular. Splash in the wine or sherry around the side of the wok. When the sizzling dies down, pour in the well-stirred sauce. Continue to toss for a few seconds more. Add salt to taste, if necessary. Transfer the mixture to a warm serving plate. Serve immediately.

Edible Jellyfish with Cucumber

Do not be put off by the initial rubbery appearance of the jellyfish, which is sold in sheets, folded and packed into plastic bags with large grains of salt in between the folds. When properly prepared, edible jellyfish gives great pleasure to those who enjoy food as much for texture as for taste. This is certainly why the Chinese like it.

1. Shake all the sandy salt from the jellyfish. Wash in 3 changes of water, squeezing to get rid of some of the excess saltiness.

2. Put into a large, deep bowl and fill with cold water. Soak for 3 to 4 days, changing the water twice a day and squeezing the jellyfish each time. At the end of the soaking, it should be totally free of salt.

3. *Prepare the dressing:* Mix together the vinegar, soy sauce, sugar, oil and mustard.

4. Squeeze excess water from the jellyfish. Put on a board and cut into thin strips about ⅛ inch wide. Drain well.

5. Cut the cucumber diagonally into slices about ⅛ inch thick. Stack a few pieces together at a time (a) and cut into sticks about ⅕ inch wide (b).

INGREDIENTS
1 pound preserved edible jellyfish
½ long cucumber

FOR THE DRESSING
1 teaspoon rice or cider vinegar
2 tablespoons thin soy sauce
½ teaspoon sugar
1 tablespoon sesame oil
½ teaspoon prepared mustard

Serves 4

Illustrated on page 47

a

b

6. Arrange the cucumber sticks in a circle on the serving plate and place the jellyfish in the center.

7. Just before serving, add the well-stirred dressing to the jellyfish.

Shredded Chicken with Tientsin Fen Pi

雞
絲
粉
皮

INGREDIENTS

1 pint clear stock or water
2 small chicken breasts, skinned and boned, or chicken breast fillet
4 pieces Tientsin fen pi, each about 9 inches in diameter
½ long cucumber, about 8 ounces

FOR THE SAUCE

1 tablespoon rice or white wine vinegar
2 teaspoons hot prepared mustard
½ teaspoon salt
½ teaspoon sugar
4 tablespoons thin soy sauce
8 turns white pepper mill
1 tablespoon sesame oil
3 tablespoons peanut or corn oil

Serves 6

Illustrated opposite

This pleasant Northern dish is served cold with a slightly tangy sauce, and because it can be prepared completely in advance it is very handy for entertaining. The fen pi, *literally meaning the skin of flour, must not be soggy if the dish is to be successful.*

1. Put the stock or water in a saucepan and bring to a boil. Add the chicken and simmer, covered, for about 5 minutes. Remove from the heat and let steep in the liquid for 15 minutes without disturbing. Remove and let cool.

2. *Prepare the sauce:* Mix together the vinegar, mustard, salt, sugar, soy sauce, pepper and oils.

3. Bring a large pan of water, about 3 pints, to a fast boil. Put in the fen pi, one by one, so that they will not stick to each other. Cover and remove from the heat for 5 minutes. Drain. Then, handling with care, put the fen pi into a pan of cold water.

4. Fold each fen pi into 3, then cut crosswise at ½ inch intervals. Transfer to a serving plate.

5. Cut the cucumber diagonally into thin slices, leaving them in an ordered pile. Cut the pile into thin strips. Place on top of the fen pi.

6. Going with the grain, tear the chicken by hand into thin strips and put on top of the cucumber.

7. Just before serving, pour the sauce over it, mix well and serve.

Note: If the dish is not to be served right away, the ingredients can be individually refrigerated, covered, and assembled just prior to serving.

Facing page, clockwise from the top: Shredded chicken with Tientsin fen pi (see above); Steamed scallops in the shell (see page 53); Spiced salt spareribs (see page 52)

椒
盐
排
骨

Spiced Salt Spareribs

You can also use boneless shoulder or chops to make this dish. You will find the result just as deliciously satisfying.

INGREDIENTS

1½ to 2½ pounds meaty
    spareribs
1½ to 2½ tablespoons cornstarch
peanut or corn oil for deep-frying
1 to 1½ teaspoons spice salt

FOR THE SPICED SALT

2 tablespoons salt
¾ teaspoon ground roasted
    Szechwan peppercorns
½ teaspoon five-spice powder

FOR THE MARINADE

¾ to 1¼ teaspoons spiced salt
1½ to 2½ tablespoons thin soy
    sauce
1 to 1½ teaspoons sugar
8 to 10 turns black pepper mill
2 to 3 teaspoons Shaohsing wine
    or medium-dry sherry

Serves 6 to 8

Illustrated on page 51

1. Ask the butcher to separate the spareribs, and then chop them into pieces about 2 inches long. This can also be done at home if you possess a heavy kitchen cleaver, a thick chopping board and a strong arm. Put the meat into a dish.

2. *Prepare the spiced salt:* Add the salt to a dry wok and stir-fry over moderate heat for about 4 minutes, or until it takes on color slightly. Remove from the heat and add the Szechwan peppercorns and five-spice powder. Mix well and let cool. (Spiced salt can be kept in a covered jar for a long time.)

3. *Prepare the marinade:* Add the spiced salt, soy sauce, sugar, pepper and wine or sherry to the spareribs. Blend well. Let marinate for about 2 hours, turning the pieces over 2 or 3 times for better absorption.

4. Pour off any liquid marinade that has not been absorbed. Sprinkle with the cornstarch and mix well to coat.

5. Half fill a wok or deep fryer with oil. Heat to a temperature of 350°F or until a cube of stale bread browns in 60 seconds. Place the spareribs on a large hand strainer or in a deep-frying basket. Dip into the oil 2 or 3 times while you separate the pieces with a pair of long chopsticks. Slide the pieces into the oil if you are using a perforated spoon and a wok, or leave the deep-frying basket in the deep fryer. Deep-fry for about 3 minutes, or until the pieces begin to surface. Remove and set aside.

6. Reheat the oil to the same temperature. Return the spareribs to the oil and deep-fry a second time for about 1 minute, or until crisp and thoroughly cooked. Remove and drain on paper towels before placing on a warm serving plate.

7. Sprinkle with the spiced salt. Mix thoroughly, then serve.

Note: Left over spareribs can be reheated. Wrap in foil and place in a preheated oven at 375°F for 20 minutes.

Steamed Scallops in the Shell

A Cantonese dish at its simplest and best. The fresh scallops are steamed with just a touch of garlic, then served with a sauce to add zest to their natural sweetness. The details of preparation, seemingly elaborate, are nevertheless worth observing if you wish to make this simple yet sophisticated dish.

1. Ask the fishdealer to open the scallops on the cup side of the shells rather than on the flat side. If they have already been opened on the flat side, ask for the cup shells, so that you can transfer the scallop meat to them. Remove the frills or rims, sandy and black impurities and the muscles, leaving only the white meat and the corals or roes. Separate the corals from the meat and save them for another recipe or freeze them. Rinse the scallop meat and pat dry, leaving them on the shells.

2. *Prepare the sauce:* Divide the scallions into 2 portions and put into 2 serving bowls. Heat a wok until smoke rises. Add the oil and swirl it around. Lower the heat and add the ginger and chilies. Remove from the heat. After a few seconds, add the soy sauces and water and bring to simmering point. Pour this mixture over the scallions in the bowls.

3. Half fill a wok or deep fryer with oil. Heat to a temperature of 350°F or until a cube of stale break browns in 60 seconds. Put the garlic into a small wire sieve. Dip the sieve into the oil quickly 3 or 4 times, or until the garlic has taken on color. Save the oil for other deep-frying purposes.

4. Place 4 or 5 pieces of garlic and the same amount of green scallions on each scallop. Place the scallops in a wok or steamer; some shells can perch on top of other shells as long as they are not pressing down on the meat.

5. Steam over high heat for about 7 to 10 minutes. The scallops will be opaque and be just cooked. There will be juice in the shell.

6. Remove each shell, taking care not to spill the juice, and put on a large serving platter or on individual plates. Serve hot.

7. To eat, put a small amount of sauce on the meat, then break it up to absorb the sauce. As host or hostess, do encourage your guests to pick up the shell and drink the tasty juice as well.

INGREDIENTS

20 large scallops
peanut or corn oil for deep-frying
6 or 8 cloves garlic, peeled and diced
4 or 6 large scallions, green parts only, cut into rounds

FOR THE SAUCE

4 or 6 large scallions, white parts only, cut into silken threads (see page 34)
3 to 4 tablespoons peanut or corn oil
3/4 inch fresh ginger root, peeled and cut into silken threads (see page 35)
3 or 4 fresh green chilies, seeded and cut into rounds
2 tablespoons thick soy sauce
2 tablespoons thin soy sauce
2 tablespoons water

Serves 6 to 8

Illustrated on page 51

清蒸帶子

小
吃

Deep-fried Appetizers

This is not literally a menu, so never try to make all seven at once. Rather, attempt one or two at a time and you will have fun both making them and eating the delicious results with your guests.

炸
五
香
卷
Deep-fried five-spice rolls
Aromatic pork-filled rolls,
served with tomato, chili
and soy sauces
(see page 195).

百
花
釀
蟹
鉗
Stuffed crab claws
An elegant combination of
prawn and crab meat,
crisp on the outside,
tender and juicy on the
inside (see page 197).

鳳尾蝦 **Phoenix-tail prawns**
Deep-fried prawns served with deep-fried pepper (see page 198).

錦鹵雲吞 **Deep-fried wontons**
Crisp parcels of prawns, served with a sweet and sour sauce (see page 194)

 紙包蝦 **Prawns wrapped in rice paper**
Deep-fried rolls of prawns, ham and bamboo shoots, served with a chili sauce (page 199).

特式春卷 **Special spring rolls**
Delicious, deep-fried packets filled with a seafood, meat and vegetable mixture (see page 196).

炸牛奶 **Deep-fried milk**
Smooth, creamy filling of coconut cream and crab meat, with a crisp outside (see page 198).

Ginger Soup with Pork and Wood Ears

INGREDIENTS

½ ounce wood ears, reconstituted (see page 39)

6 ounces lean pork

2 to 3 tablespoons peanut or corn oil

1 to 2 ounces fresh ginger root, peeled and sliced into slivers

1 tablespoon Shaohsing wine or medium-dry sherry

½ teaspoon salt

2 teaspoons thin soy sauce

2 pints clear stock

3 scallions, cut into ½-inch pieces

Serves 6

Illustrated opposite

This is a favorite summer soup of the Hunanese, who appreciate the cooling effect that the ginger brings on a humid day.

1. Drain excess water from the wood ears but leave damp. Break up the larger pieces.

2. Slice the pork into strips, about 1½ by ½ inch and ⅒ inch thick.

3. Heat a wok over high heat until smoke rises. Add the oil and swirl it around. Add the ginger and stir a few times. Put in the pork and, sliding the wok scoop or metal spatular to the bottom of the wok, turn and toss for about 30 seconds. Add the wood ears, lowering the heat so they do not make explosive sounds or fly out of the wok. Stir and turn for another 30 seconds.

4. Add the wine or sherry, salt, soy sauce and stock. Bring to a boil. Spoon off the foam that surfaces. Lower the heat, cover and simmer for 10 to 15 minutes. Taste for seasoning, then add the scallions and immediately remove from the heat.

5. Transfer to a large warm soup tureen or individual soup bowls and serve hot.

Facing page, clockwise from the top: Dried scallop soup (see page 59); Egg drop soup (see page 58); Ginger soup with pork and wood ears (see above); Bean curd soup (see page 58)

Eggdrop Soup

This is the most basic Chinese soup and can be made in an instant with some clear stock and an egg. The soup's success, depends on the technique of adding the egg to the soup.

INGREDIENTS
1 egg
1½ pints clear stock
½ teaspoon salt
½ teaspoon sugar
1 teaspoon thin soy sauce
2 large scallions, green parts only, cut into tiny rounds

Serves 4

Illustrated on page 57

1. Beat the egg lightly.

2. Put the stock in a saucepan or wok and bring to a boil. Lower the heat to a minimum. Slowly pour in the beaten egg, either through the gap of 2 chopsticks or along the back of a fork held about 8 to 10 inches above the saucepan, moving the chopsticks or fork in a circular motion so that the egg covers the whole surface of the stock.

3. Remove from the heat and cover for 45 seconds, to allow the egg to set into tender flakes. Add the salt, sugar and soy sauce, and sprinkle on the scallions. Give the soup 2 or 3 generous stirs.

4. Transfer to a large warm soup tureen or individual soup bowls and serve.

Bean Curd Soup

A simple but refreshing soup that is also very healthy – a vegetarian's delight.

INGREDIENTS
2 cakes bean curd
4 ounces frozen small green peas
salt
1½ pints clear stock
thin soy sauce to taste
1 to 2 tablespoons peanut or corn oil

Serves 4

Illustrated on page 57

1. Cut each cake of bean curd into 32 cubes: cut lengthwise into 4 pieces, then crosswise into another 4 pieces and then halve each piece. Steep in hot water for 10 to 15 minutes. Drain, handling with care, so as not to break them.

2. Place the peas in a saucepan of boiling salted water and simmer for about 3 minutes. Drain.

3. Put the stock, bean curd and peas in a saucepan and bring to a boil. Season with salt and a little soy sauce. Add the oil. Transfer to a large warm soup tureen or individual soup bowls and serve.

Dried Scallop Soup

Dried scallops used to be relatively cheap in China and dried scallop soup was the poor man's shark's fin soup. However, times have changed, and this soup, with its contrast in texture between the tender scallops and the crisp bamboo shoots, is now one of the most sought-after first courses, second only to shark's fin and bird's nest soups.

1. Rinse the dried scallops, rubbing with your fingers to get rid of the white filmy substance sometimes found on their surface.

2. Put into a large saucepan and add about 2½ pints of water. Bring to a boil and skim off the white foam that surfaces. Reduce the heat and simmer for 1¾ to 2 hours, until the scallops are tender and the liquid has reduced to about 1¾ pints. Check the water level from time to time and add more if necessary.

3. Using a perforated spoon, transfer the scallop pieces to a dish. Shred, using a knife and fork or the fingers. Be sure to pick out and discard the hard muscles, which are whole and easily recognizable. Return the shredded scallops to the saucepan.

4. Stack the bamboo slices, a few at a time, and cut into very thin strips similar to the length of the scallops. Add to the saucepan. (The procedure up to this point can be done several hours in advance.)

5. Just before serving, bring the soup to a gentle simmer. Add the salt and well-stirred dissolved potato flour, stirring as it thickens.

6. Slowly pour in the beaten egg, either between the gap of 2 chopsticks or along the back of a fork, moving the chopsticks or fork in a circular motion at the same time. Remove from the heat and cover for 45 seconds, to allow the egg to set in tender flakes.

7. Transfer to a warm soup tureen or individual soup bowls and serve.

Note: The soup can be reheated over moderate heat.

INGREDIENTS

10 dried scallops, about 4 ounces)
4 ounces canned bamboo shoots, thinly sliced
½ teaspoon salt
2 tablespoons potato flour, dissolved in 4 tablespoons water
1 large egg, lightly beaten with ¼ teaspoon salt

Serves 4 to 6

Illustrated on page 57

Bird's Nest Soup

雞
茸
燕
窩

INGREDIENTS
4 ounces loose bird's nest
4 thickish slices fresh ginger root,
   peeled
2 large scallions
2 to 2½ pints prime stock (see
   page 225)
2 tablespoons cornstarch,
   dissolved in 2 tablespoons
   water
salt to taste
½ to 1 quantity chicken velvet
   (see page 63)
1 ounce best ham, ideally Chinua
   or Virginia, chopped finely

Serves 10

Illustrated opposite

*Like shark's fin soup, bird's nest soup reaches the heights of
Chinese cuisine, though Westerners are often put off by the name
and the fact that is is produced by swallows' saliva. Alone, bird's
nest is bland, and its function is to provide texture, rather than
taste, to the soup. A very rich, prime stock is therefore essential as
a base, as is the chicken velvet. And yet, without the bird's nest, no
amount of prime stock or chicken velvet could produce the unique
quality of this soup.*

1. Soak the bird's nest in about 2½ pints of tepid water for several
hours or overnight. Drain through a fine sieve. It will have increased
about 4 times in weight.

2. With a pair of tweezers, remove any feathers or other impurities.
Depending on the quality of the bird's nest, this can be a
time-consuming task. Rinse in cold water 2 or 3 times and drain.

3. Put into a saucepan, add the ginger, scallions and about 6 cups
of boiling water. Return to a boil, then simmer for 10 minutes.
Remove and discard the ginger and scallions. Drain but leave damp.
(The bird's nest can now be left in the refrigerator, covered, for 2 or
3 days before making the soup.)

4. Put the bird's nest and prime stock into a large saucepan and
bring to a gentle simmer. Stir in the dissolved cornstarch and let the
soup thicken. Add salt to taste.

5. Stir about 2 ladles of hot soup into the chicken velvet to make the
purée thinner. Slowly pour into the simmering soup, stirring to
make a smooth consistency. Continue to simmer until the chicken is
cooked.

6. Transfer to a warm soup tureen. Sprinkle the chopped ham on
top in the center. Serve hot.

Note: Any leftover soup can be frozen.

Facing page, clockwise from the top: Bird's nest soup (see above);
Shredded ham and bean sprouts, mustard and vinegar for Shark's fin
soup; Shark's fin soup (see page 62)

Shark's Fin Soup

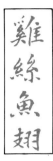

INGREDIENTS

11 to 12 ounces loose shark's fin
5 ounces chicken breast meat
4 slices fresh ginger root, each
   abut ¼ inch thick
3 large scallions, halved crosswise
1 ounce lard
3 tablespoons Shaohsing wine or
   medium-dry sherry
1 tablespoon peanut or corn oil
2¼ to 2½ pints prime stock (see
   page 225)
salt to taste
thin soy sauce to taste

FOR THE MARINADE

½ teaspoon salt
¼ teaspoon sugar
3 to 4 turns white pepper mill
1 teaspoon Shaohsing wine or
   medium-dry sherry
1 teaspoon cornstarch
1½ tablespoons egg white, lightly
   beaten
1 tablespoon peanut or corn oil

FOR THE SAUCE

3 to 4 tablespoons water chestnut
   flour or potato flour
3 tablespoons water
2 teaspoons thick soy sauce

TO SERVE

2 ounces lean ham, Virginia or
   Chinhua
8 ounces bean sprouts
Chinese red vinegar
hot prepared mustard

Serves 6

Illustrated on page 61

The Chinese are unanimous in their appreciation of shark's fin soup, and this very nutritious soup is rightly considered to be one of the most exotic examples of Chinese cuisine. A fin of the best quality is, however, extremely expensive and takes four days to prepare. The fin used in this recipe is sold in a package consisting of the cartilage with some fin needles and is already processed and then dried again. By itself, shark's fin has little taste, but when combined with other ingredients in a prime stock, it makes the perfect soup.

1. Put the shark's fin in a large container and pour over it about 2½ pints of hot water. Soak overnight or for a minimum of 6 hours.

2. Rub with fingers. Drain through a fine sieve, so as not to lose any of the precious shark's fin needles while getting rid of fine sand. Repeat as many times as necessary. Put into a large saucepan.

3. Add about 3 pints of water. Bring to a boil and simmer gently for about 2 hours, replenishing the water if it evaporates too quickly.

4. Test to see if the fin needles are ready: they should be tender yet still firm. A way to test is to press one between thumb and index finger: if it breaks easily, it is ready. Drain. If the fin is still hard, let the water cool, then drain. Return to the saucepan, add the same amount of water and boil gently for another hour, or longer. Drain, taking care not to lose the needles.

5. Meanwhile, cut the chicken into matchstick-sized pieces. Put into a small bowl.

6. *Prepare the marinade:* Add the salt, sugar, pepper, wine or sherry and cornstarch to the chicken. Stir in the egg white in the same direction and let marinate for 20 to 30 minutes. Blend in the oil.

7. Place about 1¾ pints of water in a saucepan with the ginger, scallions, half the lard and 2 tablespoons of the wine or sherry. Bring to a boil. Add the shark's fin and boil gently for about 15 minutes. This curing process rids the fin of any remaining rank odor. Drain, discarding the ginger and scallion.

8. Cut the ham into matchstick-sized pieces.

9. Pluck the bean heads off the bean sprouts and discard them. Blanch in boiling water until the water returns to a boil. Drain, then refresh under cold running water. Drain thoroughly.

10. Arrange the ham and bean sprouts in bunches on 1 or 2 small serving dishes. Put the vinegar and mustard into separate saucers on the table.

11. *Prepare the sauce:* Mix the flour, water and soy sauce thoroughly.

12. Heat a wok or saucepan over high heat until hot. Splash in the remaining wine or sherry. As it sizzles, add the remaining lard and the oil. Pour in the prime stock, add the shark's fin and stir to mix. Slowly bring to a boil, then add the chicken, stirring to separate the pieces. Reduce the heat. Gradually add the well-stirred sauce to the soup, stiring as the soup thickens. Remove from the heat. Taste for seasoning; add salt and thin soy sauce, if necessary.

13. Transfer to a warm soup tureen and serve. To eat, each person puts some bean sprouts and ham into his bowl before adding the shark's fin soup. Some may also like to add a little vinegar or mustard to the soup.

Chicken Velvet

A preparation of finely minced chicken breast, which is made light and fluffy by the addition of egg white. It is used to add taste, texture and substance to soups, such as winter melon soup (see page 65) and bird's nest soup (see page 60).

1. Turn the chicken breasts inside out and pull off the 2 fillets.

2. Hold the end of the white tendon of each fillet with the fingers of one hand and scrape the flesh away from it with a Chinese cleaver or knife. Discard the tendons.

3. Holding the large end of one chicken breast, scrape the flesh, going with the grain, from the small end all the way to the large end, discarding membranes and fat as you go. Repeat with the other breast and then with the 2 fillets.

4. Gather the chicken pieces, sprinkle with the salt and start chopping, adding drops of ice water and folding the pieces back to the center from time to time. Chop for about 3 minutes, or until the chicken is very finely minced.

5. Transfer the meat to a bowl. Blend in the cornstarch and egg white, and stir until a light purée – the velvet – is achieved. This can be refrigerated, covered, for a few hours before it is used.

Note: Steps 3 and 4 can be done in a food processor or blender, adding all the ice water and salt to the roughly cut-up chicken breast before mincing.

INGREDIENTS
2 chicken breasts, about 1 pound
    skinned and boned
½ teaspoon salt
2 teaspoons ice water
2 teaspoons cornstarch
1 egg white, lightly beaten

Sweet-Corn Soup

雞茸粟米湯

INGREDIENTS

1 chicken breast, 6 ounces
  skinned and boned, or 4
  ounces chicken fillet
8- to 10-ounce can sweet-corn
  kernels, drained
1 or 2 eggs
¼ teaspoon salt
2 teaspoons peanut or corn oil
10¾-ounce can condensed cream
  of chicken soup
3 soup cans cold water
8- to 10-ounce can cream-style
  sweet-corn

FOR THE MARINADE

¼ teaspoon salt
2 teaspoons thin soy sauce
6 turns white pepper mill
1 tablespoon Shaohsing wine or
  medium-dry sherry
1 teaspoon cornstarch
4 tablespoons water
1 teaspoon sesame oil
1 teaspoon peanut or corn oil

Serves 6 to 8

Illustrated on page 67

This Cantonese soup, like sweet and sour pork, is tremendously popular with non-Chinese, especially Westerners. Canned products are used here for labor-saving purposes. The soup will still be delicious if you want to make it very simple and omit the chicken.

1. Mince the chicken finely in a food processor or mincer. Put into a bowl.

2. *Prepare the marinade:* Add the salt, soy sauce, pepper and wine or sherry to the chicken. Sprinkle with the cornstarch and stir in the water, 1 tablespoon at a time, until the chicken becomes a smooth paste. Let stand for 15 minutes. Blend in the oils.

3. Roughly chop the sweet-corn kernels in a food processor or blender, or by hand. (They can be left whole).

4. In a small bowl, beat the eggs lightly with the salt and oil. Set aside.

5. Pour the marinade into a large saucepan and add the cold water gradually, stirring with a wooden spoon until smooth.

6. Stir in the sweet-corn kernels and cream-style sweet corn.

7. Bring the soup mixture to just below boiling point over moderate heat, stirring occasionally.

8. Combine about 6 tablespoons of the hot soup liquid with the chicken paste, breaking up any lumps. Add to the rest of the soup, stirring in well, and gradually bring to the boil. Simmer for 1 minute, to make sure that the chicken is cooked.

9. Slowly pour in the beaten egg through the gap of a pair of chopsticks or along the back of a fork, moving the chopsticks or fork in a circular motion at the same time. Remove from the heat and cover for 45 seconds, to allow the egg to set in tender flakes. Give the soup a final stir and then serve hot.

Note: Leftover soup can be reheated; it can also be frozen. Instead of condensed soup, 1¾ pints clear stock (see page 225) can be used, with 2 cans of cream-style sweet corn and only 2 cans of water.

Winter Melon and Chicken Velvet Soup

In Hong Kong and China, some restaurants specialize in a very sophisticated dish, Winter Melon Pond. A whole winter melon of the perfect size is partially hollowed, filled with such delicacies as crab meat, diced duck, pork, Chinese mushrooms and bamboo shoots and then steamed for hours to produce the most delectable soup. But it is not a practical dish to make at home. This recipe, however, is, and the melon is succulent in the soup.

1. Cut the winter melon into pieces that are easy to work with. Seed only, leaving the pulpy flesh alone. Cut off the hard skin and discard. Dice all the pieces, including the pulpy parts.

2. Put the winter melon and stock in a large saucepan and bring to a boil. Lower the heat and simmer, covered, for about 25 to 30 minutes, or until the melon is tender and looks transparent.

3. Put the chicken velvet into a bowl and add several spoonfuls of boiling broth. Stir to blend, then pour into the boiling soup. Stir the soup to break up any lumps of the chicken velvet as it cooks and turns opaque. Taste, and add salt if necessary.

4. Pour the soup into a large warm soup tureen, sprinkle with the ham and serve.

Note: If desired, about 8 ounces cooked white crab meat can be added to the soup at the end of step 3. Fuzzy melon, though not the traditional ingredient for this soup, is a satisfactory substitute.

INGREDIENTS

1 small winter melon or part of a large one, about 2¾ to 3 pounds
2 pints prime stock (see page 225)
1 quantity chicken velvet (see page 63)
salt to taste
2 ounces best ham, ideally Chinhua or Virginia, chopped finely

Serves 8

Illustrated on page 67

冬瓜雞茸湯

Wonton Wrapper Crisps Soup

片兒麵湯

INGREDIENTS

peanut or corn oil for deep-frying
60 wonton wrappers, halved and
    folded in 2
8 ounces Cantonese roast duck
    with some skin, diced (see page
    209)
10 ounces cooked crab meat,
    broken into chunks
4 ounces canned bamboo shoots,
    sliced or diced thin
8 ounces canned straw
    mushroom, drained and
    halved or quartered
4½ pints prime or clear stock
    (see page 225)
1 to 2 teaspoons salt
pepper to taste
1 to 2 tablespoons thin soy sauce
12 scallions, cut diagonally into
    ½-inch pieces, white and green
    parts separated

Serves 10 to 12

Illustrated opposite

*The tender wonton wrappers, deep-fried to a crisp before being
dunked in the soup, lend special character to this dish. The color of
the ingredients, suspended in the clear soup, is especially attractive.*

1. Half fill a wok or a deep fryer with oil. Heat to a temperature of
about 350°F, or until a cube of stale bread browns in 60 seconds.
Add a batch of wonton wrappers, about 20 at a time; they will sizzle
and expand at once. Transfer to paper towels before they turn
brown, using a hand strainer or perforated spoon. Repeat until all
are done.

2. Put the duck, crab meat, bamboo shoots and straw mushrooms
into the stock and bring to a boil. Add the salt, pepper and soy
sauce. Add the white scallions and, finally, the wonton wrappers. (It
is always better to add the wonton wrappers at the last moment so
that they retain their crispness.) Dunk them with a wooden spoon.
Remove from the heat and add the green scallions.

3. Serve immediately, either from a communal bowl or in individual
bowls.

Note: Wonton wrappers can be deep-fried ahead of time and, if
kept in an airtight container, will remain crisp for more than a
week. With some salt sprinkled on them, they are quite a novelty to
serve with drinks. Cantonese roast duck (page 209), is available in
some Cantonese restaurants, whole or in portions.

Facing page, clockwise from the top: Wonton wrapper crisps soup (see
above); Cantonese wonton soup (see page 68); Sweet Corn soup (see page
64); Winter melon and chicken velvet soup (page 65)

Cantonese Wonton Soup

INGREDIENTS

12 ounces pork, with about 2
    ounces fat
4 ounces raw shelled shrimp
6 scallions, cut into tiny rounds
2 to 3 ounces canned bamboo
    shoots, chopped fine
1 egg yolk
90 wonton wrappers, each about
    3 inches square
1 egg white, lightly beaten
salt
6 to 8 leaves romaine lettuce or
    Chinese celery cabbage,
    shredded crosswise into 1-inch
    pieces
1½ quarts prime and clear
    stocks, mixed together (see
    page 225)
16 teaspoons peanut or corn oil

FOR THE MARINADE

1 teaspoon salt
½ teaspoon sugar
1 tablespoon thin soy sauce
1 teaspoon thick soy sauce
10 turns freshly milled black
    pepper
1½ teaspoons Shaohsing wine or
    medium-dry sherry
1 teaspoon potato flour
3 to 4 tablespoons water
2 teaspoons sesame oil

TO SERVE

freshly ground pepper
sesame oil
thin soy sauce

*Makes 80 to 90 wontons; serves
    8 as lunch*

Illustrated on page 67

*Wontons, or small dumplings, served in broth, are a national
Chinese snack. The main ingredient for wonton filling is pork, but
in Kwangtung shrimp and prawns are also used, because they are
so readily available. This addition gives the wontons a much more
interesting taste and texture.*

1. Chop the pork by hand or mince it. Put into a large bowl.

2. Pat dry the shrimp. Cut into the size of small peas and add to the
pork.

3. *Prepare the marinade:* Add the salt, sugar, soy sauces, pepper,
wine or sherry and potato flour to the pork. Stir in the water, 1
tablespoon at a time.

4. Pick up the pork mixture with one or both hands and throw it
back into the bowl or onto a flat surface. Repeat this action about
100 times to achieve the desired light and yet firm texture.

5. Add half the scallions and all the bamboo shoots to the pork
mixture, mix well and let marinate for 20 to 30 minutes. Then blend
in the sesame oil.

6. Just before ready to wrap the wontons, stir in the egg yolk,
which will bind the filling to the wrappers.

7. Wrap the wontons. There are 2 ways to do this:

a.   *The quick way:* Put about 1 teaspoon of filling in the center of
1 wrapper placed on the palm of the hand. Gather together the
corners of the wrapper with the other hand and give it a twist in he
middle to secure the wrapping. Repeat until all the filling is used up.

a   b

b   *The classic way:* Put about 1 teaspoon of filling in the center
of 1 wrapper placed at an angle, like a diamond, on the palm of the
hand or on a surface. Fold the bottom half upward to make a
triangle, then turn the triangle to point toward you. Fold the 2 side

corners backward and, using one finger, smear a little egg white on one corner and put the other corner on top, pressing to secure them. Turn up the front flaps to make the wonton look like a hat.

c

d

e

f

g

h

8. Bring a large saucepan of salted water to a boil. Blanch the lettuce or cabbage for about 1 minute, remove with a hand strainer or perforated spoon and transfer to a bowl.

9. Put the stock in another saucepan and bring to simmering point.

10. Bring the water in the large saucepan to a boil again. Plunge in the wontons, no more than 20 at a time, and return to a boil, stirring gently to separate them. Continue to boil, uncovered, for about 3 minutes, or until the wontons are cooked and float to the surface.

11. Transfer with a hand strainer to individual serving bowls, allowing about 10 wontons per bowl. To each bowl, add a pinch of the remaining scallions, a few pieces of lettuce or cabbage and 2 teaspoons of oil, and then pour a ladleful of stock (about 6 ounces) over it. Everyone can help themselves to ground pepper, sesame oil and soy sauce placed on the table.

Note: Wontons freeze well and can therefore be made in advance up to step 8 and frozen. Make sure, however, to cook the defrosted wontons a little longer in the boiling water.

Varation: Wonton soup can also be served with cooked egg noodles in the stock. Allow fewer wontons per bowl when served in this way.

Cantonese Fire Pot

打邊爐

INGREDIENTS

12 ounces to 1 pound fresh or
   frozen medium raw prawns in
   the shell, without heads
1 Dover sole, or sea bass, about 1
   pound, skinned and boned
10 large scallops, white meat only
2 chicken breasts, skinned and
   boned
12 ounces to 1 pound beef, rump,
   skirt steak or fillet
1 pound Chinese celery cabbage
1 large romaine lettuce
1 pound spinach, washed and
   trimmed
1 bunch watercress, washed and
   trimmed
4 cakes bean curd
1 pound dried egg noodles or 1½
   pounds fresh noodles
about 4 to 5 pints clear stock
peanut or corn oil

FOR THE DIPS

8 eggs
thick or thin soy sauce
peanut, corn or sesame oil
salt
freshly ground black pepper
hot prepared mustard
chili sauce

Serves 8 as dinner

Illustrated opposite

A Cantonese fire pot reflects what's easily available in the region, and it therefore consists of seafood as well as meat and vegetables. If you don't have a traditional charcoal-burning fire pot for cooking at the table, use a fondue set or heatproof bowl and burner or an electric pot.

1. Shell and devein the prawns (see page 39). Halve lengthwise.

2. Cut the fish fillets across into 1 inch pieces.

3. Wash and pat dry the scallops. Remove and discard the hard muscles. Place each one on its side and cut into 3 or 4 pieces.

4. Cut the chicken into thin slices, about ⅛ inch thick.

5. Cut the beef across the grain into slices abut 2 by 1½ inches and ¼ inch thick.

6. Cut each Chinese celery cabbage stalk across at about 1-inch intervals.

7. Break up the lettuce leaves into large pieces.

8. Steep the bean curd in hot water for 15 minutes. Drain, handling with care. Cut each into 8 pieces.

9. Bring a large pan of water to a boil. Add the noodles, return to a boil and continue to cook for a few minutes, or until *al dente*. Pour into a colander and refresh under cold running water. Drain thoroughly.

10. Arrange all the ingredients on individual plates or together on several plates. The meat and seafood slices can be laid overlapping each other. Put on the table.

11. Arrange all the dips in small dishes and put on the table, reserving the center for the fire pot.

12. To serve, provide each person with one bowl and a side plate, one pair of bamboo chopsticks and one small wire strainer.

13. Crack 1 egg into each bowl and beat lightly. Pour 2 teaspoons of soy sauce on each saucer and add ½ teaspoon of oil. This can be replenished by individuals later.

14. Have the stock simmering in a saucepan.

Facing page, top left to right: Lamb for Mongolian fire pot (see page 72); buckwheat and cellophane noodles; Chinese celery cabbage; coriander leaves; scallions; sesame paste dip. *Bottom left to right:* prawns, white fish and scallops for Cantonese fire pot (see above); bean curd and fresh noodles; lettuce and Chinese celery cabbage; egg, mustard, chili sauce, pepper, salt, sesame oil; soy sauce; beef and chicken. *Center:* traditional fire pot with stock and strainers

15. If a traditional fire pot is used, heat the charcoal and put into the chimney in the middle of the pot. Put on the table on top of a thick heatproof mat. An electric pot may be used. In either case, pour sufficient stock into the heated pot to come about halfway up the sides, and bring back to a boil. Add about 3 tablespoons of oil.

16. To eat, everyone picks up one or two morsels of either meat or seafood, places them in the strainer and then lowers it into the fire pot to cook. If you have no strainers, chopsticks can be used to hold and dip the food into the boiling stock to cook. The food is removed after a few seconds, or as soon as it is cooked, dipped into the egg and seasoned with the other condiments before eating. (If you dislike the raw egg idea, dispense with it.)

17. When a fair amount of meat and seafood has been eaten, put the vegetables and the bean curd, in stages, into the pot. Let everyone help themselves from the pot.

18. Whenever necessary, replenish the stock level with more stock or water. Add more oil and bring to a boil again before cooking more food in the pot.

19. When most of the dishes, vegetables and bean curd have been eaten and the broth is getting richer and richer, add the noodles. The broth and noodles can then be enjoyed by everyone.

Mongolian Lamb Fire Pot

This Mongolian dish, which has long since become part and parcel of Peking food, ranks second in fame only to Peking duck (see page 209).

1. Ask the butcher to bone the lamb for you. If possible, freeze for 3 or 4 hours, so that the meat becomes firm and easier to cut into paper-thin slices.

2. Meanwhile, soak the cellophane noodles in plenty of boiling water in a bowl, for a minimum of 20 to 30 minutes, so they expand. Drain. Make 2 or 3 cuts with scissors to shorten them. Transfer to a serving bowl.

3. Slice the celery cabbage at 1-inch intervals. Put on a plate.

4. Plunge the noodles into plenty of boiling water, return to a boil, then continue to cook for several minutes, until they are soft yet *al dente*. Drain and rinse under cold running water. Put on a plate or into as bowl.

5. *Prepare the dip:* Put the sesame paste into a fairly large serving bowl and gradually add about 4 ounces of water to dilute, stirring until smoothly blended. Add 3 or 4 tablespoons of water to the red bean curd and blend to a creamy consistency. Pour into the

INGREDIENTS

½ leg of lamb, ideally, spring lamb, about 2½ pounds
4 ounces cellophane noodles
1 Chinese celery cabbage, about 1¾ pounds, trimmed
8 ounces dried egg or buckwheat noodles

FOR THE DIP

8 tablespoons sesame paste, well stirred in the jar
2 cakes fermented red bean curd or about 4 tablespoons and 2 tablespoons own juice
6 tablespoons Shaohsing wine or medium-dry sherry
3 tablespoons sugar
8 tablespoons thin soy sauce
3 to 4 tablespoons hot chili oil (see page 225)
3 to 4 tablespoons sesame oil
4 tablespoons fish sauce

serving bowl, then add the wine or sherry, sugar, soy sauce, the oils and fish sauce and stir until well mixed.

6. Take the lamb out of the freezer. Trim excess fat and cut into slices, as paper-thin as you can possibly manage. Ideally, each slice should be about 4 by 1½ inches. Arrage them on several serving plates in single layers but overlapping each other. Refrigerate, covered, until ready to eat.

7. Put all the ingredients on the dining table.

8. If a traditional fire pot is used, heat the charcoal and put into the chimney in the middle of the pot. Put on the table on top of a thick heatproof mat. An electric pot may be used. In either case, pour boiling water into the heated pot to come about halfway up the sides, and bring back to a boil. The feast is now ready.

9. To serve, provide each person with a pair of bamboo chopsticks (not plastic or lacquered ones), a small wire strainer made especially for fire-pot feasts (optional), a bowl and a small plate.

10. To eat, each person spoons some sauce into his bowl and adds some coriander leaves and scallions. Everyone then picks up 1 or 2 slices of lamb at a time, puts them into the strainer (or uses chopsticks) and immerses them in the water in the pot. The meat is removed after a few seconds (or longer if very well-done meat is preferred) and dipped into the sauce before eating.

11. After about half of the lamb has been consumed and the water in the pot has become a tasty broth, put in some of the cabbage and cellophane noodles for everyone to share. They are dipped into the sauce before eating. Whenever necessary, replenish the water level in the pot.

12. After about three-quarters of the lamb has been consumed, put in half or all of the remaining noodles.

13. At the end of the feast, the broth in the pot is shared. Each person spoons some into his bowl, mixes it with the remaining sauce and drinks it.

4 ounces coriander leaves, chopped into small pieces
10 or 12 large scallions, cut into small rounds

Serves 6 as dinner

Illustrated on page 71

四川菜

A Western or Szechwan Menu

This menu for eight, with its delicious tastes and aftertastes, offers the full spectrum of Szechwan flavors, from spicy and numbing to *salty, sweet and vinegary. The dishes can be prepared and enjoyed individually, or two or three at a sitting.*

银丝卷 **Silver thread buns**
Steamed buns, always served with Fragrant and crispy duck (see page 201).

荷叶夹 **Lotus leaf buns**
Steamed buns for Fragrant duck (see page 200).

香酥鸭 **Fragrant and crispy duck**
Marinated and steamed before being deep-fried, the meat in this dish simply melts off the bone (see page 200).

酸
辣
湯

Hot and sour soup
Spicy-hot soup with pork, mushrooms and bean curd (see page 202).

魚
香
肉
絲

Fish fragrant shredded pork
Finely sliced pork combined with chili paste, garlic, ginger and scallions (see page 203).

乾
煸
四
季
豆

Dry-fried four-season beans
Delicious hot or cold, this dish combines deep-fried beans with a tangy flavoring (see page 203).

棒
棒
雞

Pang pang chicken
Peppery-hot dish served cold with cucumber and scallions (see page 204).

FISH AND SEAFOOD

Sautéed Mackerel

INGREDIENTS
1 large mackerel, about 1½ to
  1¾ pounds, cleaned, with
  head left on
½ teaspoon salt
8 ounces peanut or corn oil
6 thin slices fresh ginger root,
  peeled
½ inch fresh ginger root, peeled
  and cut into silken threads (see
  page 35)
4 to 6 scallions cut into small
  rounds

FOR THE SAUCE
1 tablespoon thin soy sauce
1 tablespoon thick soy sauce
½ teaspoon sugar
2 teaspoons Shaohsing wine or
  medium-dry sherry

*Serves 2 as main course; 4 with 2
  other dishes*

Illustrated opposite

*To sauté or shallow-fry is one of the basic Chinese methods of
cooking fish; the technique is explained in this recipe for mackerel.
Another fish that lends itself to sautéing is pomfret, which abounds
off South China, India and Southeast Asia. Red snapper, red mullet
and whiting, among others, are also delicious sautéed.*

1. Halve the mackerel, which at this weight is probably long,
crosswise. Rub the salt all over the skin, crevices and cavity. Let
stand for about 15 minutes.

2. *Prepare the sauce:* Mix together the soy sauces, sugar and wine
or sherry.

3. Heat a wok or a heavy flat frying pan over high heat until smoke
rises. Pour in the oil, tip the wok carefully to swirl it around the
sloping edges, then pour all but about 3 tablespoons into a container.
Reheat the oil, add the ginger slices and fry until brown, then
discard. Lower the heat, wait until the oil is less hot and then add
both pieces of mackerel. Fry for about 5 minutes, to brown the skin.
Turn over and brown the other side for about 5 minutes. Turn over
again and continue to shallow-fry for about another 3 minutes,
adding about 1 tablespoon of oil around the edges of the fish. Repeat
with the other side.

4. Pour the sauce over the fish and sprinkle on the silken threads of
ginger. Cover and continue to cook for about 3 minutes. Sprinkle on
some of the scallions and cook, covered, for a few more seconds.
Transfer to a warm serving plate and pour the sauce from the wok
or frying pan over the fish.

5. Put the 2 pieces of mackerel side by side or join to form a
"whole" mackerel. Sprinkle the remaining scallions on top and
serve.

Facing page, from the top: Abalone with Chinese mushrooms (page 74);
Steamed prawns in mixed bean sauce (page 78); Sautéed mackerel (see
above)

Steamed Prawns in Mixed Bean Sauce

INGREDIENTS

12 ounces medium or large prawns in the shell, without heads

a few coriander leaves, torn into pieces

FOR THE SAUCE

1 tablespoon fermented black beans

1 tablespoon salted yellow beans

½ teaspoon sugar

1 teaspoon sesame oil

4 to 5 tablespoons peanut or corn oil

4 to 6 cloves garlic, peeled and chopped fine

½ to ¾ inch fresh ginger root, peeled and chopped fine

½ to 1 fresh green or red chili, seeded and sliced into tiny rounds

1 to 1½ tablespoons Shaohsing wine or medium-dry sherry

Serves 4 to 6 with 2 or 3 other dishes

Illustrated on page 77

I first tasted this dish in 1980 in one of the famous restaurants of my hometown, Hong Kong, and thought it tasted heavenly. There was no question of their letting me into their cookery secret, so I experimented and came up with this concoction. I think you will enjoy it, too.

1. *Prepare the sauce:* Mash the black beans and salted yellow beans together with the sugar and sesame oil into a paste.

2. Heat a wok over high heat until smoke rises. Add the oil and swirl it around. Add the garlic, and as soon as it takes on color, put in the ginger. Stir. Quickly add the mashed bean paste, stir well, and then add the chili. Splash in the wine or sherry around the side of the wok. As soon as the sizzling dies down, lower the heat, stir well and then pour the sauce into a container and allow to cool.

3. Remove and discard the prawn legs. Pat dry. Split lengthwise into 2, except for the tails (a). Discard the veins (b). Arrange around a heatproof serving dish with a slightly raised edge.

a   b

4. Spoon the sauce on the prawns, scraping up every bit of oil as well.

5. Steam in a wok or steamer, over moderately high heat for 3 or 4 minutes (see page 44). Check to see if the prawns are cooked. Scatter the coriander leaves over the prawns. Replace the lid and steam for a brief moment, to cook the coriander leaves partially.

6. Remove from the heat and again spoon the sauce on the prawns and coriander leaves. Serve immediately from the dish in which they were cooked.

Abalone with Chinese Mushrooms

Dried abalone, which ranks with shark's fin and bird's nest in gastronomic prestige, is sadly out of the question for most people's pockets; these days canned abalone graces even the best tables. Although it lacks the depth of taste found in dried abalone, its subtle taste and slightly chewy texture satisfy the palate of many a gourmet.

1. Put the mushrooms in a saucepan and pour over them 1½ pints of boiling water. Return to a boil, then lower the heat and simmer for 1 hour, until tender. When cool, clip off the stems and discard. Squeeze out excess water but leave damp. (They can be prepared hours ahead of time.)

2. Tear the lettuce leaves into large pieces.

3. Drain the abalone, reserving the juice. Slice it into pieces about ⅛ inch thick.

4. Pour the can juice into a saucepan, add 1 tablespoon of the oil and bring to a boil. Immerse the lettuce in it, return to a boil and cook for 1 minute; the lettuce will be cooked yet still crisp. Transfer with a perforated spoon to a sieve placed over a bowl, so that it will continue to drain. Pour the drained stock back into the saucepan.

5. Heat a wok over high heat until smoke rises. Add the remaining oil and swirl it around. Add the white scallions and stir a couple of times. Splash in the Shaohsing wine or sherry around the side of the wok, then add the stock saved from the lettuce, the oyster sauce, thick soy sauce, to enhance the coloring, and sugar. Bring to a boil.

6. Add the mushrooms and abalone and slowly return to a boil. Cover, lower the heat and simmer for about 2 minutes, to let the abalone and mushrooms absorb the flavor.

7. Spread the lettuce on a warm serving plate.

8. Trickle the well-stirred dissolved potato flour into the sauce, stirring as it thickens. Tip in the green scallions.

9. Transfer the ingredients to the serving plate, arranging the mushrooms on the lettuce, cap side up, then the abalone. Pour the sauce over them. Serve hot.

INGREDIENTS

16 dried Chinese mushrooms (the thick and floral ones are best), washed

1 medium iceberg lettuce, washed and trimmed

1 can best abalone, 15 to 16 ounces

drained can juice from abalone

5 tablespoons peanut or corn oil

3 scallions, cut into 1-inch sections, white and green parts separated

1 tablespoon Shaohsing wine or medium-dry sherry

3 tablespoons oyster sauce

1½ teaspoons thick soy sauce

½ teaspoon sugar

1 tablespoon potato flour, dissolved in 2 tablespoons water

Serves 4 with 2 other dishes

Illustrated on page 77

鮑
魚
燜
冬
菇

One Fish for Two Dishes:

Stir-fried Fish Fillet

INGREDIENTS

1 pound 2 ounces to 1¼ pounds
    fillet from 1 small halibut
    weighing 2¾ to 3 pounds
salt
peanut or corn oil for deep-frying
8 ounces sugar peas, trimmed
2 cloves garlic, peeled and cut
    diagonally into slivers
6 thin slivers fresh ginger root,
    peeled
1 or 2 shallots, skinned and
    chopped
1 tablespoon Shaohsing wine or
    medium-dry sherry

FOR THE MARINADE

1 inch fresh ginger root, peeled
    and chopped fine
¼ teaspoon salt
¼ teaspoon sugar
6 turns white pepper mill
1 teaspoon Shaohsing wine or
    medium-dry sherry
1½ teaspoon cornstarch
1 tablespoon egg white, lightly
    beaten

FOR THE SAUCE

½ teaspoon potato flour
3 tablespoons clear stock
2 tablespoons oyster sauce
1 teaspoon thin soy sauce

*Serves 4 to 5 with the soup and 2
other dishes*

*When a fish of firm texture is large enough, the Chinese often make
two dishes out of it: stir-frying the fillet and making a soup with the
head and carcass. This practice is especially common in the South
of China, where the yield from the sea enriches the table with such
delicious fish as grouper and perch. Small turbot and other flat fish
are also suitable for this purpose.*

1. Ask the fishdealer to fillet the halibut for you, removing the skin
as well. Take the head and carcass home to make soup (see following
recipe).

2. Pat the fillet dry. Cut into pieces of similar size, about 1 by 1½
inches (a) and (b). Put into a dish.

a   b

3. *Prepare the marinade:* Put the chopped ginger in a garlic press
in 2 batches with 2 drops of water each time and squeeze the juice
over the fish. Discard the pulp. Add the salt, sugar, pepper, wine or
sherry, cornstarch and egg white to the fish. Mix well to coat. Let
marinate for 15 minutes.

4. *Prepare the sauce:* Mix together the potato flour, stock, oyster
sauce and soy sauce.

5. Bring a large pan of water to a boil. Add 1 teaspoon of salt and
1 tablespoon of oil. Plunge in the sugar peas and, once the water
returns to a boil, pour into a colander and refresh under cold
running water. Drain thoroughly.

6. Half fill a wok or deep fryer with oil. Heat to a temperature of
350°F or until a cube of stale bread browns in 60 seconds. Let the
fish "go through the oil" carefully for about 10 seconds, using a pair
of long chopsticks to separate the pieces. With a large hand strainer,
quickly transfer to a dish. The fillet is now half cooked.

7. Pour the oil into a container to be used again, leaving only about 3 tablespoons in the wok.

8. Reheat the oil over high heat. Add the garlic and, as it sizzles, add the ginger slices and shallots and stir for a few seconds, to release their aroma. Return the fish to the wok and toss and turn for about 30 seconds, or until very hot. Splash in the wine or sherry around the side of the wok, continuing to turn and stir as it sizzles. Pour in the well-mixed sauce, stirring as it thickens. Return the sugar peas to the wok; turn and toss to mix. Transfer the fish mixture to a warm serving plate. Serve immediately.

Note: Other vegetables, like broccoli, Chinese broccoli or fresh mushrooms, can also be used as complementary ingredients to the fish.

Bean Curd Soup with Fish Stock

1. Wash the fish head and carcass thoroughly. Put into a large saucepan.

2. Add the water, ginger and scallions, and bring to a boil. Skim off the scum that surfaces. Reduce the heat to maintain a fast simmer for 30 minutes. Drain and discard all the solids. Season with salt.

3. Meanwhile, slice the pork into thin slivers. Put into a bowl.

4. *Prepare the marinade:* Add the salt, sugar, soy sauce, pepper, wine or sherry, potato flour and water to the pork. Stir to coat. Let marinate for 15 minutes. Blend in the oil.

5. Slice the bean curd into thin strips or pieces of the same size.

6. Return the fish stock to a boil. Add the oil. Add the bean curd and sugar peas and bring to a boil again. Add the pork, using a pair of chopsticks or a fork to separate the pieces. Reduce the heat and simmer for 1 or 2 minutes, depending on the thickness of the pork.

7. Remove from the heat. Add the scallions.

8. Transfer to a warm soup tureen or individual bowls and serve piping hot.

INGREDIENTS

1 pound 10 ounces to 1¾ pound
    head and carcass of 1 small
    halibut
2 pints water
1 inch fresh ginger root, peeled
    and bruised
2 large scallions, quartered
½ teaspoon salt
4 ounces lean pork
2 cakes bean curd, drained
2 tablespoons peanut or corn oil
1 ounce sugar peas, trimmed (or
    blanched small green peas
2 or 3 scallions, green parts only,
    cut into small rounds

FOR THE MARINADE

½ teaspoon salt
¼ teaspoon sugar
2 teaspoons thin soy sauce
3 or 4 turns white pepper mill
2 teaspoons Shaohsing wine or
    medium-dry sherry
½ teaspoon potato flour
1 tablespoon water
1 tablespoon peanut or corn oil

Serves 4 to 5 with the stir-fried
*   fillet and 2 other dishes*

Illustrated on page 83

Braised Fish Hunan-Szechwan Style

乾
煸
鱸
魚

INGREDIENTS

1 sea bass, gray mullet or trout, about 1 pound 6 ounces to 1 pound 8 ounces, cleaned, with head left on
½ teaspoon salt
8 ounces peanut or corn oil
3 or 4 cloves garlic, peeled and chopped fine
1 inch fresh ginger root, peeled and chopped fine
2 to 4 tablespoons Szechwan chili paste (see page 226) or hot soybean paste
1 tablespoon Shaohsing wine or medium-dry sherry
½ teaspoon sugar
4 ounces clear stock or water
1 tablespoon hot chili oil (see page 225)
6 to 8 scallions, green parts only, cut into small rounds

Serves 4 with 2 other dishes

Illustrated opposite

The essence of this dish is the gradual absorption of the Szechwan chili paste, a favorite seasoning in Hunan-Szechwan cuisine. The dish is made all the more aromatic by the addition of garlic and ginger.

1. Blot the fish dry. Rub salt all over it, including the cavity. Let stand for about 15 minutes.

2. Heat a wok over high heat until smoke rises. Pour in the oil. Tip the wok carefully to swirl it all around the sloping edges. Pour all but 2 tablespoons into a container.

3. Lower the heat. Add the fish at once and brown for about 2 minutes. Slip 2 metal spatulas underneath the fish and turn over carefully. Brown the other side for about 2 minutes. Transfer to a plate.

4 Turn up the heat. Add another 2 tablespoons of oil to the wok and heat until smoke rises. Now add the garlic and ginger and, as they sizzle, add the Szechwan chili or hot soybean paste, wine or sherry and sugar. Pour in the stock or water and bring to a boil, stirring to mix. Return the fish to the wok, lower the heat, cover and simmer in the sauce for 12 to 15 minutes. Turn the fish over carefully and simmer, covered, for another 12 to 15 minutes, until the fish is cooked and some of the sauce has been absorbed.

5. Remove the cover. Turn up the heat to reduce the sauce, spooning it over the fish continually. Transfer only the fish to a warm serving plate.

6. Add the hot chili oil to the sauce, then the scallions. Stir and cook for a few seconds, then scoop the sauce over the fish. Serve immediately.

Facing page, clockwise from the top: Bean curd soup with fish stock (page 81); Braised fish Hunan-Szechwan style (see above); Stir-fried scallops in oyster sauce (page 84); Stir-fried fish fillet (page 80)

Stir-fried Scallops in Oyster Sauce

INGREDIENTS

4 large dried Chinese
 mushrooms, reconstituted (see
 page 39)
10 to 12 large scallops, fresh or
 frozen
5 tablespoons peanut or corn oil
4 cloves garlic, peeled and
 chopped fine
6 thin slices fresh ginger root,
 peeled
4 scallions, cut into 1-inch
 sections, white and green parts
 separated
1 tablespoon Shaohsing wine or
 medium-dry sherry
4 to 6 sticks celery, cut diagonally
 into thin slices
sesame oil to taste

FOR THE MARINADE
white pepper to taste
1 teaspoon cornstarch
½ egg white, lightly beaten

FOR THE SAUCE
½ teaspoon potato flour
1 teaspoon water
¼ teaspoon salt
2 tablespoons oyster sauce
3 tablespoons juice from cooked
 scallops

*Serves 4 to 6 with 2 or 3 other
 dishes*

Illustrated on page 82

*Another classic Cantonese dish. You may think it gilding the lily to
add the sweet-tasting oyster sauce to the inherently sweet scallops,
but your palate will be delighted with the result.*

1. Drain and squeeze out excess water from the mushrooms but
leave damp. Quarter them.

2. Wash the scallops, remove and discard the hard muscle. Pat dry
and separate the corals from the scallops. Place each scallop on its
side and slice into 2 or 3 pieces. Pat dry again and put into a dish.
Halve the corals horizontally and put into another dish.

3. *Prepare the marinade:* Add the white pepper, half the
cornstarch and a little over half of the egg white to the scallops and
stir to coat. Add the remaining cornstarch and egg white to the
corals. Let marinate for 10 minutes.

4. *Prepare the sauce:* Dissolve the potato flour in the water. Stir in
the salt and oyster sauce and set aside.

5. Heat a wok over high heat until smoke rises. Add 2½ tablespoons
of the oil and swirl it around. Add half the garlic and, as soon as it
sizzles and takes on color, add half the ginger, then half the white
scallions. Stir and tip in the scallops immediately. Sliding the wok
scoop or metal spatula to the bottom of the wok, turn and toss for 30
to 60 seconds, or until the scallops are barely cooked, and have
become whitish. Splash half the wine or sherry around the side of
the wok and continue to stir. As soon as the sizzling dies down,
drain in a sieve placed over a bowl, to catch the juice that will
continue to drip from the scallops.

6. Add 1½ tablespoons of oil to the wok and swirl it around. Stir in
the rest of the garlic, ginger and white scallions. Add the coral and
stir and toss as before for about 1 minute. Splash the remaining
wine or sherry around the side of the wok, stir, cover, lower the
heat and cook for about 2 more minutes, or until the corals become
firm to the touch. Transfer to the sieve over the bowl. While the
corals are being cooked, add 3 tablespoons of scallop juice to the
sauce. Blend thoroughly and set aside.

7. Turn up the heat again, add the remaining 1 tablespoon of oil to
the wok and swirl it around. Tip in the celery, stir, and then add the
mushrooms. Stir and toss for 30 to 60 seconds; the celery should
remain crisp. Make a well; pour in the well-stirred sauce and when
it bubbles add the scallops and corals. Add the green scallions and
then transfer to a warm serving plate. Sprinkle on some sesame oil
to enhance the flavor. Serve immediately.

Deep-fried Fish with Sweet and Sour Sauce

A sweet and sour sauce goes especially well with deep-fried food, not just because it whets one's appetite but, more important, because it counteracts any trace of grease. Such is, indeed, the case with fish. There are regional variations and personal preferences, but mainly a sweet and sour sauce is a mixture of vinegar and sugar, balanced by salt, and made more interesting by the addition of other condiments. Try this one, and then concoct your own.

1. If the wok in which the fish will be deep-fried is large enough (14 inches or over) leave the fish whole; otherwise, cut it in half. Make 2 or 3 diagonal slashes across the thickest part of both sides of the fish, taking care not to go right to the edges.

2. *Prepare the marinade:* Squeeze the ginger in a garlic press with 2 drops of water and mix the juice with the wine or sherry and salt. Rub both sides of the fish, including the crevices and the cavity, with the mixture. Let marinate for about 15 to 30 minutes. Discard any excess liquid.

3. *Prepare the sweet and sour sauce:* Drain and squeeze out excess water from the mushrooms but leave damp. Cut into small cubes. Cook the peas in boiling water for 2 minutes, drain. Mix together the dissolved potato flour, vinegar, sugar, ketchup, salt, soy sauce, wine or sherry and water. Heat a wok (if you have a second small one), or a saucepan, over high heat until smoke rises. Add 3 tablespoons of the oil and swirl it around. Add the garlic, then the onion or shallots and fry for about 1 minute, stirring. Add the mushrooms, peas and bamboo shoots. Stir the sauce mixture once more to blend, then pour into the wok or saucepan. Bring to a boil, stirring continuously as it thickens. Set aside.

4. Half fill a wok or deep fryer with oil. Heat to a temperature of 375°F, or until a cube of stale bread browns in 50 seconds.

5. While the oil is heating, brush the egg yolk over both sides of the fish, then sift the cornstarch over it, smoothing it for evenness.

6. Lower the fish into the oil and deep-fry for about 7 or 8 minutes, or until the skin is crisp. Turn over carefully and deep-fry the other side for about the same time.

7. Remove with a hand strainer or perforated spoon and drain on paper towels. Transfer to a warm serving dish. If the fish has been cut into halves, put together to look whole again.

8. Reheat the sauce until simmering, stir in the remaining 1 teaspoon of oil and pour over the fish. Serve immediately.

INGREDIENTS

1 red snapper or gray mullet, about 2¼ to 2½ pounds, cleaned with head left on
peanut or corn oil for deep-frying
1 egg yolk
about 3 tablespons cornstarch

FOR THE MARINADE

1 inch fresh ginger root, peeled and chopped fine
1 teaspoon Shaohsing wine or medium-dry sherry
1 teaspoon salt

FOR THE SWEET AND SOUR SAUCE

3 dried Chinese mushrooms, reconstituted (see page 39)
2 ounces small peas
2 teaspoons potato flour, dissolved in 2 tablespoons water
4 tablespoons rice or wine vinegar
4 tablespoons sugar
4 tablespoons tomato ketchup
1 teaspoon salt
1½ teaspoons thick soy sauce
2 teaspoons Shaohsing wine or medium-dry sherry
½ pint water
4 tablespoons peanut or corn oil
1 clove garlic, peeled and chopped fine
1 small onion or 3 shallots, skinned and diced
2 ounces canned bamboo shoots, diced

Serves 6 with 3 other dishes

Illustrated on page 87

糖醋炸魚

Stir-fried Squid in Shrimp Paste

蝦
醬
鮮
魷

INGREDIENTS

1 large squid, about 1½ pounds
    or body pouch pieces only
2 teaspoons thin soy sauce
1 teaspoon potato flour
4 tablespoons water
peanut or corn oil for deep-frying
1½ tablespoons shrimp paste
3 to 4 cloves garlic, peeled and
    chopped fine
1 ounce fresh ginger root, peeled
    and chopped fine
6 scallions, cut into ½-inch
    diagonal slices, white and
    green parts separated
1 tablespoon Shaohsing wine or
    medium-dry sherry

Serves 4 to 5 with 3 other dishes

Illustrated opposite

Shrimp paste has a strong, almost unpleasant, odor, and squid is very bland. However, when stir-fried together, with garlic, this peasant dish, although an acquired taste, can delight even the most sophisticated palate.

1. Cut off the head of the squid from the body pouch and discard. Cut off the eyes and discard. Rinse in cold water, then cut the tentacles into 1½-inch sections.

2. Slit the body pouch open lengthwise as far as the innards. Pull these out and discard. Remove the transparent bone and peel off the reddish skin; discard. Rinse in cold water.

3. Turn the body pouch inside out. Lay it flat on a board and, using the sharp edge of a knife, score in a crisscross pattern. Cut into pieces about 2 by 1 inches.

4. Immerse the squid briefly in plenty of boiling water. As soon as the pieces curl up, pour into a colander and rinse under cold running water. This makes the squid crisp and tender. Drain thoroughly and dry.

5. Mix together the soy sauce, potato flour and water. Set aside.

6. Half fill a wok or deep fryer with oil. Heat until just hot, about 300°F. Add the squid and let it "go through the oil" for about 10 seconds. Remove with a hand strainer and set aside. Pour all but about 3 tablespoons of the oil into a container and save for other uses.

7. Dilute the shrimp paste with 1 tablespoon of water, stirring to blend.

8. Reheat the oil until it smokes. Add the garlic, and when it sizzles, add the ginger. Stir a couple of times and add the white scallions. Stir a few more times, then pour in the shrimp sauce. Cook for a few seconds, stirring. Return the squid to the wok. Sliding the wok scoop or metal spatula to the bottom of the wok, turn and toss for about 10 to 20 seconds, or until thoroughly hot. Splash in the wine or sherry around the side of the wok. When the sizzling dies down, add the well-stirred dissolved potato-flour mixture. Continue to stir while this thickens. Tip in the green scallions.

9. Transfer to a warm serving plate. Serve immediately.

Note: Steps 1 to 6 can be prepared several hours in advance. Instead of 1 large squid, small squid can be used.

Facing page, clockwise from the top: Stir-fried squid in shrimp paste (see above); Stir-fried clams in black bean sauce (see page 88); Deep-fried fish with sweet and sour sauce (see page 85)

Stir-fried Clams in Black Bean Sauce

INGREDIENTS

24 clams, about 3 pounds
3 tablespoons peanut or corn oil
4 or 5 cloves garlic, peeled and chopped fine
½ inch fresh ginger root, peeled and chopped fine
4 or 5 scallions, cut into 1-inch sections, white and green parts separated
1½ tablespoons fermented black beans, rinsed, mashed with 1½ teaspoons sugar
2 tablespoons Shaohsing wine or medium-dry sherry
1 tablespoon thick soy sauce
3 tablespoons clear stock or water
1 teaspoon potato flour, dissolved in 1 tablespoon water
sesame oil to taste (optional)

Serves 4 to 6 as a first course

Illustrated on page 87

Black bean sauce and clams go together for the Chinese the way horseradish and roast beef do in the West.

1. Leave the clams in water with a little salt until ready to use. Scrub the shells very thoroughly.

2. Heat a wok over high heat until smoke rises. Add the oil and swirl it around. Add the garlic, ginger and white scallions. Stir and let them sizzle for a few moments to release their aroma. Add the mashed black beans and stir to mix. Tip in the clams. Sliding the wok scoop or metal spatula to the bottom of the wok, turn and toss for 30 to 45 seconds. Splash in the wine or sherry around the side of the wok, continuing to turn and stir. When the sizzling dies down, add the soy sauce and stock or water. Bring to a boil, cover, lower the heat to medium and cook for about 8 minutes.

3. Transfer the opened clams with a pair of chopsticks or tongs to a warm serving platter and keep warm. Stir and turn the remainder a few times and cook, covered, for another 4 to 5 minutes, so that they will open. Transfer the rest to the serving platter, leaving the sauce in the wok. Discard any clams that do not open.

4. Lower the heat, add the well-stirred potato flour to the sauce, stirring as it thickens. Tip in the green scallions.

5. Scoop the sauce over the clams and serve immediately. Sesame oil may be sprinkled on if desired.

Lobster with Ginger and Scallions

The species of lobster found along the Chinese coast is the spiny lobster or crayfish and, significantly, the Chinese name for it is dragon prawn. The meat, compared to that of the true lobster, is slightly coarser, but cooking methods and recipes are the same for both. Only fresh lobsters are fit for consumption; they can be kept alive up to 3 days in the vegetable compartment of the refrigerator.

1. *Prepare the sauce:* Mix together the flour, water, soy sauce and oyster sauce. Set aside.

2. Kill and chop up the lobsters. Before starting, make sure that strong rubber bands are around the pincers. Lay the lobsters flat, one at a time, on a chopping board, and steady them with one hand. Pierce the center of the head, where there is a cross, with the pointed end of a strong knife, pressing firmly all the way down in order to paralyze the nerve and hence kill the lobster instantly. Split it in half along the back, all the way to the tail, cutting through both the shell and the flesh. Remove and discard the pouch of grit from the head, as well as the dark gut running along the body. Remove the tiny eggs, if any, and the greenish creamy substance (tomalley), which can be cooked separately if you like it. Twist the joints to dislodge the 2 claws from the body. Lay each half of the body flat and, using a kitchen cleaver, chop each into 3 pieces. Remove the gill from the head, close to the shell. Lay the claws on the board and bang them, one by one, with either the broad side of the cleaver or a hammer until the shell is cracked at various points so that it will not be necessary to use crackers when eating them. Cut each claw in 2 at its obvious joint.

3. Put all the head and claw pieces into one large bowl and the body pieces into another. Pat dry with paper towels.

4. Half fill a wok or deep fryer with oil. Heat to a temperature of 350°F, or until a cube of stale bread browns in 60 seconds. Carefully lower all the head and claw pieces into the oil and let them "go through the oil" for 20 to 30 seconds, so that their juices are sealed in. Remove immediately with a large hand strainer and put on a large platter.

5. Reheat the oil and let the body pieces "go through the oil" for about 10 seconds.

6. Empty the oil into a container and save it for other purposes. Wash and dry the wok.

7. Heat the wok over high heat until smoke rises. Add 3 tablespoons of oil and swirl it around. Add the ginger, stir, and let it sizzle for about 1 minute, to release its aroma fully. Add the white scallions

INGREDIENTS
2 lobsters, each about 1½ pounds
peanut or corn oil for deep frying
3 tablespoons peanut or corn oil
3 ounces fresh ginger root, peeled and cut into thin slices
10 to 12 large scallions, cut diagonally, white and green parts separated
1½ tablespoons Shaohsing wine or brandy
¼ pint prime stock (see page 225)

FOR THE SAUCE
1 teaspoon potato flour
4 tablespoons water
½ tablespoon thin soy sauce
1½ tablespoons oyster sauce

Serves 6 as a first course

Illustrated on page 91

薑
蔥
焗
龍
蝦

and stir a few times. Now return *all* the lobster and, sliding the wok scoop or metal spatula to the bottom of the wok, turn and toss the pieces until thoroughly hot. Splash in the wine or brandy around the side of the wok, continuing to stir as it sizzles.

8. Pour in the stock, cover and cook for about 2 minutes, at the end of which most of the liquid will have been absorbed. Add the well-stirred sauce, tip in the green scallions and stir and toss until the sauce thickens.

9. Transfer to a large warm serving platter. Serve immediately.

Spiced-Salt Prawns

This dish, with its subtly spicy flavor, is very popular in Hong Kong, one of the leading capitals of Chinese food. The prawns are left with their shells on because this protects the meat from the intense heat of deep-frying, thereby making it succulent when cooked.

INGREDIENTS
1 pound fresh or frozen medium
    raw prawns in the shell,
    without heads
2 tablespoons salt
1 teaspoon five-spice powder
1 teaspoon ground roasted
    Szechwan peppercorns
1 teaspoon ground black pepper
peanut or corn oil for deep frying

Serves 6 with 3 other dishes

Illustrated opposite

1. If frozen prawns are used, defrost thoroughly. Wash the shells well; remove and discard the legs.

2. Devein: Using a bamboo stick or a strong needle, pierce the flesh at the joints of the shell sections and remove the black veins.

3. To make the spiced salt, heat a wok over medium heat until hot but not smoking. Add the salt and stir continuously for about 4 minutes, or until very hot and slightly grayish in color. Transfer to a small bowl. Add the five-spice powder, ground roasted Szechwan peppercorns and pepper. Mix well.

4. Half fill a wok or deep fryer with oil. Heat to a temperature of 350°F, or until a cube of stale bread browns in 60 seconds. Add the prawns and deep-fry for 30 to 45 seconds, or until they have curled up and turned red, indicating that they are cooked. Remove with a large hand strainer or perforated spoon and drain.

5. Empty the oil into a container and save it for other cooking purposes. Wash and dry the wok.

6. Reheat the wok until hot. Add 1 tablespoon of the spiced salt and return the prawns to the wok. Over medium heat flip and turn the prawns in the salt for about 30 seconds, so that the salt permeates them. Transfer to a warm serving plate. Put the remaining salt on a small saucer for additional dipping, with chopsticks, at the table.

Facing page, from the top: Lobster with ginger and scallions (page 89); Spiced-salt prawns (see above)

Stir-fried Prawns in Tomato Sauce

番
茄
炒
蝦
球

INGREDIENTS

8 ounces fresh or frozen raw prawns, in the shell, without heads
¼ teaspoon salt
8 ounces tomatoes
5 tablespoons peanut or corn oil
4 to 5 cloves garlic, peeled and chopped fine
4 scallions, cut into 1-inch sections, white and green parts separated
2 teaspoons thin soy sauce
½ teaspoon sugar
½ teaspoon potato flour, dissolved in 1 tablespoon water

Serves 2 with 1 other dish

Illustrated opposite

The Cantonese like to bite into prawns that are "crisply firm," and to achieve this texture Cantonese chefs leave out ginger and wine when preparing them, as we have here.

1. If frozen prawns are used, defrost thoroughly. Shell and devein the prawns (see page 39). Pat dry with paper towels and put into a bowl.

2. Sprinkle with half the salt, which will firm up the prawns. Let sit for about 15 minutes.

3. Plunge the tomatoes into a bowl of very hot water and leave for 5 to 10 minutes. Peel off the skins. Cut the flesh into slices.

4. Heat a wok over high heat until smoke rises. Add the oil, swirl it around and heat until very hot. Add the garlic and half the white scallions. Stir a few times to release their aroma and add the prawns. Sliding the wok scoop or metal spatula to the bottom of the wok, flip and turn in rapid succession for about 1 minute, or until the prawns have curled up and turned pink in color. Scoop to a warm plate, leaving behind as much oil as possible.

5. Add the remaining white spring onion to the wok. Tip in the tomatoes and stir well. Season with the remaining salt, the soy sauce and sugar. Cover and cook over a medium heat for 2 or 3 minutes.

6. Add the well-stirred dissolved potato flour.

7. Return the prawns to the wok and tip in the green scallions. Turn up the heat, stir and turn until the prawns are very hot. Transfer to a warm serving plate.

Facing page, clockwise from the top: Steamed trout with black beans and garlic (see page 95); Stir-fried prawns in tomato sauce (see above); Sizzling rice with shrimp and tomato sauce (see page 94)

Sizzling Rice with Shrimp and Tomato Sauce

蝦
仁
鍋
巴

INGREDIENTS
8 ounces raw peeled shrimp
peanut or corn oil for deep frying
12 to 14 ounces canned tomatoes,
    chopped
½ teaspoon salt
½ to 1 teaspoon sugar
2 to 3 teaspoons thin soy sauce
1 tablespoon Shaohsing wine or
    medium-dry sherry
1 pint clear stock
1½ to 2 tablespoons cornstarch,
    dissolved in 4 tablespoons
    clear stock or water
12 pieces guoba

FOR THE GUOBA
13 to 14 ounces cooked rice
1 to 2 tablespoons peanut or corn
    oil

FOR THE MARINADE
½ teaspoon salt
2 teaspoons cornstarch
½ egg white or 1 tablespoon

Serves 4 with 3 other dishes

Illustrated on page 93

In many Chinese households, rice, the staple food, used to be cooked in a large, round copper pot. When there was a layer of cooked rice stuck to the bottom of the pot, it would be carefully removed, roasted over a slow fire and then used again. These roasted rice pieces, called guoba, *led to the invention of sizzling rice dishes in Eastern regional cuisine. This dish is also called "Thunder bolt out of the blue," because of the sizzle caused by the boiling sauce when poured on the crispy* guoba.

1. *Prepare the guoba:* Loosen the rice and let dry for 4-5 hours.

2. Lightly brush 2 baking pans with the oil. Form the rice into 14 to 16 thin cakes, squares or circles, about 2½ inches across, and place in the baking pans (a).

3. Put them, one pan at a time, if necessary, on the top shelf of a preheated over, at 425°F, and roast for about 20 minutes, or until the bottom side of the cakes is brown. If the surface still looks pale, loosen the cakes with a spatula, turn them over and roast for another 5 minutes.

4. Take the pans out of the oven and let the guoba cool. Store in an airtight container. (They can also be eaten alone if sprinkled with a little salt.)

5. If frozen shrimp are used, defrost thoroughly. Wash twice in cold water to make them as white as possible. Drain well or pat semidry with paper towels. Put into a bowl.

6. *Prepare the marinade:* Add the salt, cornstarch and egg white to the shrimp. Stir to coat evenly. Let marinate in the refrigerator for a minimum of 3 hours or overnight.

7. Half fill a wok or deep fryer with oil. Heat until just hot, about 300°F. Add the shrimp and let them "go through the oil" for about 30 seconds, separating them with a pair of long chopsticks or a wooden spoon. The shrimp, having turned pinkish, will be almost cooked. Remove with a large hand strainer and set aside.

8. Heat 2 casseroles or ovenproof soufflé dishes in a preheated oven at about 275°F. One is for serving the sizzling rice at the table, the other is for the boiling sauce.

9. Put the chopped tomato, salt, sugar, soy sauce, wine or sherry and stock in a saucepan and slowly bring it almost to a boil. Reduce the heat and stir in the dissolved cornstarch. Leave over a low flame or on a hot plate.

10. Reheat the oil until it reaches 375°F, or until a cube of stale

bread browns in 50 seconds. Carefully add the pieces of guoba and deep fry for about 2 minutes, or until they are golden (b). Remove and transfer to the serving dish. Keep warm in the oven.

a   b

11. Add the shrimp to the tomato sauce and bring to a fast boil.

12. Take the serving dish containing the guoba to the table. Take the other dish out of the oven and pour the boiling sauce into it. Pour the sauce over the guoba at the table – there will be a great deal of sizzling. Serve as soon as the sizzling subsides.

Steamed Trout with Black Beans and Garlic

When condiments are needed to enhance the flavor of a fish, it is often steamed with fermented black beans and garlic and then garnished with scallions. Rainbow trout and gray mullet, among others, are delicious steamed this way.

1. Pat the fish dry. Lay them on a heatproof serving dish with slightly raised sides. Place 2 slices of ginger in the cavity of each fish.

2. Mix together the black beans and garlic, and spread on the fish.

3. Steam in a wok or steamer over high heat for 6 to 8 minutes, until the fish is cooked and the flesh flakes easily (see page 45).

4. Remove from the heat and sprinkle with the scallions.

5. Heat the oil in a small saucepan over high heat until smoke rises. Pour it over the scallions. The sizzling oil partially cooks them, enhancing the flavor.

6. Remove the fish from the wok or steamer. Add the soy sauce.

7. To serve, scrape the condiments on the fish to the side. Peel and discard the uppermost skin. Spoon some of the condiments and sauce back on the fish and serve.

INGREDIENTS
2 trout, about 12 ounces each, cleaned with heads left on
4 thin slices fresh ginger root, peeled
2 tablespoons fermented black beans, rinsed and partially mashed with ½ teaspoon sugar and 1 teaspoon Shaohsing wine; leave some beans whole
4 to 6 cloves garlic, peeled and chopped fine
2 or 3 scallions, cut into small rounds
4 tablespoons peanut or corn oil
2 tablespoons thick soy sauce

Serves 4 with 2 other dishes

Illustrated on page 93

豆
豉
蒸
魚

A Southern or Cantonese Menu

Cantonese and Fukinenese cuisines, the two distinctive representatives of the Southern region, specialize in seafood. Hence this predominantly seafood menu for eight. However for those less *fond of seafood there are more than enough classic meat and poultry dishes from the south from which to choose.*

蟹扒蘆筍 **Asparagus with crab meat**
Sweet-tasting combination of firm asparagus and tender crab meat
(see page 205).

紅豆沙 **Red bean fool**
Purée of red beans and rice, traditionally served hot
(see page 208).

香芒牛肉 **Stir-fried fillet of beef with mango**
Colorful dish combining sweet and piquant tastes
(see page 207).

干燒明蝦 **Dry-fried prawns**
Prawns lightly fried in a tangy sauce of ginger, garlic, chili and soy sauce
(see page 206).

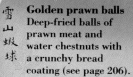

雪山蝦球 **Golden prawn balls**
Deep-fried balls of
prawn meat and
water chestnuts with
a crunchy bread
coating (see page 206).

清蒸鱸魚 **Clear-steamed sea bass**
Simply steamed, then
served with scallions,
ginger, garlic and oil
poured on top
(see page 205).

POULTRY AND EGGS

Stir-fried Chicken with Sugar Peas

INGREDIENTS
2 chicken breasts, about 1
    pound, when skinned and
    boned
8 ounces sugar peas, trimmed
salt
peanut or corn oil for deep frying
3 or 4 thin slices fresh ginger
    root, peeled
3 or 4 cloves garlic, peeled and
    chopped fine
4 scallions, cut into 1-inch
    sections, white and green parts
    separated
1 tablespoon Shaohsing wine or
    medium-dry sherry

FOR THE MARINADE
¼ teaspoon salt
2 teaspoons thin soy sauce
4 turns white pepper mill
2 teaspoons Shaohsing wine or
    medium-dry sherry
1 teaspoon cornstarch
1½ tablespoons egg white, lightly
    beaten
1 tablespoon peanut or corn oil

FOR THE SAUCE
1 teaspoon potato flour
6 tablespoons clear stock or
    water
2 tablespoons oyster sauce
½ tablespoon thick soy sauce

*Serves 4 to 6 with 2 or 3 other
    dishes*

Illustrated opposite

*This is a pleasant Southern stir-fried dish of tender and tasty
chicken with crunchy sugar peas. The oyster sauce, a special
condiment of the South, adds a pleasing taste to the dish.*

1. Cut the chicken into large cubes. Put into a bowl.

2. *Prepare the marinade:* Add the salt, soy sauce, pepper, wine or
sherry, cornstarch and egg white to the chicken and stir to coat. Let
marinate for 15 to 30 minutes. Blend in the oil so that the cubes of
chicken will not stick to each other.

3. Bring a pan of water (about 3 pints) to a boil. Add 1 teaspoon of
salt and 1 tablespoon of oil. Plunge in the sugar peas and as soon as
the water returns to a boil, pour into a colander and refresh under
cold running water. Drain. They will remain crisp and retain their
color for 2 or 3 hours.

4. *Prepare the sauce:* Mix together the potato flour, stock or water,
oyster sauce and soy sauce.

5. Half fill a wok or deep fryer with oil. Heat to a temperature of
350°F, or until a cube of stale bread browns in 60 seconds. Let the
chicken "go through the oil" for about 30 seconds, separating the
pieces with a pair of long chopsticks (see page 43). Remove with a
large hand strainer and set aside.

6. Transfer all but about 1 tablespoon of oil to a container and save
for later use. Reheat the oil and add the ginger. When it sizzles, add
the peas. Reduce the heat to medium and stir and turn until the
peas are very hot. Season with salt to taste, then transfer to a warm
serving plate and keep warm.

7. Wipe the wok clean. Turn the heat to high, add 2 tablespoons of
oil and swirl it around. Add the garlic, let it sizzle, then add the
white scallions and stir to release the aroma. Return the chicken to
the wok and turn and toss with the wok scoop or metal spatula for
30 to 45 seconds. Splash in the wine or sherry around the side of the
wok, stirring continuously as it sizzles. Pour the well-stirred sauce
over the chicken. Lower the heat and continue to stir while the sauce
thickens. Add the green scallions, stir, then scoop the chicken
mixture on top of the peas. Serve immediately.

*Facing page, clockwise from the top: Duck stuffed with myriad condiments
(see page 100); Sauce for duck; Stir-fried chicken with sugar peas (see above)*

Duck Stuffed with Myriad Condiments

INGREDIENTS
12 to 15 scallions, white parts
  only, made into brushes (see
  page 34)
1 pound taro, peeled
1 oven-ready duck, 4 to 4½
  pounds
1 tablespoon thick soy sauce

FOR THE SAUCE STUFFING
¼ of whole dried tangerine peel,
  soaked in cold water, then cut
  into small pieces
4 cloves garlic, peeled and
  chopped fine
2 inches fresh ginger root, peeled
  and chopped fine
3 shallots, skinned and chopped
  fine
2 whole star anise (16 segments)
6 tablespoons crushed yellow
  bean sauce
5 tablespoons hoisin sauce
1 tablespoon sesame paste
1 teaspoon five-spice powder
2 teaspoons ginger powder
2 teaspoons salt
2 tablespoons sugar
1 tablespoon Mei-kuei-lu wine or
  gin

Serves 6 with 3 or 4 other dishes

Illustrated on page 99

The best time to serve this famous Cantonese dish is in the autumn and winter. The sauce resulting from this subtly balanced blend of seasonings is delicious.

1. *Prepare the sauce stuffing:* Mix together the tangerine peel, garlic, ginger, shallots, star anise, sauces, sesame paste, five-spice powder, ginger powder, salt, sugar and wine or gin. (This can be done hours in advance.)

2. Make the scallion brushes and put them in a bowl of water and refrigerate. (This can also be done hours in advance.)

3. Slice the taro into pieces about ½ inch thick. Lay them on a large heatproof dish with raised edges.

4. The duck must be at room temperature, otherwise the steaming will take much longer. Dry both skin and cavity with paper towels. Chop off the pinions of the wings; save them for the stockpot.

5. Spoon the sauce stuffing into the cavity. To seal the tail end, fold the parson's nose inward. If necessary, use a thin poultry skewer or bamboo stick to thread through the skin. To seal the neck end, fold the flap of neck skin over the neck cavity.

6. Lay the duck on top of the taro on the heatproof dish, breast side up. Put the dish into a wok or steamer and steam (see page 45), tightly covered, for 1¼ to 1½ hours, or until the duck is tender yet still firm.

7. Drain the scallion brushes and pat dry.

8. Remove the dish from the steamer and transfer the duck to another dish. Brush the thick soy sauce over the skin to give it color.

9. Turn the parson's nose outward or remove the skewer. Spoon the sauce stuffing into a saucepan.

10. Transfer the taro to a warm serving platter and keep warm. Degrease the liquid remaining in the heatproof dish and pour it into the saucepan.

11. Stir to blend the liquid and the sauce stuffing in the saucepan and simmer over low heat for 5 to 10 minutes. Strain through a sieve and discard the solids. Return this sauce to the saucepan and bring to a simmer again.

12. Chop the duck either in the Chinese way (see opposite) or by your usual method. Arrange the pieces on top of the taro.

13. Pour some of the sauce over the meat. Garnish with scallion brushes. Pour the remaining sauce into a bowl and serve.

CHOPPING POULTRY CHINESE-STYLE

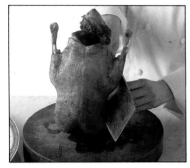

1 Slice off the wing on each side, cutting through the joint close to the body.

2 Slice off the leg on each side, cutting down through the joint close to the body.

3 On each leg cut the drumstick and thigh apart. Cut both the thigh and drumstick in two.

4 Split the carcass in half lengthwise so that the back and breast form two separate pieces.

5 Remove the breastbone with a knife, sliding it between the bone and the meat.

6 Using a pair of kitchen scissors cut the backbone out of the back piece, and discard.

7 Cut the back pieces crosswise into 1 inch pieces.

8 Halve the breast meat lengthwise then cut crosswise into 1 inch pieces.

9 Reassemble the bird with the breast meat on top of the back pieces.

Smoked Duck, Szechwan Style

INGREDIENTS

1 scant teaspoon saltpeter
1 oven-ready duck, about 5
    pounds
1¾ tablespoons salt
6 ounces plain flour
4 ounces brown sugar
4 tablespoons black tea leaves
2 pieces fresh ginger root, each ½
    inch, peeled and bruised
2 large scallions
1 whole star anise (8 segments)
1½ teaspoons Szechwan
    peppercorns
2 tablespoons Shaohsing wine or
    medium-dry sherry
peanut or corn oil for deep frying
1 tablespoon sesame oil

Serves 6 with 3 other dishes

Illustrated opposite

The various cooking processes used in this dish may seem too time-consuming, but the duck is made once crispy and moist, smoky and aromatic.

1. Rub the salt thoroughly over the skin of the duck and inside the cavity, then rub the cavity only with saltpeter. Leave the duck in a cool place for about 10 hours or overnight.

2. Rinse the duck, especially the cavity, in plenty of hot water. Wipe dry. The duck is now ready for smoking.

3. Line a large wok with heavy-duty foil and place the flour, sugar and tea in the bottom. Place a metal trivet or bamboo stand on top. Place the duck on that, breast side up, and make sure that there is a gap between it and the smoking ingredients, to allow free circulation of smoke. Put the wok cover on tightly.

4. Turn the heat on high until you see smoke coming out, then adjust it, making sure that plenty of smoke continues to come out. Smoke for 15 minutes, turn the duck over and smoke, breast side down, for another 15 minutes. Remove from the heat.

5. When cool enough to handle, transfer to a large heatproof dish, breast side up. Put half of the ginger, scallions, star anise, peppercorns and wine or sherry into the cavity; put the other half on the breast.

6. Steam in a steamer or another wok for 1 to 1¼ hours (see page 45).

7. When cool enough to handle, transfer the duck to a rack and let cool. Remove and discard all the condiments. Dry with paper towels.

8 Half fill a wok or deep fryer with oil. Heat to a temperature of 375°F, or until a cube of stale bread browns in 50 seconds. Carefully lower the duck into the oil, breast side down, and deep fry for 3 or 4 minutes, or until brown. With a wooden spoon or spatula in one hand and another inside the cavity, turn the duck over and deep-fry the other side until brown. Hot oil can also be spooned over the skin. Remove to a chopping board. Brush the sesame oil over the breast. The duck can be carved either in the Chinese way (see page 101) or by your usual method. Serve warm.

Note: If the duck is prepared in advance, it can be reheated in a preheated oven at 300°F for 30 to 45 minutes, or until it's hot and the skin is crisp.

Facing page, from the top: Lettuce-wrapped chicken (see page 104); Smoked duck Szechwan style (see above)

Lettuce-wrapped Chicken

生
菜
包

INGREDIENTS

2 large iceburg lettuce heads
8 medium dried Chinese
    mushrooms, reconstituted (see
    page 39)
2 to 3 ounces Szechwan
    preserved vegetable, rinsed
    and dried
6 to 8 water chestnuts, fresh
    peeled or canned, drained
4 to 6 chicken breasts, about 2 to
    2½ pounds, skinned and
    boned
2 ounces walnuts or blanched
    almonds
10 tablespoons peanut or corn oil
4 or 5 cloves garlic, peeled and
    chopped fine
6 scallions, cut into tiny rounds,
    white and green parts
    separated
1½ tablespoons Shaohsing wine
    or medium-dry sherry

FOR THE MARINADE

¾ to 1 teaspoon salt
¾ to 1 teaspoon sugar
1 tablespoon thin soy sauce
8 to 10 turns white pepper mill
2 teaspoons Shaohsing wine or
    medium-dry sherry
1½ teaspoons cornstarch
1 egg white, lightly beaten
2 to 3 tablespoons water
2 tablespoons peanut or corn oil
2 teaspoons sesame oil

FOR THE SAUCE

1½ teaspoons potato flour
9 tablespoons clear stock
1 to 2 teaspoons thick soy sauce
    (for coloring)
2 tablespoons oyster sauce

Serves 6 with 2 other dishes

Illustrated on page 103

Although this chicken recipe is delicious, an arguably more elegant (although more expensive) version of this Southern dish uses quail's meat and dried oysters.

1. Wash and dry the lettuce. Refrigerate to maintain crispness until almost ready to cook the chicken. Then arrange the leaves on 1 or 2 plates.

2. Drain and squeeze out excess water from the mushrooms but leave damp. Dice into the size of small peas.

3. Finely chop the Szechwan preserved vegetable, removing stringy fibers at the same time.

4. Mince the water chestnuts in a food processor or blender.

5. Chop the chicken by hand or mince coarsely. Put into a large bowl.

6. *Prepare the marinade:* Add the salt, sugar, soy sauce, pepper, wine or sherry, cornstarch and egg white to the chicken. Stir to coat until well blended. Add the water, 1 tablespoon at a time, and stir vigorously to make the chicken lighter in texture.

7. Stir in the mushrooms, preserved vegetable and water chestnuts. Let marinate for 30 minutes. Blend in the oil and sesame oil.

8. *Prepare the sauce:* Dissolve the potato flour in a small bowl with 2 tablespoons of the stock. Stir in the remaining stock and add the soy sauce and oyster sauce.

9. Heat a wok until hot. Add the walnuts or almonds and stir continuously over low to medium heat for about 3 minutes, until crisp and fragrant. Remove and chop. Wash and dry the wok. (This step can be done several hours ahead.)

10. Reheat the wok over high heat until smoke rises. Add the oil and swirl it around until very hot. Add the garlic, which will sizzle and take on color almost instantly. Add the white scallions, stir a couple of times and add the chicken. Sliding the wok scoop or metal spatula to the bottom of the wok, flip and toss for 2 or 3 minutes, or until the chicken turns white, breaking up lumps at the same time. Splash in the wine or sherry around the side of the wok, stirring as it sizzles.

11. As soon as the sizzling dies down, lower the heat, push the ingredients to the side of the wok and pour the well-stirred sauce into the middle. When it bubbles, stir in the surrounding chicken, add the green scallions and walnuts or almonds, still stirring to blend well. Transfer to a warm serving plate and put in the center of the table with the prepared lettuce (a).

12. To eat, each person takes 1 piece of lettuce at a time (b), spoons some chicken onto the lettuce (c), folds it to encase the chicken (d) and then eats it with the fingers.

a

b

c

d

Willow Chicken in Black Bean Sauce

豉
椒
雞
柳

INGREDIENTS

about 1¾ pounds, pieces chicken thigh, skinned and boned
2 small green peppers, seeded
1 to 2 fresh green chilies, seeded (optional)
6 tablespoons peanut or corn oil
5 or 6 cloves garlic, peeled and cut into silken threads (see page 35)
4 scallions, cut into 1-inch sections, white and green parts separated
3 tablespoons fermented black beans, rinsed and mashed
1 tablespoon Shaohsing wine or medium-dry sherry
little sesame oil (optional)
chili sauce (optional)

FOR THE MARINADE

½ teaspoon salt
½ teaspoon sugar
1 tablespoon thin soy sauce
8 turns black pepper mill
2 teaspoons Shaohsing wine or medium-dry sherry
1 teaspoon cornstarch
2 tablespoons egg white, lightly beaten
1½ tablespoons peanut or corn oil

FOR THE SAUCE

1 teaspoon cornstarch
4 tablespoons clear stock or water
2 teaspoons oyster sauce or 1 teaspoon thick soy sauce

Serves 6 with 3 other dishes

Illustrated on page 109

This dish takes its name from the willowy strips of the chicken and pepper.

1. Cut the chicken into strips, about ⅕ inch thick. Put into a bowl.

2. *Prepare the marinade:* Add the salt, sugar, soy sauce, pepper and wine or sherry to the chicken. Sprinkle with the cornstarch, add the egg white and stir to coat. Let marinate for 15 to 30 minutes. Blend in the oil.

3. Slice the peppers into long and narrow strips.

4. Slice the chilies into strips.

5. *Prepare the sauce:* Mix together the cornstarch, stock or water, oyster or soy sauce.

6. Heat a wok until hot. Add 1 tablespoon of the oil and swirl it around. Add the pepper and stir and toss with the wok scoop or metal spatula constantly for about 2 minutes. When tender yet crunchy, transfer to a warm plate and keep warm.

7. Wash and dry the wok.

8. Heat the wok over high heat until smoke rises. Add the remaining oil and swirl it around. Add the garlic and when it sizzles and takes on color, add the chilies, white scallions and then the black bean paste. Stir to blend with the garlic. Put in the chicken and stir and toss the strips for 2 minutes, or until they turn whitish, scraping the paste from the bottom of the pan to coat.

9. Splash in the wine or sherry around the side of the wok and let it sizzle, stirring continuously. When the sizzling dies down, lower the heat and add the well-stirred sauce to the chicken. Continue to stir as the sauce thickens. Add the pepper and green scallions and mix well. Remove to a warm plate and serve immediately. A little sesame oil can be sprinkled on top. For those who like an extra-hot flavor, chili sauce can be served at the table.

Note: In pursuit of gastronomic excellence, you can let the chicken "go through the oil" (see page 40) before stir-frying it in step 8. In that case, simply stir-fry for a shorter time.

Chicken in Yunnan Steam Pot

A Yunnan steam pot is, basically a pottery casserole dish about 8 inches in diameter and 4 inches high with a cone-shaped chimney in the center of the bowl. The pot, with its tightly fitting lid, is placed in boiling water so that steam rises through the chimney to circulate inside and cook the ingredients. Chicken cooked in this way is tender and succulent, and the accompanying soup is pure and flavorful. The pot is available in some Chinese shops, but, in a pinch, a double boiler can be used.

INGREDIENTS

12 medium dried Chinese mushrooms, reconstituted (see page 39)
8 ounces best ham, trimmed of fat
1 oven-ready chicken, 3 to 3¼ pounds
1 to 1¼ teaspoons salt
4 to 6 turns white pepper mill
2 thickish slices fresh ginger root, peeled
2 scallions, quartered
1 tablespoon Shaohsing wine or medium-dry sherry
thin soy sauce (optional)

Serves 6 with 3 other dishes

Illustrated on page 109

1. Drain and squeeze out excess water from the mushrooms but leave damp. Reserve the soaking liquid.

2. Slice the ham into large pieces.

3. Chop the chicken through the bones into serving pieces, using a kitchen cleaver, a mallet and kitchen scissors, if necessary. Cut the wings, thighs and drumsticks at the joints and slit the whole breast off from the back. Cut and discard the pinions, then halve each wing at the joint. Halve each thigh and drumstick crosswise. Halve the breast lengthwise, then cut each half crosswise into 3 or 4 pieces. Do not use the back; save it for the stockpot.

4. Bring a large saucepan of water to a boil and add the chicken pieces. Return to a boil and continue to boil for about 2 minutes, so that the scum rises. Pour into a colander and rinse the chicken to get rid of any remaining scum.

5. Line the steam pot with the mushrooms, ham and chicken. Add the salt, pepper, ginger, scallions and wine or sherry. Add sufficient water (including the mushroom water) to come within 1 inch of the top of the chimney of the pot. Put the lid on.

6. Over moderate heat, place the steam pot on the rim of a small saucepan with boiling water inside, leaving a gap between the water level and the bottom of the steam pot. Cook for 1 to 1¼ hours without disturbing. Replenish the water in the saucepan from time to time, removing the steam pot to do so if necessary.

7. Remove from the heat. Spoon off excess fat, if any, on the surface.

8. Take the steam pot to the dining table and serve from it. Use the soy sauce as a dip if you like.

Red-braised Chicken with Chestnuts

INGREDIENTS

20 medium dried Chinese mushrooms, reconstituted (see page 39)
1 pound chestnuts
8 ounces canned bamboo shoots
1 oven-ready chicken, 4 to 4½ pounds
3 to 4 tablespoons peanut or corn oil
3 tablespoons Shaohsing wine or medium-dry sherry
4 thickish slices fresh ginger root, peeled
2 whole star anise (16 segments)
1-inch cinnamon stick
1½ teaspoons salt
1 teaspoon brown sugar
4 to 5 tablespoons thick soy sauce
½ pint clear stock

Serves 6 to 8 as main course

Illustrated opposite

A popular national dish during autumn and winter, when chestnuts are in season.

1. Drain and squeeze out excess water from the mushrooms but leave damp.

2. Make a cross in the shell of each chestnut and put into a saucepan of cold water. Bring to a boil and boil for 3 to 5 minutes, depending on the size of the chestnuts. Remove from the heat but leave the chestnuts in the water. Shell and peel the chestnuts as best you can.

3. Cube the bamboo shoots in the size of a small chestnut.

4. Chop the chicken through the bones into serving pieces, using a kitchen cleaver, a mallet and kitchen scissors, if necessary. Cut the wings, thighs and drumsticks at the joints and slit the whole breast off from the back. Cut and discard the pinions, then halve each wing at the joint and chop each piece crosswise into 2. Chop each thigh and drumstick crosswise into 2 or 3. Halve the breast lengthwise, then chop each half into 3 or 4 pieces. Do likewise with the back.

5. Heat a large, deep and heavy saucepan over high heat until very hot. Add the oil and swirl it around. Add the dark meat of the chicken, turn and toss to brown for about 3 minutes. Add the white meat, mushrooms and bamboo shoots and toss and turn for another 2 or 3 minutes.

6. Add the wine or sherry, ginger, star anise and cinnamon, continuing to stir until the sizzling dies down.

7. Add the salt, brown sugar and soy sauce. Adjust the heat, turning and stirring so that the chicken will be dyed by the soy sauce.

8. Pour in the stock and add the chestnuts. Bring to a boil and simmer fast for about 30 minutes, until the ingredients are tender. (The cooking up to this point can be done up to a day in advance.)

9. Just before serving, bring slowly to a boil. Turn up the heat to maximum, and as the sauce bubbles, spoon it over the ingredients. Repeat until the sauce has reduced and thickened, and the flavor has become richer. Transfer to a warm serving dish and serve piping hot.

Facing page, clockwise from the top: Chicken in Yunnan steam pot (see page 107); Willow chicken in black bean sauce (see page 106); Red-braised chicken with chestnuts (see above)

Chicken Glazed in Hoisin Sauce

醬爆雞丁

INGREDIENTS

2 or 3 chicken breasts, about 1 pound, skinned and boned
6 tablespoons peanut or corn oil
5 or 6 cloves garlic, peeled and chopped fine
4 or 5 scallions, cut into 1-inch sections, white and green parts separated
1 to 1½ tablespoons Shaohsing wine or medium-dry sherry
3 tablespoons hoisin sauce
2 ounces roasted cashew nuts

FOR THE MARINADE

½ teaspoon salt
8 turns white pepper mill
2 teaspoons Shaohsing wine or medium-dry sherry
1 teaspoon cornstarch
½ egg white, lightly beaten
2 teaspoons sesame oil

Serves 4 to 6 with 2 or 3 other dishes

Illustrated opposite

The hoisin sauce adds color and flavor to the chicken in this Northern dish, and the cashew nuts provide a pleasing contrast of texture.

1. Dice the chicken into ¾-inch cubes. Put into a bowl.

2. *Prepare the marinade:* Add the salt, pepper and wine or sherry to the chicken. Sprinkle with the cornstarch and stir in the egg white to coat. Let marinate for 15 to 30 minutes. Blend in the sesame oil.

3. Heat a wok over a high heat until smoke rises. Pour in 5 tablespoons of the oil and swirl it around. Add two-thirds of the garlic and the white scallions. Stir with the wok scoop or metal spatula a few times, then add the chicken. Sliding the scoop or spatula to the bottom of the wok, turn and toss for about 2 minutes, lowering the heat so that the chicken does not become tough. Splash in the wine or sherry around the side of the wok. As soon as the sizzling dies down, transfer the chicken, still a little undercooked, to a warm plate.

4. Increase the heat, add the remaining 1 tablespoon of oil and swirl it around. Add the remaining garlic, and as it sizzles, add the hoisin sauce and stir well. Return the chicken to the wok and toss in the sauce to glaze until just cooked. Mix in the cashew nuts and green scallions. Transfer to a warm serving plate. Serve immediately.

Facing page, from the top: Duck stuffed with glutinous rice (see page 112); Chicken glazed in hoisin sauce (see above)

Duck Stuffed with Glutinous Rice

INGREDIENTS

1 oven-ready duck, 4½ to 5
  pounds
1½ tablespoons thick soy sauce
5 or 6 tablespoons peanut or corn
  oil for deep frying
1 teaspoon salt
1½ tablespoons Shaohsing wine
  or medium-dry sherry
1 whole star anise or 8 segments
1 teaspoon Szechwan
  peppercorns
¼ preserved tangerine peel,
  soaked in cold water for 20
  minutes, drained
2 or 3 teaspons potato flour,
  dissolved in 3 tablespoons
  water
1 to 2 tablespoons oyster sauce
12 ounces broccoli spears,
  trimmed

FOR THE STUFFING

½ ounce dried shrimp, rinsed
3 tablespoons peanut or corn oil
2 cloves garlic, peeled and
  chopped fine
3 scallions, cut into small rounds
2 ounces pork, diced into size of
  matchstick heads
8 small dried Chinese
  mushrooms, reconstituted (see
  page 39) and chopped into size
  of matchstick heads
2 ounces canned bamboo shoots,
  chopped into size of
  matchstick heads
3 ounces glutinous rice, soaked in
  cold water for 2 hours,
  drained
½ teaspoon salt
1½ tablespoons thin soy sauce
8 turns pepper mill

Serves 6 with 3 other dishes

Illustrated on page 111

Duck stuffed with glutinous rice is popular with most Chinese, irrespective of the region they come from. The stuffing can be made a day in advance and refrigerated, but if it is, bring it out so that it will be at room temperature before being stuffed into the duck.

1. Soak the shrimp in just enough boiling water to cover them, for 20 minutes. Drain, but save the liquid.

2. *Prepare the stuffing:* Heat a wok over high heat until smoke rises. Add the oil and swirl around. Add the garlic and scallions and stir for a few seconds. Add the shrimp, stir, the pork, stir, and then the mushrooms, bamboo shoots, glutinous rice and the shrimp liquid. Mix and stir for about 1 minute, partially cooking the mixture. Season with the salt, thin soy sauce and pepper. Transfer to a bowl. Wash and dry the wok.

3. Boil a kettle of water. Pour over the duck, turning it over several times to ensure even scalding. Wipe off excess water.

4. While the skin is still warm, brush all over with the thick soy sauce, not missing the wings and legs. Put on a wire rack.

5. Heat a wok over high heat, add the oil, swirl it around and heat until smoke rises. Carefully lower the duck into the oil, breast side down, and fry for 1 or 2 minutes, or until brownish in color. With a wooden spoon or spatula held in one hand and another put inside the cavity, turn the duck over and fry the other side for another 1 or 2 minutes, or until brownish. Turn off the heat. Transfer to a larger plate. Discard the oil.

6. As soon as the duck has cooled a little, rub all over with the salt and wine or sherry. Pack the cavity loosely with the stuffing; there is no need to sew up either end.

7. Put into a large dish with about 1-inch raised edges. Add the star anise, peppercorns and tangerine peel. Steam in a wok or steamer for 1¾ to 2 hours (see page 44). Transfer carefully to a large heatproof serving platter. Keep warm in a low oven.

8. Spoon off most of the fat in the steaming dish. Strain the juices into a saucepan, discarding the spices: there should be about ½ pint. Slowly bring to a simmer. Trickle in the well-stirred dissolved potato flour, stirring as it thickens. Taste for flavor. Add the oyster sauce. Remove from the heat and keep hot.

9. Put the broccoli into a pan of boiling water with about 1 teaspoon of salt and 1 tablespoon of oil. Return to a boil and cook for 2 or 3 minutes, until tender but still crisp. Drain thoroughly. Take the

duck out of the oven and arrange the broccoli around it. Pour the hot sauce over the duck and broccoli.

10. To eat it the Chinese way, everyone helps himself and picks from the duck. It is so tender that the meat will come away from the bones when pressure from the chopsticks is applied. The stuffing can be spooned out of the cavity and served with the meat.

Note: After the duck is steamed (step 7), if it is left in a preheated oven of 300° to 350°F for 45 to 60 or 30 to 45 minutes, the skin will be crisp again. This time gap allows for drinks or other dishes to be served.

Scrambled Egg with Chinese Chives

1. Pick over the Chinese chives, snip off and discard both the hard top ends and the wilted tail ends. Wash and dry them well. Cut into 1-inch lengths.

2. Beat the eggs lightly in a large bowl with 1 tablespoon of the oil until well blended and frothy. Add the salt and pepper and beat a few more times.

3. Heat a wok over high heat until smoke rises. Add the remaining oil, swirl it around and heat until very hot. Add the Chinese chives, stir for about 20 seconds, then pour in the egg. Sliding the wok scoop or metal spatula to the bottom of the wok, keep turning and letting the egg go under to blend with the oil and chives. Continue in this way until all the egg is just set.

4. Remove from the heat and scoop the egg-and-chives mixture to a warm serving plate. Serve immediately.

Note: A small bunch of chives can be used as a substitute for Chinese chives.

INGREDIENTS

3 or 4 ounces Chinese chives
6 large eggs
8 tablespoons peanut or corn oil
½ to ¾ teaspoon salt
several turns pepper mill

Serves 6 with 2 or 3 other dishes

Illustrated on page 115

Whampoa Stir-fried Egg

黄埔炒蛋

INGREDIENTS

6 eggs

¼ to ½ teaspoon salt

½ pint peanut or corn oil (only about 7 tablespoons actually used)

Serves 4 to 6 with 2 or 3 other dishes

Even if someone arrives unannounced, the Chinese will extend an immediate invitation to stay for dinner with the stock phrase: "We'll just add another pair of chopsticks to the table." However, in the kitchen there will be a stir to whip up a quick and easy dish to add to those ready to be served. This egg dish fills the bill. It takes its name from Whampoa, a port near Canton, where the technique for stir-frying eggs was orginally invented. The tenderness of the egg has earned much fame for this Cantonese dish.

1. Beat the eggs lightly with the salt and 2 tablespoons of the oil until well amalgamated.

2. Heat a wok over medium heat until hot but not smoking. Add all the oil and swirl around 2 or 3 times to reach over halfway up the sloping edges. Pour the oil back into a container and then return the wok to the burner. There will be some oil left in the wok.

3. Add 2 tablespoons of oil and heat until hot but not smoking. Pour in the egg slowly, stirring and folding with the wok scoop or metal spatula. As soon as all the egg has been poured in, start slowly pouring in another 2 or 3 tablespoons of oil, little by little, around the side of the wok, while continuing to stir and fold. When the egg has set into tender flakes, remove from the heat and scoop at once to a warm serving dish.

Facing page, clockwise from the top: Soy sauce chicken (see page 116); Scrambled egg with Chinese chives (see page 113); Whampoa stir-fried egg (see above)

Soy Sauce Chicken

INGREDIENTS

2 whole star anise (16 segments)
1 teaspoon Szechwan
    peppercorns
1 tablespoon peanut or corn oil
6 scallions, halved crosswise
2 or 3 slices fresh ginger root,
    about ⅛ inch thick, peeled
1 oven-ready chicken, 3 pounds,
    at room temperature
½ pint thick soy sauce
2 tablespoons Shaohsing wine or
    medium-dry sherry
4 or 5 tablespoons brown sugar

*Serves 6 with 3 other dishes; or 4
as a main course*

Illustrated on page 115

*This is a whole chicken dish, beloved of the Southern Chinese. If the
chicken is hand-plucked in the old-fashioned way, it will be colored
an even russet brown by the soy sauce and sugar mixture. When a
chicken is machine-plucked, as it usually is in the West, the coloring
will not be as successful. Fortunately, the aromatic soy sauce taste
is not affected in any way.*

1. To make the spiced liquid, put the star anise and peppercorns in
a saucepan with 12 ounces of water and bring to a boil. Lower the
heat and simmer for about 15 minutes, reducing the liquid to 6
ounces. Drain and discard the spices.

2. Heat a wok over high heat until smoke rises. Add the oil and
swirl it around. Add the scallions and ginger, stir for about 10
seconds, or until they have released their aroma. Remove from the
heat. Transfer the scallions and ginger to the chicken cavity.

3. Wash the wok, then add the spiced liquid, soy sauce, wine or
sherry and sugar. Bring to a boil, stirring to make sure that the
sugar has dissolved.

4. Put the chicken in on its side. Using a large spoon, pour the
simmering sauce repeatedly over the chicken for 10 minutes.

5. With a spatula held in one hand and a wooden spoon put inside
the cavity, turn the chicken over to lie on the other side. Spoon the
simmering sauce over for another 10 minutes.

6. If too much sauce has evaporated, replenish with about 2 ounces
of water. Bring to simmering point again.

7. Cover and simmer for 20 minutes. Turn the chicken over again,
cover and continue to simmer for another 20 minutes, until the
chicken is cooked. To test, pierce the thickest part of the thigh with
a chopstick. If no pink juices run out, the chicken is cooked.

8. Remove the chicken from the wok, tipping out the soy sauce from
the cavity. Put some of this sauce on the table to use as a dip. The
rest can be stored in the refrigerator and used to season other
ingredients.

9. To serve the chicken, carve either Chinese style (see page 101) or
in your usual way.

Variation: Soy sauce drumsticks or chicken wings:
12 drumsticks or chicken wings or 6 of each. Pour the sauce
repeatedly over the drumsticks or wings for 10 minutes, then
simmer, covered, for 20 to 30 minutes, until cooked.

Kung Pao Chicken

A famous Szechwan dish that tempts the palate with a full range of tastes and aftertastes: peppery hot and spicy, savory and slightly sweet and sour. It is said that this was a favorite dish of a Szechwan governor during the Ch'ing dynasty (1644-1911), after whose official title, "Kung Pao," the dish was named. The governor must have been fond of peanuts, for it is unthinkable not to add them.

1. Cut the chicken into thin strips (a). Cut into cubes about ½ inch square (b). Put into a bowl.

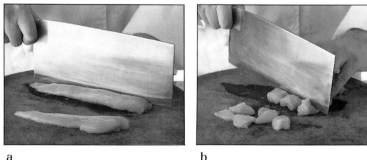

a   b

2. *Prepare the marinade:* Add the salt, soy sauce, wine or sherry, cornstarch and egg white to the chicken. Mix well and let marinate for 15 to 30 minutes.

3. *Prepare the sauce:* Mix together the soy sauce, chili sauce, vinegar, sugar, cornstarch, and stock or water.

4. Heat a wok over high heat until smoke rises. Add the oil and swirl it around. Add the dried chili, stir, then add the garlic and ginger and stir to release their aroma. Add the chicken. Sliding the wok scoop or metal spatula to the bottom of the wok, turn and toss for about 60 seconds. Splash in the wine or sherry around the side of the wok, stirring and tossing continuously. Add the scallions and continue to stir for another 30 to 45 seconds. The chicken should be almost cooked by now.

5. Add the well-stirred sauce to the wok. Continue to stir while it thickens.

6. Add the peanuts, stir to mix for a few times, then transfer to a warm serving plate. Serve immediately.

INGREDIENTS

12 ounces chicken breast meat
4 tablespoons peanut or corn oil
2 or 3 long (about 3 inches or more each) dried red chilies, or 4 or 5 smaller, seeded and cut into pieces
2 cloves garlic, peeled and diagonally sliced
4 to 6 thin slices fresh ginger root
1 tablespoon Shaohsing wine or medium-dry sherry
3 scallions, cut into small rounds
2 ounces roasted peanuts

FOR THE MARINADE
⅓ teaspoon salt
2 teaspoons thin soy sauce
2 teaspoons Shaohsing wine or medium-dry sherry
1 teaspoon cornstarch
1 tablespoon egg white, lightly beaten

FOR THE SAUCE
1 tablespoon thick soy sauce
1 or 2 tablespoons chili sauce
2 teaspoons rice or white wine vinegar
2 teaspoons sugar
1½ teaspoons cornstarch
6 tablespoons clear stock or water

Serves 4 with 3 other dishes

Illustrated on page 119

宮
保
雞
丁

Sautéed Chicken Livers

In this simple dish, with its slightly piquant taste, the livers are partially browned, so that they're crispy on the outside, but pink inside. As one of the dishes in a Chinese meal, rice would be served with it as usual, but as a main course, noodles or spaghetti would do equally well. A green salad could be served afterward.

INGREDIENTS

1½ pounds chicken livers, trimmed
1½ teaspoons cornstarch
6 or 7 tablespoons peanut or corn oil
2 to 2½ inches fresh ginger root, peeled and cut into slices
9 or 10 large scallions, sliced diagonally into ½ inch sections, white and green parts separated
1½ tablespoons Shaohsing wine or medium-dry sherry

FOR THE MARINADE

¾ teaspoon salt
¾ teaspoon brown sugar
1 tablespoon thick soy sauce
10 turns black pepper mill
2 teaspoons Worcestershire sauce
2 teaspoons Shaohsing wine or medium-dry sherry

FOR THE SAUCE

1½ teaspoons cornstarch
6 tablespoons clear stock or water
2 teaspoons thick soy sauce
1 teaspoon Worcestershire sauce

Serves 4 as a main course; 8 with 3 or 4 other dishes

Illustrated opposite

1. Slice each liver into 2 or 3 pieces. Place in a colander to wash and drain well. Put into a large bowl.

2. *Prepare the marinade:* Add the salt, sugar, soy sauce, pepper, Worcestershire sauce and wine or sherry to the livers. Stir to mix well and let marinate for 1 to 2 hours, stirring occasionally.

3. *Prepare the sauce:* Put the cornstarch in a small bowl, stir in 2 tablespoons of the stock or water and blend until smooth. Add the soy and Worcestershire sauces, and stir in the remaining stock or water.

4. Just before ready to cook, sprinkle the livers with the cornstarch and stir to coat well.

5. Heat a wok over high heat until smoke rises. Add the oil and swirl it around. Add the ginger and white scallions and let them sizzle. As soon as the scallions take on color, add the livers and brown for about 2 minutes, turning once or twice with a wok scoop or metal spatula to prevent sticking. Sprinkle with the wine or sherry, and when the sizzling has died down, lower the heat, cover and cook for about 2 minutes. Turn the livers over, add the green scallions, cover and continue to cook for about 2 more minutes.

6. Pour the well-stirred sauce over the livers and stir until it thickens. Transfer to a warm serving plate. Serve immediately.

Note: If pressed for time, instead of marinating the livers, pierce them with a fork to let the marinade permeate.

Facing page, clockwise from the top: Paper-wrapped chicken (see page 121); Dragon flying and phoenix dancing (see page 120); Sautéed chicken livers (see above); Kung Pao chicken (see page 117)

A Chicken for Two Dishes:

Dragon Flying and Phoenix Dancing

INGREDIENTS

2 chicken breasts from a 3 to 3½
    pound chicken, skinned and
    boned
8 ounces medium raw prawns,
    without heads, shelled, halved
    and deveined
1¼ teaspoons salt
4 ounces sugar peas, trimmed
peanut or corn oil for deep frying
2 or 3 cloves garlic, peeled and
    chopped fine
3 or 4 scallions, cut into 1 inch
    sections, white and green parts
    separated
2 ounces red-in-snow, rinsed
1 tablespoon Shaohsing wine or
    medium-dry sherry

FOR THE MARINADE

1½ teaspoons salt
½ teaspoon sugar
6 turns white pepper mill
1 teaspoon Shaohsing wine or
    medium-dry sherry
1 teaspoon cornstarch
1 tablespoon egg white, lightly
    beaten

FOR THE SAUCE

¾ teaspoon potato flour
5 tablespoons clear stock
1 tablespoon oyster sauce

*Serves 4 to 6 with 2 or 3 other
    dishes*

Illustrated on page 119

*The dragon and phoenix of the title are metaphors for the two main
ingredients: chicken and prawns. Because it is a very elegant dish,
it is worth the trouble to use the "going through the oil" technique to
seal in the juices of the ingredients before stir-frying them.*

1. Cut the chicken into large even-sized pieces. Put into a bowl.

2. *Prepare the marinade:* Add the salt, sugar, pepper, wine or
sherry, cornstarch and egg white to the chicken. Stir to mix well. Let
marinate for 20 to 30 minutes.

3. Add ¼ teaspoon of the salt to the prawns.

4. Blanch the sugar peas in plenty of boiling water with 1 teaspoon
of the salt and 1 tablespoon of oil until the water returns to a boil.
Pour into a colander and refresh under cold running water.

5. *Prepare the sauce:* Mix together the potato flour, stock and
oyster sauce.

6. Half fill a wok or deep fryer with oil. Heat to a temperature of
350°F, or until a cube of stale bread browns in 60 seconds. Add the
chicken and, using a long pair of chopsticks, separate the pieces and
let them "go through the oil" for about 20 seconds (see page 40).
Remove with a hand strainer and put on a plate. Do not turn off the
heat.

7. Add the prawns to the oil for about 20 seconds, separating the
pieces with chopsticks. Transfer to another plate. Turn off the heat.

8. Pour the oil into a container for future use, leaving about 5
tablespoons in the wok.

9. Reheat the wok over high heat until smoke rises. Add the garlic,
and as it sizzles, add the white scallions and stir. Add the
red-in-snow and stir until hot. Return the chicken to the wok and,
sliding the wok scoop or metal spatula to the bottom of the wok,
turn and toss until almost cooked. Return the prawns to the wok,
continuing to turn and stir. Splash in the wine around the side of the
wok, stirring as it sizzles: both chicken and prawns will be cooked
by now. Add the sugar peas. Sprinkle in the well-stirred sauce,
stirring as it thickens. Add the green scallions. Transfer to a warm
serving dish. Serve immediately.

Paper-wrapped Chicken

*The wind-dried sausage in this dish makes the chicken, already
highly seasoned in the marinade, even spicier and richer in taste.*

1. Skin and bone the drumsticks and thighs. Discard the pinions of
the wings and chop each wing into 3 pieces. Scrape out the 2 oysters.
Put into a bowl.

2. *Prepare the marinade:* Add the soy sauce, sugar, wine or sherry,
ginger, five-spice powder and oil to the chicken. Mix well. Let
marinate for a minimum of 1 hour, turning the pieces occasionally.

3. Squeeze out excess water from the mushrooms but leave damp.
Halve if small ones are used, quarter if large ones are used.

4. Slice the bamboo shoots into 24 pieces, each about 1/5 inch thick.

5. Rinse the Chinese sausages and pat dry. Slice each diagonally
into 8 pieces, making a total of 48.

6. About 10 minutes before the wrapping, add the mushrooms and
bamboo shoots to the chicken, so that they can absorb some of the
marinade.

7. Using a brush, thoroughly oil one side of 1 square of greaseproof
paper. Put on a plate or work surface at an angle, like a diamond,
and layer on it 1 piece of chicken between 2 slices of Chinese
sausage, then 1 piece of bamboo shoot, and, finally, 1 piece of
mushroom with a coriander leaf on top.

8. To wrap in the classic Chinese way, fold the bottom flap up
toward the center, then fold the 2 side flaps inward on top of each
other and finally fold the top flap down and tuck it squarely inside
the opening. Repeat this process until all have been wrapped.

9. Half fill a wok or deep fryer with oil. Heat to a temperature of
350° to 375°F, or until a cube of stale bread browns in 50 to 60
seconds. Slip 12 parcels into the oil, unsealed side down, and
deep-fry for about 5 minutes if you like the chicken just done, or for
about 8 minutes if you like it much more cooked and slightly
charred. Turn them over for the last minute of cooking.

10. Remove with a large hand strainer and, holding it carefully
above the oil, let excess oil from the parcels drain back into the wok
or deep fryer. Put the parcels on a warm serving plate. Reheat the
oil and deep-fry the remainder as before.

11. Serve hot. As soon as the fingers can stand the heat, open a
parcel and savor its contents.

Note: Any leftover parcels can be deep-fried again momentarily or
put into a preheated oven of 350°F for 10 minutes.

INGREDIENTS

the rest of the chicken (or 6
   drumsticks or thigh pieces),
   over 2 pounds
12 small or 6 large dried Chinese
   mushrooms, reconstituted (see
   page 39)
4 to 6 ounces canned bamboo
   shoots
6 wind-dried Chinese sausages,
   liver or pork or both
24 pieces greaseproof paper, each
   8 inches square
24 large pieces coriander leaves
   (optional)
peanut or corn oil for deep-frying

FOR THE MARINADE
3 tablespoons thin soy sauce
2 teaspoons sugar
2 teaspoons Shaohsing wine or
   medium-dry sherry
1 teaspoon ginger powder
1/4 teaspoon five-spice powder
1 tablespoon sesame oil

*Serves 8 as a first course; 4 as a
   main course with a salad*

Illustrated on page 119

A Northern or Peking Menu

The main feature of this menu for six is, without doubt, the Peking duck, with its pancake accompaniment. In fact, they alone, with any one of the other dishes, should make four people feel well fed and contented.

北京菜

薄餅 **Mandarin pancakes**

北京填鴨 **Peking duck**
Tender duck served, traditionally, wrapped in a Mandarin pancake with hoisin sauce and scallions (see page 209).

賽
干
貝
鬆

"Seaweed"
Deep-fried cabbage greens
garnished with sugar and
almonds (see page 211).

酒
溜
魚
片

Fish in wine sauce
Delicate-tasting dish with
firm white fish and cloud
ears in a wine sauce
(see page 211).

北
京
泡
菜

**Pickled cabbage Peking
style**
Spicy dish served cold as an
hors d'oeuvre or side dish
(see page 212).

奶
油
津
白

**Chinese celery cabbage in cream
sauce**
An unusual dish, one of the few Chinese
recipes using dairy produce
(see page 212).

MEAT

Rustic Steamed Beef

A delicious family dish that is equally good to serve when entertaining.

INGREDIENTS

12 ounces steak, beef, fillet, rump or skirt, trimmed
2 tablespoons cloud ears, reconstituted (see page 39)
1 small handful golden needles, about ⅕ ounce, reconstituted (see page 39)
4 medium dried Chinese mushrooms, reconstituted (see page 39)
1½ teaspoons thick soy sauce
3 tablespoons peanut or corn oil
1 ounce Szechwan preserved vegetable, rinsed
3 or 4 scallions, cut into 2-inch sections, shredded lengthwise
2 or 3 coriander leaves, torn into pieces (optional)

FOR THE MARINADE

½ inch fresh ginger root, peeled and grated fine
¼ teaspoon salt
¼ teaspoon sugar
1 tablespoon thick soy sauce
6 turns black pepper mill
2 teaspoons Shaohsing wine or medium-dry sherry
2 teaspoons potato flour
2 tablespoons water
1 tablespoon peanut or corn oil

Serves 4 with 2 other dishes

Illustrated opposite

1. Slice the beef into pieces about 1 by 1½ inches and ¼ inch thick. Put into a bowl.

2. *Prepare the marinade:* Add the ginger, salt, sugar, soy sauce, pepper, wine or sherry and potato flour to the beef. Add the water, 1 tablespoon at a time, and stir in to coat the meat. Let marinate in the refrigerator for 20 to 30 minutes. Blend in the oil just before ready to steam.

3. Drain the cloud ears and golden needles and squeeze out excess water from the mushrooms but leave damp. Break up or cut the cloud ears into similarly-sized pieces. Split the golden needles in half lengthwise or crosswise. Slice the mushrooms into thin strips.

4. Put the cloud ears, golden needles and mushrooms together. Mix in the soy sauce and 1 tablespoon of the oil.

5. Slice the preserved vegetable into very thin pieces.

6. Mix the cloud ears, golden needles, mushrooms and preserved vegetable. Spread out on a heatproof dish with sloping edges.

7. Steam the beef in a wok or steamer over high heat for 10 minutes for medium-done beef or 13 to 15 minutes for well-done (see page 44). Remove from the heat. Put the scallions and coriander leaves, if used, on top of the dish.

8. Heat the remaining 2 tablespoons of oil in a small saucepan until just smoking. Pour over the scallions to cook partially.

9. Remove the dish from the wok or steamer and serve immediately.

Facing page, clockwise from the top: Rustic steamed beef (see above); Twice-cooked pork (see page 126); Sweet and sour pork (see page 127)

Twice-cooked Pork

INGREDIENTS

1 pound pork in one piece, 2½ to
   3 inches wide (middle section
   of belly with alternating lean
   and fat layers is ideal)
1 leek, trimmed
2 or 3 cloves garlic, peeled and
   sliced thin
3 tablespoons peanut or corn oil
salt to taste

FOR THE SAUCE

1½ tablespoons hot soy bean
   paste
1 tablespoon thick soy sauce
¼ teaspoon salt
1 teaspoon sugar
1 tablespoon Shaohsing wine or
   medium-dry sherry

*Serves 4 to 6 with 2 or 3 other
   dishes*

Illustrated on page 125

*One of the most popular Szechwan pork dishes, it is cleverly
produced by combining two very different cooking methods: boiling
and stir-frying.*

1. Neatly remove the spareribs, if any, from the pork. Put the
whole piece, rind and all, in a saucepan, cover with boiling water
and simmer over moderate heat for about 20 to 25 minutes. The
pork is not expected to be thoroughly cooked. Remove and leave to
cool. Store in the refrigerator for about 2 hours to firm up the meat.
It can be left overnight, covered.

2. When ready to cook, remove the rind and slice crosswise into
very thin pieces, not more than ¹⁄₁₀ inch thick, if possible.

3. Cut the leek lengthwise into 2 and wash thoroughly to remove any
grit caught between the leaves. Cut diagonally into ½-inch sections.

4. *Prepare the sauce:* Mix together the paste, soy sauce, salt, sugar
and wine or sherry in a small bowl and set aside. (Those who like it
really hot and spicy can use more hot soy bean paste.)

5. Heat a wok over moderate heat until hot. Add 1 tablespoon of
the oil and swirl it around. Add the leek and stir-fry with the wok
scoop or metal spatula for about 2 minutes. Season with salt to taste
and transfer to a warm plate. The leek should be moist but not
swimming in liquid. Drain if there is any excess water.

6. Dry the wok and reheat over high heat until smoke rises. Add the
remaining oil and swirl it around. Add the garlic, and as soon as it
sizzles and takes on color, add the pork. Stir and spread the pieces
into more or less a single layer, so that the fat fries in the oil. Turn
over, pressing gently, to fry until the fat is transparent. Lower the
heat if necessary; if excess fat oozes out, spoon from the wok and
discard.

7. Pour in the sauce and stir to let it permeate the pork. Add the
leek and stir until the sauce is almost absorbed. Transfer to a warm
serving plate. Serve immediately.

Sweet and Sour Pork

To many people, sweet and sour pork is synonymous with bad Chinese takeout food: lumps of chewy pork wrapped in thick batter, covered with a gluey and sickening sweet and sour sauce. However, when well made – crisp outside yet tender inside, topped with a well-balanced sweet and sour sauce – this is one of the most appetizing Cantonese dishes.

1. Cut the pork into pieces about 1 by 1¼ by ¾ inches. Put into a bowl.

2. Add the salt and soy sauce and let marinate for 30 to 60 minutes. Stir in the egg to coat thoroughly.

3. Dredge the pork, piece by piece, with the cornstarch, making sure it is evenly coated. It is not necessary to use up all the cornstarch.

4. Half fill a wok or deep fryer with oil. Heat to a temperature of 350°F, or until a cube of stale bread browns in 60 seconds. Add the pork and deep-fry for about 1 minute in 1 or 2 batches; separate the pieces with a pair of chopsticks or a wooden spoon if they stick together. Drain on paper towels. This step can be done ahead of time.

5. *Prepare the sauce:* In a bowl, dissolve the potato flour in the water and pineapple juice. Add the vinegar, sugar, salt, soy sauce, ketchup and Worcestershire sauce and stir to blend. (This can be made in advance.)

6. Heat a frying pan or saucepan (unless you have another wok) until hot. Add 1½ tablespoons of oil and swirl it around. Add the garlic and onion, stir a few times and then add the green pepper. Stir-fry for about 2 minutes over medium heat and season with salt, if desired. Add the pineapple chunks. Pour in the well-stirred sauce and bring to a boil slowly, stirring constantly.

7. Reheat the oil for deep-frying to a higher temperature, 375°F, or until a cube of stale bread browns in 50 seconds. Add the pork and again deep-fry in one batch for about 2 or 3 minutes, to ensure that the outside is crisp and golden without the pork inside getting dry. Drain on paper towels and transfer to a warm serving plate. Reheat the sweet and sour sauce and stir in the remaining 1 tablespoon of oil. This prevents the sauce from being gluey. Pour the sweet and sour sauce over the pork. Serve immediately.

Note: When reheated, sweet and sour pork will be soggy but it will still taste good.

INGREDIENTS

1 pound lean pork belly, skinned and trimmed of excess fat
½ teaspoon salt
1 teaspoon thin soy sauce
½ egg, lightly beaten
3 tablespoons cornstarch
peanut or corn oil for deep-frying
2½ tablespoons peanut or corn oil
1 clove garlic, peeled and minced
1 onion, skinned and roughly chopped
1 green pepper, halved, seeded and diced
4 ounces canned pineapple chunks, drained, juice reserved

FOR THE SAUCE

2 teaspoons potato flour
4 tablespoons water
4 tablespoons pineapple juice
3 tablespoons rice or wine vinegar
4 to 4½ tablespoons sugar
¼ teaspoon salt
2 teaspoons thin soy sauce
2 tablespoons tomato ketchup
1½ teaspoons Worcestershire sauce

Serves 4 to 6 with 2 or 3 other dishes

Illustrated on page 125

咕
嚕
肉

蒜
子
牛
肉

Braised Beef with Garlic

Do not be put off by the large amount of garlic used in this recipe: the Chinese way of sizzling the garlic in hot oil burns off the garlic odor, and instead produces a heavenly aroma, which is absorbed by the beef.

INGREDIENTS

2½ pounds beef, shin and chuck steak, trimmed
4 tablespoons peanut or corn oil
8 ounces garlic cloves, peeled
3 tablespoons Shaohsing wine or medium-dry sherry
¼ teaspoon salt
1 teaspoon sugar
2 tablespoons thick soy sauce
1 tablespoon thin soy sauce
1 pint clear stock
½ to 1 teaspoon potato flour, dissolved in 1 tablespoon water
8 scallions, cut into 1-inch sections

Serves 6 as a main course

Illustrated opposite

1. Cut the beef into cubes of about 1½ inches.

2. Heat a wok over high heat until smoke rises. Add the oil and swirl it around. Add the garlic, turn and toss until it takes on color. Add the beef, turn and flip with a wok scoop or metal spatula to brown it with the garlic for 2 or 3 minutes. Splash in the wine or sherry around the side of the wok, stirring continuously as it sizzles and reduces to about half. Remove from the heat.

3. Transfer the wok contents to a large, heavy saucepan or flameproof casserole, scraping all the juices from the wok as well. Season with the salt, sugar and soy sauces, and pour in the stock. Bring to a boil, reduce the heat to maintain a moderate simmer and continue to cook, covered, for 1½ to 1¾ hours, or until the beef is tender and most of the garlic has been assimilated into the sauce. Check the water level from time to time and replenish whenever necessary; also stir thoroughly a few times to make sure that the beef has not stuck to the bottom. When ready, there should be more than ½ pint of sauce. (This dish can be prepared and cooked to this stage several hours or even a day in advance. The taste actually improves overnight.)

4. Just before serving, bring to a boil, then add the well-stirred dissolved potato flour, to thicken the sauce slightly. Add the scallions, replace the lid and cook for a few seconds more. Transfer to a warm serving dish and serve.

Facing page, clockwise from the top: Braised beef with garlic (see above); Beef in oyster sauce (see page 130); Beef with preserved tangerine peel (see page 131)

Beef in Oyster Sauce

INGREDIENTS

1 pound beef, rump, fillet or
    skirt steak
8 ounces asparagus
5 to 6 tablespoons peanut or corn
    oil
3 or 4 cloves garlic, peeled and
    chopped fine
¼ inch fresh ginger root, peeled
    and chopped fine
3 or 4 scallions, cut into 1-inch
    sections, white and green parts
    separated
1 tablespoon Shaohsing wine or
    medium-dry sherry
sesame oil to taste (optional)

FOR THE MARINADE

¼ teaspoon salt
¼ teaspoon sugar
2 teaspoons thick soy sauce
6 turns pepper mill
2 teaspoons Shaohsing wine or
    medium-dry sherry
1 teaspoon potato flour
1 to 2 tablespoons water
2 teaspoons peanut or corn oil

FOR THE SAUCE

1 teaspoon potato flour
6 tablespoons clear stock or
    water
2½ to 3 tablespoons oyster sauce

Serves 4 with 2 other dishes

Illustrated on page 129

Although the Cantonese enjoy pork as much as all the other Chinese, they tend to eat more beef than many of their compatriots. Beef in oyster sauce is perhaps the most basic of all the Cantonese beef dishes. It is delicious also with other vegetables, such as mushrooms, celery, bamboo shoots or bean sprouts. In stir-frying beef, the Cantonese believe that it is most important to make it tender and "velvety," and to achieve this they add bicarbonate of soda to the marinade. This tenderizing process is unnecessary in the West.

1. Pat the beef dry. Cut across the grain into rectangular slices about 1 by 1½ inches and ¼ inch thick. Put into a fairly large, deep bowl.

2. *Prepare the marinade:* Add the salt, sugar, soy sauce, pepper, wine or sherry to the beef. Stir to blend. Sprinkle with the potato flour. Add 1 tablespoon of the water and stir, to coat the beef, until it is too difficult to continue. Add the remaining water and stir again. This process will make the beef velvety and tender when cooked. Let marinate in the refrigerator for 30 minutes. Blend in the oil.

3. *Prepare the sauce:* Put the potato flour in a small bowl, stir in the stock or water to blend thoroughly. Add the oyster sauce.

4. Wash and trim the asparagus. Cut diagonally into thin slices, so that they can be cooked quickly and can absorb the sauce easily.

5. Heat a wok over high heat until smoke rises. Add the oil and swirl it around. Add the garlic, ginger and white scallions in rapid succession. Stir several times to release their aroma and then add the beef. Sliding the wok scoop or metal spatula to the bottom of the wok, flip and toss for up to 1 minute. Splash in the wine or sherry around the side of the wok, just above the beef and, while it sizzles, continue to stir. Transfer to a warm plate as soon as the sizzling is over, but leave some oil behind.

6. Without washing the wok, add 1 tablespoon of oil. Add the asparagus and stir-fry for 1 minute. Season with salt, sprinkle with drops of water, lower the heat, cover and steam for about 1 more minute.

7. Push the asparagus around the sides of the wok and pour the well-stirred sauce into the center. As soon as it bubbles, return the beef, add the green scallions and stir together with the asparagus until hot. Transfer to a warm serving plate. Serve immediately. Sprinkle with sesame oil at the table, if desired.

Beef with Preserved Tangerine Peel

True to form, this Hunan dish is spicy hot, savory and slightly sweet. As if the flavors are not complex enough, tangy tangerine peel is added to provide a further dimension in taste. The orange rind is not a traditional ingredient for this dish, but it is used here because it compliments rather than detracts from the tangerine peel.

1. Soak the tangerine peel in cold water for about 2 hours, or until soft. Drain and slice into strips about ⅕ inch wide.

2. Peel the orange rind lengthwise and blanch in boiling water for 5 minutes to remove its bitterness. Drain and rinse in cold water. Slice into strips similar to the tangerine strips.

3. Cut the beef into thickish slices, about 1 by 1½ inches and put into a bowl.

4. *Prepare the marinade:* Add the salt, sugar, soy sauces, wine or sherry and potato flour to the meat. Add the water, 1 tablespoon at a time, and stir in the same direction until all is absorbed. Mix in the chopped chili and let marinate for 30 to 60 minutes. Blend in the hot chili oil.

5. Heat a wok over high heat until smoke rises. Add the oil and swirl it around. Add the ginger, stir, then add the white scallions and let sizzle. Add the tangerine and orange peel and fry for a few seconds. Put in the beef and, sliding the wok scoop or metal spatula to the bottom of the wok, flip and turn for 1 or 2 minutes or until very hot. Splash in the wine or sherry around the side of the wok, continuing to stir. When the sizzling dies down, add the chili sauce. Cover, lower the heat and cook for about 2 minutes, so that the flavor of the tangerine peel can permeate the beef.

6. *Prepare the sauce:* Mix together the potato flour, water or stock and soy sauce.

7. Dribble into the wok and stir as the sauce thickens. Add the green scallions and stir to mix. Transfer to a warm serving dish. Serve immediately.

INGREDIENTS

- 5 or 6 pieces preserved tangerine peel
- 1 sweet orange
- 1½ pounds beef, rump, fillet or skirt steak, trimmed
- 4 tablespoons peanut or corn oil
- 1 inch fresh ginger root, peeled and cut into silken threads (see page 35)
- 6 scallions cut into 2-inch sections, white and green parts separated
- 1 tablespoon Shaohsing wine or medium-dry sherry
- 2 to 3 tablespoons chili sauce

FOR THE MARINADE

- ¾ teaspoon salt
- 1 teaspoon sugar
- 2 teaspoons thin soy sauce
- 2 teaspoons thick soy sauce
- 2 teaspoons Shaohsing wine or medium-dry sherry
- 1½ teaspoons potato flour
- 2 tablespoons water
- 1 dried red chili, seeded and chopped
- 1 tablespoon hot chili oil (see page 225)

FOR THE SAUCE

- ½ teaspoon potato flour
- 2 tablespoons water or clear stock
- 1 tablespoon thick soy sauce

Serves 4 with 2 other dishes

Illustrated on page 129

陳皮牛肉

White-cut Pork

白切肉

INGREDIENTS

1 to 1¼ pounds lean pork belly

SZECHWAN-STYLE SAUCE

2½ teaspoons garlic chopped very fine

2 tablespoons fresh coriander leaves, chopped

2 large scallions, cut into small rounds

1 fresh green or red chili, about 3 inches long, seeded and chopped

3 tablespoons thick soy sauce

1 tablespoon sesame oil

1½ teaspoons rice or wine vinegar

¾ teaspoon sugar

1½ teaspoons hot chili oil

PEKING-STYLE SAUCE

4 teaspoons very finely chopped garlic

2½ tablespoons thick soy sauce

2 teaspoons sesame oil

Serves 4 to 6 with 2 or 3 other dishes

Illustrated opposite

This dish, popular in both Szechwan and Peking cuisines, either as family fare or for entertaining, can be made one day ahead. It is so named because the pork is simply boiled in a pot of clear tap water, or "white water," as the Chinese call it. True to form, the Szechwan-style sauce evokes a wide range of tastes and aftertastes; the Peking counterpart is laden with garlic.

1. Put the piece of pork in a large saucepan and cover with water. Bring to a boil.

2. Lower the heat and simmer gently for 1 hour, or until the pork is thoroughly cooked. To test, insert a chopstick or fork into the thickest part; if no pink juices run out, the pork is cooked.

3. Transfer the pork to a colander, saving the water, for the stockpot. Rinse under cold water for 10 minutes, to firm up the texture.

4. Refrigerate, covered, for several hours or overnight.

5. *Prepare the sauce:* Mix together the chosen sauce ingredients and set aside.

6. Put the chilled pork on the chopping board. Slide a sharp knife between the rind and the fat and slice off the rind. Discard.

7. Slice the pork along the grain into paper-thin pieces, about 2½ inches wide. Arrange the slices on a round serving plate, overlapping each other. Pour the sauce over them and serve.

Facing page, clockwise from the top: White-cut pork (see above); Pearly pork balls (see page 135); Char-siu (see page 134)

Char-siu: Cantonese Roast Pork

INGREDIENTS

2½ pounds pork without bone or
   rind, shoulder or leg cuts
about 2 tablespoons runny honey

FOR THE MARINADE

2 tablespoons hoisin sauce
2 tablespoons ground yellow bean
   sauce
4 tablespoons thin soy sauce
6 tablespoons sugar
1 tablespoon Shaohsing wine or
   medium-dry sherry
1 teaspoon salt

*Serves 4 as a main course; 8 with
   4 other dishes*

Illustrated on page 133

*As a contribution to Chinese gastronomy, this dish is arguably as
notable as Peking Duck, and it's certainly easier to make. When
roasted, this fragrant and succulent pork looks reddish brown with
slightly burned edges, especially around the fat. Delicious hot or
cold, it's a versatile ingredient and can be stir-fried with vegetables,
or mixed with fried rice and used as a topping on noodles.*

1. Divide the pork into 4 strips (a). Leave any fat on, because it is
delicately succulent when roasted.

2. Make 3 or 4 diagonal cuts from opposite directions, cutting
three-quarters through the width of a strip without cutting it into
pieces (b). This allows for better absorption of the marinade and
gives the pork the traditional char-siu look.

a   b

3. *Prepare the marinade:* In a large bowl mix together the sauces,
sugar, wine or sherry and salt. Put the pork in and let marinate for
4 hours, turning it over every 30 minutes.

4. Place the strips of pork side by side on a wire rack in the top
third of the oven with a tray of water ½ inch deep underneath to
catch the drippings. (The water prevents the juices that drip from
the pork from burning; steam from it also keeps the pork from
drying.) Roast in a preheated oven at 375°F, for 25 to 30 minutes, at
the end of which time the top side will be reddish brown. Remove
from the oven, dip each piece into the marinade and return to the
rack with the bottom side up. Lower the oven temperature to 350°F,
and continue to roast for another 25 to 30 minutes. Insert a
chopstick or fork into the thickest part of one piece: if no pink juices
run out, the pork is cooked.

5. Transfer to a wire rack. Immediately brush all over with honey,
making sure not to neglect the crevices.

6. Carve into slices and serve immediately.

Note: This dish can be frozen. To reheat, place on a rack in a preheated oven at 350°F for about 12 minutes. The leftover marinade can be cooked to make a dipping sauce for the pork. If it is too sweet, add more salt to it.

Variation: Roast spareribs
Use one whole side of spareribs (about 3 pounds). Divide it in half and roast in the same manner as char-siu.

Pearly Pork Balls

It is a misconception to think that every Hunan dish is spicy hot. On the contrary, many are not, and this dish, that derives its name from the glutinous rice that shines like little pearls on the pork balls, is one of them.

1. Rinse the rice, rubbing gently with your fingers in 3 or 4 changes of water, or until it is no longer milky. Drain.

2. Soak in plenty of cold water for about 4 hours. Drain well and spread out in a shallow pan.

3. Drain and squeeze out excess water from the mushrooms but leave damp. Chop into the size of matchstick heads.

4. Soak the shrimp, in just enough boiling water to cover them, for 10 to 15 minutes. Drain them, reserving the soaking liquid.

5. Chop fine or mince the shrimp and the water chestnuts.

6. Chop the fat and lean pork by hand or mince coarsely.

7. Combine the mushrooms, dried shrimp, water chestnuts and pork in a large bowl. Add the salt, pepper and potato flour. Stir in, a spoonful at a time, 3 tablespoons of water and the soaking liquid from the shrimp.

8. Cut the ham into pieces the size of matchstick heads and mix with the rice in the pan.

9. Pick up about 1 tablespoon of the pork mixture, roll it between your palms into a ball about the size of a Ping-Pong ball. Roll this ball over the rice and ham, making sure it is completely covered, and put it on a heatproof plate. Repeat until all the pork mixture is used. The pork balls will fill more than one plate.

10. Steam the pork balls in a wok or steamer for 15 minutes (see page 44).

11. Serve the pearly balls hot, either piled up neatly in a bowl or arranged on a warm serving plate.

INGREDIENTS

5 ounces white glutinous rice
4 medium dried Chinese mushrooms, reconstituted (see page 39)
2 tablespoons dried shrimp, rinsed
4 water chestnuts, fresh peeled or canned, drained
12 ounces pork, about 3 ounces fat and 9 ounces lean
½ teaspoon salt
8 turns white pepper mill
1 tablespoon potato flour
2 ounces lean ham

Serves 6 with 3 other dishes

Illustrated on page 133

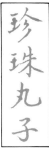

珍珠丸子

Stir-fried Pork with Szechwan Preserved Vegetable

榨
菜
肉
絲

INGREDIENTS

8 ounces pork tender loin
2 ounces Szechwan preserved
    vegetable, rinsed
4 tablespoons peanut or corn oil
1 large clove garlic, peeled and
    cut into silken shreds (see page
    35)
5 or 6 scallions, halved
    lengthwise, then cut into
    2-inch sections

FOR THE MARINADE

large pinch salt
½ teaspoon sugar
½ teaspoon thin soy sauce
1 teaspoon Shaohsing wine or
    medium-dry sherry
½ teaspoon potato flour
1 tablespoon water
1 teaspoon sesame oil

Serves 2 with 1 other dish

Illustrated opposite

Since preserved Szechwan vegetable is a regional product and pork is the national Chinese meat, it is hardly surprising that a standard Szechwan dish combines the two. In fact, this simple stir-fried dish is popular family fare all over China, eaten as much in the South as in the North.

1. Slice the pork into matchstick-sized strips. Put into a bowl.

2. *Prepare the marinade:* Add the salt, sugar, soy sauce, wine or sherry, potato flour and water to the pork. Stir until absorbed. Let marinate for about 15 minutes. Blend in the sesame oil.

3. Slice the preserved vegetable into very thin pieces, stack them up and slice them into very thin strips.

4. Heat a wok over high heat until smoke rises. Add the oil and swirl it around. Add the garlic, and as it sizzles, add the preserved vegetable and stir a few times. Before it begins to "bounce," add the pork. Sliding the wok scoop or metal spatula to the bottom of the wok, turn and toss in rapid succession for about 1 minute, separating the strips at the same time. Splash in the wine or sherry around the side of the wok and continue to stir as it sizzles. Add the scallions and stir together for another minute, or until the pork has become opaque and is cooked. Transfer to a warm serving plate. Serve immediately.

Facing page, clockwise from the top: Stir-fried pork with Szechwan preserved vegetable (see above); Mu-shu pork (see page 139); Stir-fried beef with pickled mustard green (see page 138)

Stir-fried Beef with Pickled Mustard Green

咸酸菜炒牛肉

INGREDIENTS

8 ounces canned pickled mustard green, rinsed
2¼ tablespoons sugar
12 ounces beef, skirt, steak, rump or fillet
1 teaspoon potato flour
6 tablespoons water
5 tablespoons peanut or corn oil
4 or 5 cloves garlic, peeled and chopped fine
4 scallions, cut into 1-inch sections, white and green parts separated
1 tablespoon Shaohsing wine or medium-dry sherry
¼ to ½ inch fresh ginger root, peeled and chopped fine or sliced

FOR THE MARINADE

¼ teaspoon salt
scant 1 tablespoon thick soy sauce
8 turns black pepper mill
2 teaspoons Shaohsing wine or medium-dry sherry
1 teaspoon potato flour
2 tablespoons water
1 teaspoon sesame oil

Serves 4 with 2 other dishes

Illustrated on page 137

This Cantonese dish, with its mouth-watering combination of pungent, savory, sweet and sour tastes, comes from the area along the Eastern River in Kwangtung province.

1. Shred the pickled mustard green into narrow pieces. Put into a bowl, add the sugar and mix well. Let stand at room temperature for up to 1 hour.

2. Cut the beef across the grain into slices about 1 by 1½ inches and ¼ inch thick. Put into a bowl.

3. *Prepare the marinade:* Add the salt, soy sauce, pepper and wine or sherry to the beef. Sprinkle with the potato flour and add the water, 1 tablespoon at a time, stirring until it is difficult to continue before adding another spoonful. This process will make the beef velvety and tender. Put in the refrigerator for 30 minutes. Blend in the sesame oil.

4. Mix the 1 teaspoon of potato flour and the water in a small bowl and put aside.

5. Heat a wok over high heat until smoke rises. Add 4 tablespoons of the oil and swirl it around. Add the garlic, and as soon as it takes on color, add the white scallions and stir. Add the beef. Sliding the wok scoop or metal spatula to the bottom of the wok, turn and toss vigorously for 30 to 60 seconds, or until partially cooked. Splash in the wine or sherry around the side of the wok, continuing to turn and toss until the sizzling dies down. Transfer to a warm plate.

6. Add the remaining 1 tablespoon of oil to the wok and swirl it around. Tip in the ginger, stir, and then add the pickled mustard green. Stir and turn until piping hot and then push to the edge, leaving a well in the middle.

7. Return the beef to the middle and immediately pour in the well-stirred dissolved potato flour. Continue to toss the beef until this thickening has cooked. Stir in the green scallions. Transfer to a warm serving plate. Serve immediately.

Mu-shu Pork

Some Chinese dishes have a time-honored formula for the ingredients, and this Northern dish, consisting of golden needles, cloud ears, pork and egg, is one of them. Mu-shu is the Chinese name for golden needles, which, in this dish, rank in equal importance with the pork. Mu-shu is also said to refer to the egg pieces, because their yellow color, reminds one of the tinge of the golden needles.

1. Drain the cloud ears (for extra slipperiness, soak in boiling water for another 20 to 30 minutes). Squeeze out excess water but leave damp.

2. Drain the golden needles; soak in boiling water for another 20 to 30 minutes for extra tenderness. Drain and squeeze out excess water but leave damp. Split each one lengthwise with the fingers.

3. Slice the pork into thin, even-sized rectangular pieces. Put into a bowl.

4. *Prepare the marinade:* Add the salt, sugar, soy sauces, pepper, wine or sherry, potato flour and water to the pork. Stir to coat. Let marinate for about 20 minutes. Stir in the oil.

5. Beat the eggs lightly with 1 tablespoon of the oil and ¼ teaspoon of the salt.

6. Heat a wok over high heat until smoke rises. Add 2 tablespoons of the oil and swirl it around. Add the cloud ears and stir for about 30 seconds, lowering the heat if they jump in the air and make popping noises. Add the golden needles and continue to stir and turn until very hot. Season with ¼ teaspoon salt, the soy sauce and the sugar. Transfer to a warm dish and set aside.

7. Wipe the wok and reheat until hot. Add 2 tablespoons of the oil and swirl it around. Pour in the egg and, sliding the wok scoop or metal spatula to the bottom of the wok, fold and turn until the egg forms into lumps. Transfer to a warm plate and set aside. Wash and dry the wok.

8. Reheat the wok until smoke rises. Add the remaining oil and swirl it around. Add the white scallions, stir and let them sizzle for a few seconds. Add the pork and turn and toss in rapid succession for about 1 minute or until partially cooked and turning opaque. Splash in the wine or sherry around the side of the wok, continuing to stir and turn as it sizzles. Return all the other ingredients to the wok. Stir and mix for another minute, so that the pork is thoroughly cooked, the egg firmer and all the ingredients piping hot. Add the green scallions. Transfer to a warm serving dish. Sprinkle with the sesame oil and serve immediately.

INGREDIENTS

½ ounce cloud ears, reconstituted (see page 39)
1 ounce golden needles, reconstituted (see page 39)
10 to 12 ounces lean pork
4 eggs
8 tablespoons peanut or corn oil
½ teaspoon salt
1 tablespoon thick soy sauce
¼ teaspoon sugar
3 or 4 large scallions, sliced diagonally, white and green parts separated
1 tablespoon Shaohsing wine or medium-dry sherry
2 teaspoons sesame oil or to taste

FOR THE MARINADE

¼ teaspoon salt
½ teaspoon sugar
1 teaspoon thin soy sauce
1 teaspoon thick soy sauce
6 turns white pepper mill
1 teaspoon Shaohsing wine or medium-dry sherry
1 teaspoon potato flour
1 tablespoon water
1 tablespoon peanut or corn oil

Serves 6 with 3 other dishes

Illustrated on page 137

木樨肉

Stir-fried Pork with Red-in-snow

雪菜肉絲

INGREDIENTS
12 ounces lean pork
4 ounces canned red-in-snow, drained
½ teaspoon sugar
4 ounces canned bamboo shoots, drained
4 or 5 tablespoons peanut or corn oil
1 tablespoon Shaohsing wine or medium-dry sherry
1 teaspoon sesame oil

FOR THE MARINADE
2 teaspoons thin soy sauce
6 turns white pepper mill
1 teaspoon Shaohsing wine or medium-dry sherry
1 teaspoon cornstarch
1 tabelspoon egg white
1 teaspoon sesame oil

Serves 4 with 2 other dishes

Illustrated opposite

The preserved vegetable, red-in-snow, lends a special fragrance to the pork in this dish. As in many other Shanghai or Eastern stir-fried dishes, neither garlic nor scallions are used.

1. Slice the pork into matchstick-sized strips. Put into a bowl.

2. *Prepare the marinade:* Add the soy sauce, pepper, wine or sherry, cornstarch and egg white to the pork. Stir in the same direction until absorbed. Let marinate for about 15 minutes. Blend in the sesame oil.

3. Roughly chop the red-in-snow. Mix in the sugar.

4. Slice the bamboo shoots into matchstick-sized strips.

5. Heat a wok over high heat until smoke rises. Add the oil and swirl it around. Add the red-in-snow and stir a few times to enhance its fragrance. Add the bamboo shoots and stir a few more times. Add the pork and turn and toss for about 1 minute, separating the strips as you do so. Splash in the wine or sherry around the side of the wok, continuing to stir as it sizzles. When the pork, having turned opaque, is cooked, transfer to a warm serving plate. Serve immediately.

Facing page, from the top: Dry-fried beef (see page 143); Green pepper beef in black bean sauce (see page 142); Stir-fried pork with red-in-snow (see above)

Green Pepper Beef in Black Bean Sauce

INGREDIENTS

1 pound beef, rump, skirt steak or fillet trimmed
1 teaspoon potato flour
6 tablespoons water
5 tablespoons peanut or corn oil
8 ounces green pepper, seeded and roughly chopped
salt to taste
5 cloves garlic, peeled and chopped fine
4 scallions, cut into 1-inch sections, white and green parts separated
2½ tablespoons fermented black beans, rinsed and mashed with ¼ teaspoon sugar and 1 teaspoon oil
½ to 1 fresh red chili, seeded and sliced (optional)
1 tablespoon Shaohsing wine or medium-dry sherry

FOR THE MARINADE

¼ teaspoon salt
¼ teaspoon sugar
2 teaspoons thick soy sauce
8 turns black pepper mill
2 teaspoons Shaohsing wine or medium-dry sherry
1½ teaspoons potato flour
3 tablespoons water
1 teaspoon peanut or corn oil
1 teaspoon sesame oil

Serves 4 with 2 other dishes

Illustrated on page 141

This is one of the most celebrated Cantonese dishes using the versatile black bean as an essential ingredient. It is served as much at home as in restaurants.

1. Cut the beef across the grain into rectangular slices about 1 by 1½ inches and ¼ inch thick. Put into a fairly large mixing bowl.

2. *Prepare the marinade:* Add the salt, sugar, soy sauce, pepper and wine or sherry to the meat. Sprinkle with the potato flour (a) and add the water, 1 tablespoon at a time, stirring (b), until it is difficult to continue before adding another spoonful. This process will make the beef velvety and tender. Refrigerate, covered, for 30 minutes. Blend in the oils.

a   b

3. Mix the 1 teaspoon of potato flour and 6 tablespoons of water together in a small bowl and set aside.

4. Heat a wok until hot. Add 1 tablespoon oil and swirl it around. Add the green pepper and stir-fry for about 2 minutes, lowering the heat if the pieces begin to burn. Season with salt to taste and remove to a warm plate.

5. Reheat the wok over high heat until smoke rises. Add the remaining 4 tablespoons of oil and swirl it around. Add the garlic, and as soon as it takes on color, add the white scallions and stir. Add the black bean paste and chili, and stir. Tip in the beef. Sliding the wok scoop or metal spatula to the bottom of the wok, turn and toss vigorously for 1 or 2 minutes, or until the beef is partially done. Splash in the wine or sherry around the side of the wok, continuing to turn and toss until the sizzling dies down. Still stirring, pour in the well-stirred dissolved potato flour, add the green pepper and green scallions and mix until this thickening has cooked. Transfer to a warm serving plate. Serve immediately.

Dry-fried Beef

The traditional preparation of this Szechwan dish calls for great patience, because the beef is stir-fried over low heat for about an hour, until it becomes shriveled and quite crisp. However, the same effect can be achieved in less than half that time by using the combined techniques of deep-frying and stir-frying. The beef should taste spicy hot, sweet and savory at the same time. Besides rice, it goes equally well with silver thread buns.

1. Shred the beef into long threadlike strips about 2½ to 3 inches long, ⅕ inch thick and wide. Put into a bowl.

2. *Prepare the marinade:* Add the soy sauce, sugar, wine or sherry, oil and peppercorns to the beef. Mix well. Let marinate at room temperature for 45 to 60 mintues.

3. Put the carrots into a small bowl and add ¼ teaspoon of the salt to draw out the water. Drain after 20 to 30 minutes. Pat dry, if necessary.

4. Put the celery into another bowl and add ¼ teaspoon of salt to draw out the water. Drain after 20 to 30 minutes. Pat dry, if necessary.

5. Seed the red chilies but leave whole, if possible.

6. *Prepare the sauce:* Mix together the cornstarch, sugar and water in a small bowl and set aside.

7. Half fill a wok or deep fryer with oil. Heat to a temperature of about 400°F, or until a cube of stale bread browns in 40 seconds. While the oil is being heated, stir the cornstarch into the beef to coat evenly. Add the beef gently to the oil and deep-fry for 4 or 5 minutes, or until crisp. Turn off the heat and remove with a large hand strainer or perforated spoon and drain on paper towels. Pour the oil into a container for future use. Wash and dry the wok.

8. Reheat the wok over moderate heat until hot. Add 1⅜ to 2 tablespoons of oil and swirl it around. Add the red chilies and fry until they are dark in color. Remove and discard. Add the carrots, stir and toss, and then add the celery. Stir for a few minutes, until dry, before adding the beef. Continue to stir over gentle heat for another 3 or 4 minutes, or until everything is quite dry and crisp.

9. Gradually add the well-stirred sauce, stirring continuously to coat the beef. Transfer to a warm serving plate.

10. Sprinkle with the ground Szechwan peppercorns and sesame oil.

Note: This dish can be prepared several hours in advance up to step 8. When ready to serve, simply reheat thoroughly over gentle heat and proceed with steps 9 and 10.

INGREDIENTS

1 pound beef, round, trimmed
3 to 4 ounces carrots, peeled and cut into thin strips
½ teaspoon salt
3 or 4 sticks celery, cut into thin strips
2 or 3 dried red chilies
peanut or corn oil for deep-frying
¾ teaspoon cornstarch
1½ to 2 tablespoons peanut or corn oil
½ teaspoon ground roasted Szechwan peppercorns (see page 21)
1 teaspoon sesame oil

FOR THE MARINADE

2¼ tablespoons thin soy sauce
2¼ teaspoons sugar
1 tablespoon Shaohsing wine or medium-dry sherry
1 teaspoon sesame oil
½ teaspoon ground roasted Szechwan peppercorns (see page 21)

FOR THE SAUCE

1 teaspoon cornstarch
¾ to 1 teaspoon sugar
4 tablespoons water

Serves 4 to 6 with 2 or 3 other dishes

Illustrated on page 141

乾炒牛肉絲

Ants Climbing a Tree

INGREDIENTS

3 ounces cellophane noodles
6 ounces pork loin
4 tablespoons peanut or corn oil
3 cloves garlic, peeled and
    chopped fine
3 or 4 scallions, cut diagonally
    into long slices, white and
    green parts separated
1 to 1½ tablespoons hot soybean
    paste or chili sauce
2 teaspoons Shaohsing wine or
    medium-dry sherry
½ pint clear stock
salt to taste
thin or thick soy sauce to taste

FOR THE MARINADE

½ teaspoon salt
1 tablespoon thick soy sauce
4 turns black pepper mill
1 teaspoon Shaohsing wine or
    medium-dry sherry
½ teaspoon potato flour
1 tablespoon water
2 teaspoons sesame oil

*Serves 6 with 3 or 4 other dishes
    or 4 as a first course*

Illustrated opposite

Don't be put off by the name of this dish: it is characteristic of the Szechwanese sense of humor to visualize minced pork over cellophane noodles as ants climbing up a tree, even though you may not wish to conjure the same image. Whatever the mental picture, the marinated pork cooked in a spicy sauce lends color and flavor to the otherwise bland cellophane noodles, which do, however, contribute an interesting texture to the overall effect.

1. Put the cellophane noodles in a large bowl and pour over them about 1¾ pints of boiling water. Let soak, preferably covered, for a minimum of 20 minutes.

2. Chop fine or mince the pork. Put into a bowl.

3. *Prepare the marinade:* Add the salt, soy sauce, pepper, wine or sherry, potato flour and water to the pork. Stir vigorously for 1 or 2 minutes, in order to give the pork the right consistency. Let marinate for about 15 minutes. Blend in the sesame oil.

4. Drain the cellophane noodles and make a few cuts with a pair of scissors to make them shorter and easier to handle.

5. Heat a wok over high heat until smoke rises. Add the oil and swirl it around. Add the garlic, then the white scallions. As they sizzle, add the soybean paste or chili sauce and stir a couple of times. Add the pork and, sliding the wok scoop or metal spatula to the bottom of the wok, turn and toss for about 1 minute, breaking up any lumps at the same time. Splash in the wine or sherry around the side of the wok, continuing to stir and break up any lumps.

6. When the sizzling dies down, add the noodles, stir and fold to blend. Add the stock, bring to a boil, add the salt and soy sauce to taste, then lower the heat and continue to cook, covered, for about 5 minutes.

7. Remove the wok cover. Most of the stock should have been absorbed. Add the green scallions, then scoop to a warm serving dish.

8. Arrange the pork all over the top of the noodles. Serve hot.

Note: If you cannot tolerate hot soybean paste or chili sauce, use thick soy sauce instead. This dish reheats well over low heat.

Facing page, clockwise from the top: Red-braised ox-tongue (see page 147); Ants climbing a tree (see above); Roast pork belly (see page 146); Hoisin sauce for pork

Roast Pork Belly

INGREDIENTS

3 pounds pork belly in one piece, without spareribs

about ½ teaspoon salt

2 teaspoons red food coloring (optional)

FOR THE MARINADE

1 teaspoon salt

1 teaspoon sugar

1 tablespoon ground yellow bean sauce

1 tablespoon hoisin sauce

½ teaspoon thin soy sauce

1 teaspoon five-spice powder

FOR THE DIPS

thick soy sauce

hoisin sauce

Serves 4 to 6 as a main course

Illustrated on page 145

In special Cantonese establishments, a whole pig is roasted to a rich red color in a specially built oven. A similar effect can be achieved at home by using a piece of pork from the middle section of the belly, with the skin or rind left on. Never score the skin and never use pork that has been frozen, because the skin will not get crisp enough to form the distinctive crackling of the dish.

1. Wipe the pork skin or rind dry. Using a fork with 10 close-set, sharp tines, or a similar metal piercing instrument, pierce the skin rind vigorously and repeatedly (a), for about 15 to 20 minutes, or until it is entirely covered with fine holes. Rub the salt all over the skin.

2. Lightly brush some of the food coloring over the skin (b), if used.

a   b

3. Make horizontal cuts on the flesh side, about 1 inch apart and ½ inch deep.

4. *Prepare the marinade:* Mix together the salt, sugar, yellow bean sauce, hoisin sauce, soy sauce and five-spice powder in a small bowl.

5. Using a clean brush, smear as much marinade as possible on the flesh side, particularly in the grooves. Do not smear any marinade along the sides of the pork or they will be burned when roasted.

6. Using 2 butcher's meat hooks, hang the pork up in a windy place for about 8 hours, or overnight, until the skin is very dry. The drier the skin, the better the crackling when roasted.

7. Place the pork, skin side up, on a rack in the top half of the oven over a pan of hot water to catch the drippings. Roast in a preheated oven at 400°F for 15 minutes and then reduce the oven temperature to 375°F for about 1 hour. Do not open the oven door at all until it is time to test whether the pork is done. Test by piercing the meat with a skewer or chopstick; if it goes in easily and the juices that run out are clear and not pink, the pork is done. The skin will have turned into excellent crackling.

8. Transfer the pork to a carving board to rest for a few minutes. Carve into ½-to-1-inch pieces with a cleaver or a sharp, serrated meat knife. Transfer to a warm serving dish and serve.

Red-braised Ox Tongue

A very down-to-earth dish, especially good during the autumn and winter. Ox tongue may be more readily available and cheaper but calf tongue has a more delicate flavor and texture, so by all means use 3 or 4 calves' tongues if you prefer them.

1. Place the ox tongue in a large saucepan of water and bring to a boil. Reduce the heat to a fast simmer for 1 hour. Drain and rinse in cold water. Peel and discard the hard skin that covers the tongue (This should not be difficult after boiling).

2. Heat a large heavy saucepan (an enameled casserole with a cast-iron bottom is ideal) until hot. Add 2 tablespoons of the oil and swirl it around. Add the garlic, scallions and tongue, and brown for about 1 minute on each side. Add the star anise, peppercorns, tangerine peel, stock, soy sauce, sugar, salt and wine or sherry. Cover and gradually bring to a boil. Reduce the heat and simmer fast for about 2 hours. Check the water level from time to time and add more stock or water, if necessary. There should be about 14 ounces of sauce when ready, and the ox tongue should be very tender. (This can be done several hours in advance or overnight).

3. Remove the tongue and slice into thin pieces of uniform thickness.

4. Strain the sauce through a sieve. Discard the solids.

5. Blanch the peas in boiling salted water with 1 tablespoon of oil for about 2 minutes. Drain and refresh under cold running water.

6. Just before ready to serve, return the tongue, sauce and peas to the saucepan and gradually bring to a simmer. Add the well-stirred dissolved potato flour. Continue to stir as it thickens.

7. Transfer to a large warm serving plate and serve.

Note: The cooked ox tongue freezes well, either whole or in sections. Step 2 can be cooked in a preheated oven at 400°F for 20 minutes, then at 325°F for 1¾ hours.

INGREDIENTS
1 ox tongue, about 3 pounds, unsalted
3 tablespoons peanut or corn oil
3 cloves garlic, peeled and crushed
3 large scallions, white parts only
2 whole star anise or 16 segments
1 teaspoon Szechwan peppercorns
1 piece (¼ of whole) dried tangerine peel
1 pint clear stock
5 tablespoons thick soy sauce
1½ teaspoons brown sugar
½ teaspoon salt
1½ tablespoons Shaohsing wine or medium-dry sherry
8 ounces small or regular-size peas
1 tablespoon potato flour, dissolved in 2 tablespoons water

Serves 6 as a main course

Illustrated on page 145

紅燒牛舌

上海菜

An Eastern or Shanghai Menu

This menu for eight reflects the cuisines of the two Eastern gastronomic provinces: Kiangsu and Chekiang. Between them, they boast of several of the best products in China: Chinhua ham, *Shaohsing wine and Chinkiang vinegar. In this menu, the decorative and delicate dishes are balanced by more down-to-earth dishes.*

雪菜肉絲湯
Red-in-snow soup with pork
Tasty soup with pork, cellophane noodles and crisp red-in-snow as main ingredients (see page 213).

芙蓉蛋片
Fu-yung egg slices
Tender pieces of egg served in a nourishing and tasty stock (see page 213).

揚州炒飯
Yangchow fried rice
Fried rice cooked with ham, shrimp, peas and onions, garnished with strips of egg (see page 216).

上海燻魚
"Smoked" fish Shanghai style
Cold dish, marinated, deep-fried, then steeped in a tangy sauce (see page 214).

Eight-treasure bean curd
Savory dish of puréed bean curd flavored with chicken, ham, mushrooms and nuts (see page 215).

冰糖元蹄
Crystal sugar pig's hock
Tender meat dish, spiced with ginger, scallions, soy sauce and wine, served whole (see page 214).

VEGETABLES

Fish Fragrant Eggplant

魚香茄子

INGREDIENTS

½ ounce cloud ears, reconstituted (see page 39)

2 eggplants, about 1½ pounds

peanut or corn oil for deep-frying

1½ tablespoons peanut or corn oil

4 or 5 cloves garlic, peeled and chopped fine

¼ inch fresh ginger root, peeled and chopped fine

3 scallions, cut into 1-inch sections, white and green parts separated

1 to 1½ tablespoons Szechwan chili paste (see page 226)

1 tablespoon Shaohsing wine or medium-dry sherry

1 teaspoon salt

1½ teaspoons sugar

1 tablespoon thin soy sauce

½ teaspoon potato flour, dissolved in 3 tablespoons water

1 tablespoon rice or white wine vinegar

Serves 6 with 3 other dishes

In Szechwan, many dishes which emulate the fragrance of fish because the condiments used to flavor them are the same as those traditionally used to flavor fish. This flavor is achieved by blending Szechwan chili paste with garlic, ginger and scallions in oil and then allowing this sauce to impregnate the main ingredients cooked in it. The finishing touch is the addition of wine, sugar and vinegar, which enhance the tastes and aftertastes, the hallmark of Szechwanese cooking. This dish is delicious served hot or cold.

1. Drain the cloud ears and cut into narrow strips.

2. Peel alternate strips of the eggplant skin, lengthwise. (If all the skin is peeled, eggplants shrink too much when cooked.) Slice each eggplant lengthwise into 4 or 5 pieces according to diameter, then lengthwise again into strips and then cut crosswise into several pieces.

3. Half fill a wok or deep fryer with oil. Heat to a temperature of 350°F, or until a cube of stale bread browns in 60 seconds. Put in all the eggplant and deep-fry for 2 minutes. Remove and drain well on paper towels. (This step can be done a few hours ahead.)

4. Heat a wok over high heat until smoke rises. Add 1½ tablespoons oil and swirl it around. Add the garlic, which will sizzle and take on color almost instantly, then add the ginger and white scallions, stirring a few times. Stir in the chili paste and add the eggplant and cloud ears. If the cloud ears make a cracking sound, reduce the heat. Sprinkle with the wine or sherry and stir in the salt, sugar and soy sauce to mix. Add the well-stirred dissolved potato flour and the green scallions, stirring as the sauce thickens. Remove from the heat. Sprinkle with the vinegar and quickly stir thoroughly before transferring to a warm serving plate. Serve immediately.

Facing page, clockwise from the top: Fish fragrant eggplant (see above); Dry-braised bamboo shoots and Chinese mushrooms (see page 152); Eight-treasure vegetarian assemblage (see page 153)

Dry-braised Bamboo Shoots and Chinese Mushrooms

乾燒二冬

INGREDIENTS

12 to 16 medium dried Chinese mushrooms, reconstituted (see page 39)
1½ pounds canned bamboo shoots (winter bamboo shoots are ideal), drained
peanut or corn oil for deep-frying
¼ teaspoon salt
½ teaspoon sugar
1½ tablespoons thick soy sauce
2 teaspoons thin soy sauce
2 tablespoons mushroom water

Serves 4 with 2 other dishes

Illustrated on page 151

This is a classic Eastern vegetarian dish with a play-on-words Chinese title, which, literally translated, is Dry-braised two tung. The two tungs of the pun are tung-sun *(winter bamboo shoots) and* tung-ku *(dried Chinese mushrooms).*

1. Squeeze out excess water from the Chinese mushrooms but leave damp. Save the soaking liquid.

2. Either roll-cut the bamboo shoots into fairly large pieces or cut into wedges. Pat dry with paper towels.

3. Half fill a wok or deep fryer with oil. Heat to a temperature of 375°F, or until a cube of stale bread browns in 50 seconds. Carefully add the bamboo shoots to the oil and deep-fry for about 1½ minutes, or until the edges have turned brownish. Remove with a hand strainer or perforated spoon and put on paper towels. Empty all but about 3 tablespoons of the oil into a container and save for later use.

4. Reheat the oil over high heat. When hot, add the Chinese mushrooms and, going to the bottom of the wok with a wok scoop or metal spatula, flip and toss for about 1 minute to enhance the fragrance of the mushrooms. Return the bamboo shoots to the wok and continue to stir-fry together for another minute.

5. Season with the salt, sugar, soy sauces and mushroom water. Lower the heat to medium and cook until all the liquid is absorbed, leaving only oil around the mushrooms and bamboo shoots. Transfer to a warm serving plate and serve immediately.

Bean Curd Puffs

豆腐泡

INGREDIENTS

4 cakes bean curd
peanut or corn oil for deep-frying

Makes 16

Once deep-fried, the puffs, unlike fresh bean curd, which will perish within 2 to 3 days even when refrigerated, can be kept for up to 2 weeks in the refrigerator. They are a good ingredient to use with meat, fish and vegetables, because they soak up sauces and add an interesting dimension to a dish.

1. Quarter each bean curd cake. Put the 16 cubes on changes of paper towels or cloths to drain excess water.

2. Half fill a wok or deep fryer with oil. Heat to a temperature of 400°F, or until a cube of stale bread browns in 40 seconds. Gently immerse the bean curd in the oil and deep-fry for about 15 minutes, or until golden and crisp. Remove with a hand strainer or perforated spoon and drain on paper towels.

Eight-Treasure Vegetarian Assemblage

Eight is a significant number for the Chinese, for in Buddhism, which for many centuries exerted great influence in China, there are eight treasures in life: pearl, lozenge, stone chime, rhinoceros horn, coin, mirror, books and leaf. The symbolism of these eight treasures is not lost in Chinese food: any dish comprising eight or more main ingredients can term itself an "eight-treasure" dish.

1. Drain the cloud ears and golden needles but leave damp. Break up the large pieces of cloud ears.

2. Soak the cellophane noodles in plenty of boiling water for 30 minutes. They will expand and become pliable. Drain. Cut with scissors to shorten.

3. Bring a saucepan of water to a boil and add ½ teaspoon of the salt and ½ tablespoon of the oil. Add the peas and, as soon as the water returns to a boil, drain in a colander. Refresh under cold running water and drain again.

4. Heat a wok over high heat until smoke rises. Add the remaining oil and swirl it around. Add the ginger, then the scallions and stir for a few seconds. Add the red bean curd cheese and stir to blend. Add the cloud ears, toss and stir, then adjust the heat to moderate. Add the cellophane noodles, golden needles, bean curd puffs, baby corn, straw mushrooms and ginkgo nuts and mix together. Season with the remaining salt, sugar and soy sauce. Pour in the stock and cook, covered or uncovered, until much of the stock has been absorbed. Add the peas, mix well and heat through. Sprinkle with sesame oil to taste. Transfer to a warm serving dish. Serve hot.

INGREDIENTS

2 heaped tablespoons cloud ears, reconstituted (see page 39)
½ ounce golden needles, reconstituted (see page 39)
2 ounces cellophane noodles
1 teaspoon salt
4½ tablespoons peanut or corn oil
4 ounces sugar peas, trimmed
6 thin slices fresh ginger root, peeled
6 scallions, sliced diagonally
1 tablespoon fermented red bean curd cheese, mashed with 1 teaspoon own juice or water
8 bean curd puffs, halved (see page 12)
8 canned baby corn on the cob, halved lengthwise
4 ounces canned straw mushrooms
3 to 4 ounces canned ginkgo nuts
½ teaspoon sugar
2 to 2½ tablespoons thin soy sauce
6 ounces vegetable or clear stock, mixed with ½ teaspoon potato flour
sesame oil to taste

Serves 6 with 3 other dishes

Illustrated on page 151

Sautéed Stuffed Peppers

INGREDIENTS

5 medium peppers, green and
　red, seeded and quartered
4 or 5 medium dried Chinese
　mushrooms, reconstituted (see
　page 39)
12 ounces pork with a little fat
2 tablespoons dried shrimp,
　rinsed
4 or 5 scallions, cut into tiny
　rounds
2 ounces canned bamboo shoots,
　chopped fine
1 small egg white, lightly beaten
4 tablespoons peanut or corn oil
2 teaspoons Shaohsing wine or
　medium-dry sherry

FOR THE MARINADE

½ teaspoon salt
½ teaspoon sugar
1 teaspoon thick soy sauce
1 teaspoon thin soy sauce
2 teaspoons Shaohsing wine or
　medium-dry sherry
1½ teaspoons potato flour
6 tablespoons water

FOR THE SAUCE

1½ teaspoons potato flour
9 tablespoons stock and
　mushroom water
1½ tablespoons peanut or corn
　oil
5 cloves garlic, peeled and
　chopped fine
2½ tablespoons fermented black
　beans, rinsed and mashed with
　½ teaspoon sugar and 1
　teaspoon oil
2 or 3 small fresh chilies, seeded
　and cut into small rounds
　(optional)

Serves 5 or 6 as a main course

Illustrated opposite

Tender yet still crisp pepper stuffed with pork that has a suggestion of the taste of shrimp. The black bean sauce, especially with chili, adds another dimension in taste.

1. Plunge the peppers into boiling water to blanche for 1 or 2 minutes. Drain and immediately rinse under cold running water to retain their crispness. Drain and pat dry.

2. Drain and squeeze out excess water from the mushrooms but leave damp. Shred into the thinnest possible strips and then dice. Reserve soaking water.

3. Chop or mince the pork together with the shrimp. Put into a large bowl.

4. *Prepare the marinade:* Add the salt, sugar, soy sauces, wine or sherry, potato flour and half of the water to the pork. Stir vigorously to coat the meat. Add the remaining water, a little at a time, stirring vigorously between each addition. This lightens the texture of the pork.

5. Stir in the mushrooms, scallions and bamboo shoots. Let marinate for 15 to 30 minutes. Blend in the sesame oil and egg white.

6. Fill the hollow of each piece of pepper with the stuffing until level with the edges.

7. Heat a flat frying pan or wok over high heat until smoke rises. Add 2 tablespoons of the oil and swirl it around. Put in half the pepper, stuffing side down, and brown for 1 minute. Reduce the heat to moderate or low, cover and continue to sauté for 2 more minutes. Turn and sauté for 1 or 2 more minutes.

8. Turn up the heat to high and splash in 1 tablespoon of the wine or sherry, which will sizzle. As soon as the sizzling dies down, remove to a warm serving plate and keep warm.

9. Wash and dry the frying pan or wok and repeat the process of sautéing for the remaining pepper. Wash and dry the pan or wok.

10. *Prepare the sauce:* In a small bowl, dissolve the potato flour by gradually stirring in the stock and mushroom water. Heat the wok or pan until smoke rises, add the 1½ tablespoons of oil and swirl it around. Add the garlic, which will sizzle. Add the black bean paste and chili and stir to blend. Pour in the well-stirred dissolved potato flour and stir to blend over low heat. As soon as the sauce bubbles, pour it over the pepper on the serving plate, scraping every drop from the frying pan or wok. Serve immediately.

Facing page, clockwise from the top: Red-braised gluten (see page 157); Sautéed stuffed peppers (see above); Wheat gluten – boiled and deep-fried (see page 156)

Wheat Gluten

INGREDIENTS
2 pounds wheat flour
1 tablespoon salt
1¼ pints cold or tepid water
peanut or corn oil for deep-frying

Yields about 10 to 12 ounces of
gluten

Illustrated on page 155

In Chinese, wheat gluten literally means the "sinewy essence" of wheat-flour dough. For Buddhist vegetarians in China, it is the substitute for meat and is thus an indispensable ingredient of their vegetarian dishes. Wheat gluten is sold in its cooked state in China, Taiwan and Hong Kong, but as yet it is not available elsewhere; neither is a satisfactory canned product. Fortunately, it is not difficult to make, so do try it.

1. Sift the flour into a large deep bowl. Add the salt. Gradually add the water and work into a dough, which should be firm but not hard.

2. Knead the dough. If you use your hands, knead, punch, throw and pull it as much as possible. If you use a dough hook fitted to a food mixer, knead for 4 to 6 minutes, or the maximum amount of time directed in the instructions. In either case, knead until the dough is very, very smooth and elastic, so that the maximum amount of gluten can be produced.

3. Cover the dough and let rest for about 1 hour.

4. Put the dough in a colander and stand it in the sink with the plug in. Turn on the cold water faucet start pressing and squeezing the dough with both hands. The idea is literally to wash off all the floury substance. When the water becomes too milky, change it and continue washing. After about 12 minutes, the water will become almost clear, being slightly cloudy rather than milky. The dough will have become a soft and spongy mass in the colander – this is the wheat gluten (a). Wash for 1 or 2 more minutes, then squeeze out excess water.

5. Pull with your fingers to break the gluten lump into 4 portions. Pull each portion into 10 pieces (b). Put the 40 pieces on a plate with a little space between each one so that they will not stick together.

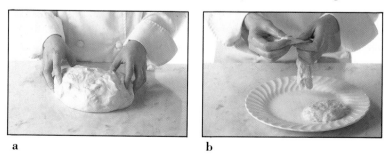

a   b

6. To cook the gluten pieces, either boil or deep-fry them. To boil: bring plenty of water in a large saucepan to a boil. Add 20 gluten pieces, continue to boil for 4 or 5 minutes, until they float to the surface, indicating that they are cooked (c). To deep-fry: half fill a

wok or deep fryer with oil. Heat to a temperature of 375°F, or until a cube of stale bread browns in 50 seconds. Put in the gluten, 1 piece at a time (10 can be deep-fried together). They will sink to the bottom, then come up to the surface, puffing bubbles all over. Turn them over repeatedly for about 2 minutes until light brown in color (d). Remove and drain on paper towels.

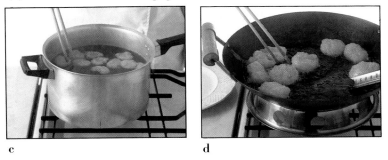

c   d

Note: Boiled gluten keeps well in the refrigerator for about 2 days; deep-fried gluten, for 7 days. Both freeze well.

Red-braised Gluten

During the slow braising of this dish, the dark soy sauce, enriched by sugar, permeates the boiled gluten and dyes it red. The bamboo shoots give a contrasting texture to the spongy gluten and tender mushrooms. In keeping with the Buddhist tradition of vegetarian food, neither ginger, garlic, scallions, nor wine is used.

1. Drain and squeeze out excess water from the mushrooms but leave damp. Reserve the soaking liquid.

2. Squeeze excess water from the boiled gluten.

3. Heat a wok over high heat until smoke rises. Add 2 tablespoons of the oil and swirl it around. Add the mushrooms, flip and turn with a wok scoop or metal spatula until very hot. Add another 1 tablespoon of oil and put in the bamboo shoots, continuing to fold and turn until very hot and fragrant. Add the remaining oil and the gluten. Stir to mix.

4. Pour in the mushroom water. Add the salt, soy sauce and sugar. Bring to a boil, then lower the heat. Cover and simmer for 30 minutes.

5. Turn up the heat and flip and turn the ingredients continuously to absorb the remaining liquid. This adds richness to the dish.

6. Transfer to a warm serving dish. Sprinkle the sesame oil on top and serve hot.

INGREDIENTS

20 small dried Chinese mushrooms, reconstituted in 1 pint boiling water (see page 39)
20 pieces boiled gluten (see page 156)
4 tablespoons peanut or corn oil
6 ounces canned bamboo shoots, thinly sliced
¼ teaspoon salt
2½ tablespoons thick soy sauce
1 teaspoon sugar
2 or 3 teaspoons sesame oil

Serves 4 with 3 other dishes

Illustrated on page 155

Pi Pa Bean Curd

INGREDIENTS
6 medium dried Chinese
    mushrooms, reconstituted (see
    page 39)
4 cakes bean curd, drained
⅓ teaspoon salt
1 egg yolk
2 tablespoons self-rising flour
peanut or corn oil for deep-frying
2 to 2½ tablespoons peanut or
    corn oil
2 cloves garlic, peeled and
    chopped fine
¼ inch fresh ginger root, peeled
    and cut into silken threads (see
    page 35)
4 scallions, cut diagonally into
    long slivers, white and green
    parts separated
2 ounces char-siu (Cantonese
    roast pork) (see page 134) or
    ham, cut into matchstick-sized
    pieces

FOR THE SAUCE
1½ teaspoons potato flour
9 tablespoons mushroom water
1½ tablespoons oyster sauce
½ tablespoon thick soy sauce

*Serves 4 to 6 with 2 or 3 other
    dishes*

Illustrated on page 161

*Here, the mashed bean curd is shaped into halved pear-shape
pieces resembling the celebrated Chinese musical instrument the* pi pa.

1. Drain and squeeze out excess water from the mushrooms but
leave damp. Slice into the thinnest possible slivers. Reserve the
soaking liquid.

2. Using a wooden spoon, mash the bean curd, forcing it through a
sieve into a dry, clean bowl. Discard the coarse dregs in the sieve.

3. Add the salt, egg yolk and self-rising flour, and blend to a smooth
paste. Let stand for about 10 minutes.

4. *Prepare the sauce:* Mix together the potato flour, reserved
mushroom water, oyster and soy sauce.

5. Half fill a wok or deep fryer with oil. Heat to a temperature of
375°F, or until a cube of stale bread browns in 50 seconds.

6. Before the oil is ready, dip 5 or 6 Chinese soup spoons into the
oil, then pack them with the bean curd paste (a), leveling it off with
the back of a knife. When the oil is ready, hold the handles of the
spoons, lower them one by one into the oil (b) and let the paste slip
out, forming a halved pear shape. Use a knife to loosen the paste
around the edges of the spoon. Repeat until the paste is used up.

7. Deep-fry the pieces for 3 or 4 minutes, turning them over
periodically (c), until they are golden in color and floating in the oil.
As they are cooked, remove with a perforated spoon or strainer (d).
Drain on paper towels. Put on a warm serving dish and set aside.

a   b

c   d

8. Pour the oil into a container for later use. Wash and dry the wok.

9. Reheat the wok over high heat until smoke rises. Add about 2 tablespoons of oil and swirl it around. Add the garlic, ginger and white scallions. As they sizzle, add the mushrooms, stir a few times; add the char-siu or ham and stir a few more times.

10. Pour the well-stirred sauce into the wok and continue to stir over moderate heat as it thickens. Add the green scallions, then scoop the mixture over the bean curd. Serve immediately.

Pock-ma Bean Curd

This internationally famous Szechwan dish was the creation of the wife of chef Ch'en Shen-fu, who worked in the capital, Ch'eng-tu, during the second half of the 19th century. If pockmarks on her face earned her this rather derogatory nickname, "Pock-ma" or "Pock-woman," they also immortalized her bean curd dish.

1. Mince the pork and put into a bowl.

2. *Prepare the marinade:* Add the salt, sugar, soy sauces, wine or sherry and oil to the pork. Stir to coat well. Let marinate for 15 to 30 minutes.

3. Chop the Szechwan vegetable into pieces the size of matchstick heads. Dice the bean curd into ½-inch cubes. Transfer to a strainer, handling gently.

4. Mix together the potato flour and water for the thickening and put aside.

5. Heat a wok over high heat until smoke rises. Add the oil and swirl it around. Add the garlic and pork and, using a wok scoop or metal spatula, flip and toss until partially cooked. Add the Szechwan vegetable, bean paste, soy sauce and sugar, continuing to turn and toss to let the sauce permeate the meat. Pour in the stock and slowly bring to a boil over moderate heat.

6. Add the bean curd and stir gently, in order not to break it up. Cook for about 2 minutes, so the flavors of both the pork and the sauce can be absorbed. Pour in the well-stirred potato flour mixture and blend well. Transfer to a warm serving dish.

7. Add the hot chili oil and sesame oil; sprinkle with the ground Szechwan peppercorns and scallions. This garnish adds a pretty red and green contrast as well as subtle flavoring. Serve piping hot.

INGREDIENTS
4 ounces lean pork
½ to ¾ ounces preserved Szechwan vegetable, well rinsed and dried
4 cakes bean curd, drained
1 teaspoon potato flour
1 tablespoon water
4 tablespoons peanut or corn oil
3 cloves garlic, peeled and chopped fine
1 tablespoon hot soybean paste or broad bean paste (for moderately-hot flavor)
1 teaspoon thin soy sauce
1 teaspoon sugar
5 ounces prime or clear stock (see page 225)
1 teaspoon hot chili oil (see page 225)
1 teaspoon sesame oil
½ teaspoon ground roasted Szechwan peppercorns (see page 21)
2 scallions, green parts only, cut into tiny rounds

FOR THE MARINADE
⅛ teaspoon salt
¼ teaspoon sugar
1 teaspoon thin soy sauce
1 teaspoon thick soy sauce
1½ teaspoons Shaohsing wine or medium-dry sherry
1 teaspoon sesame oil

Serves 4 to 6 with 2 or 3 other dishes

Illustrated on page 161

Stir-fried Chinese Broccoli with Beef

芥
蘭
炒
牛
肉

INGREDIENTS
4 to 6 ounces beef, fillet, rump or
  skirt, steak, trimmed
1 to 1½ pounds Chinese broccoli,
  trimmed
4 to 4½ tablespoons peanut or
  corn oil
4 thin slices fresh ginger root,
  peeled
¼ to ⅓ teaspoon salt
¼ to ⅓ teaspoon sugar
1 or 2 cloves garlic, peeled and
  cut diagonally into slivers
2 scallions, cut into 1-inch
  sections, white and green parts
  separated
½ tablespoon Shaohsing wine or
  medium-dry sherry

FOR THE MARINADE
¼ to ⅓ teaspoon salt
¼ to ⅓ teaspoon sugar
1 teaspoon thick soy sauce
3 or 4 turns black pepper mill
1 teaspoon Shaohsing wine or
  medium-dry sherry
½ teaspoon potato flour
1 tablespoon water
1 teaspoon peanut or corn oil

FOR THE SAUCE
½ to ¾ teaspoon potato flour
3 to 5 tablespoons water
1 to 1½ tablespoons oyster sauce
½ tablespoon thick soy sauce

Serves 4 with 3 other dishes

Illustrated opposite

*As is so often the case in Chinese cooking, meat is used here to
complement the vegetables. The Chinese broccoli in this dish, with
its distinctive flavor, similar to asparagus, goes especially well with
the velvety beef slices. If it is not available, use broccoli as a
substitute.*

1. Cut the beef across the grain into slices about 1 by 1½ inches and
⅕ inch thick. Put into a bowl.

2. *Prepare the marinade:* Add the salt, sugar, soy sauce, pepper,
wine or sherry, potato flour and water to the beef. Stir until well
coated. Let marinate for 15 to 30 minutes. Blend in the oil.

3. Cut the Chinese broccoli into pieces about 3 or 4 inches long.

4. *Prepare the sauce:* Mix together the potato flour, water, oyster
sauce and soy sauce.

5. Heat a wok until hot. Add 1½ to 2 tablespoons of the oil and
swirl it around. Add the ginger, stir. Add the Chinese broccoli.
Sliding the wok scoop or metal spatula to the bottom of the wok,
turn and toss in rapid succession for about 1 minute, adjusting the
heat if the broccoli begins to burn. Add the salt and sugar. Now add
4 or 5 tablespoons of water, bring to a boil, continue to cook,
covered, over moderate heat for about 4 or 5 minutes. The broccoli
should be tender yet crunchy. Transfer with a perforated spoon to a
warm serving plate and keep warm.

6. Wash and dry the wok. Reheat over high heat until smoke rises.
Add the remaining oil and swirl it around. Add the garlic, then stir
in the white scallions. Add the beef and turn and toss for about 30
seconds to brown. Splash in the wine or sherry around the side of
the wok, continuing to stir as it sizzles. Add the well-stirred sauce to
the wok. Toss and stir as the sauce thickens. Add the green scallions
and remove from the heat.

7. Scoop the beef mixture over the Chinese broccoli. Serve
immediately.

Facing page, clockwise from the top: Stir-fried Chinese broccoli with beef
(see above); Pi pa bean curd (see page 158); Deep-fried bean curd in
earthen pot (see page 162); Pock-ma bean curd (see page 159)

Deep-fried Bean Curd in Earthen Pot

煲
火
仔
豆
腐

INGREDIENTS

4 large or 6 medium dried
  Chinese mushrooms,
  reconstituted (see page 39)
4 cakes bean curd, drained
4 large leaves Chinese celery
  cabbage
2½ to 3 tablespoons peanut or
  corn oil
2 thin slices fresh ginger root,
  peeled
salt to taste
peanut or corn oil for deep-frying

FOR THE SAUCE

1 teaspoon potato flour
5 tablespoons mushroom water or
  clear stock
2 teaspoons thick soy sauce
2 tablespoons oyster sauce
1 or 2 cloves garlic, peeled and
  chopped fine
2 or 3 scallions, cut into 1-inch
  sections, white and green parts
  separated

Serves 4 with 2 other dishes

Illustrated on page 161

Serving certain dishes in a flameproof earthen pot is very popular in South China and Hong Kong, especially in the winter. These dishes, which can include meat, offal, fish, seafood, vegetables and bean curd, are known as earthen-pot dishes. The main ingredient is often deep-fried and then assembled with the other ingredients in the pot, which can be heated up just before being brought to the table. Instead of an earthen pot, an enamel casserole or a copper pot can be used.

1. Drain and squeeze out excess water from the mushrooms but leave damp. Slice into thin strips.

2. Cut each cake of bean curd into 3 rectangular pieces, taking care to keep them whole. Lay on several changes of paper towel to drain excess water.

3. Cut the cabbage crosswise into 1-inch lengths.

4. Heat a wok over high heat until smoke rises. Add 1 tablespoon of the oil and swirl it around. Add the ginger, and as it sizzles, add the cabbage. Sliding the wok scoop or spatula to the bottom of the wok, turn and toss for about 30 seconds. Season with a little salt, lower the heat and continue to cook, covered, for 2 or 3 minutes, or until tender yet still crisp. Remove and drain, if necessary. Put into the warm earthen pot.

5. *Prepare the sauce:* Mix together the potato flour, mushroom water or stock, soy sauce and oyster sauce. Heat a saucepan (or another wok, if you have one) until hot. Add the remaining 1½ to 2 tablespoons of oil and swirl it around. Add the garlic, let it sizzle and take on color, then add the white scallions and the Chinese mushrooms. Stir and turn for about 30 seconds. Pour the well-stirred potato flour mixture into the saucepan or wok. Lower the heat, continuing to stir as it thickens. Remove from the heat.

6. Half fill a wok or deep fryer with oil. Heat to a temperature of 400°F, or until a cube of stale bread browns in 40 seconds. Lower the bean curd into the oil, piece by piece, and deep-fry for about 4 minutes, or until golden, turning over with a pair of long bamboo chopsticks or tongs halfway through cooking. Remove with a large hand strainer or perforated spoon and drain on paper towels.

7. Lay the bean curd on the cabbage in the pot. Add the green scallions. Reheat the sauce and pour over the bean curd.

8. Heat the pot for 1 or 2 minutes, then bring to the table and serve immediately.

Stuffed Chinese Mushrooms

A delicately flavored steamed dish much enjoyed by the Cantonese and Fukienese. The egg white lightens the pork, and the bamboo shoots or water chestnuts add just a bite to the otherwise smooth texture. The sauce glistens on the stuffing, giving a transparent effect.

1. Chop the pork by hand or mince coarsely. Put into a bowl.

2. *Prepare the marinade:* Add the ginger, salt, sugar, soy sauce, pepper, wine or sherry, potato flour and water to the pork. Stir vigorously for about 30 seconds, or until well coated. Add the egg white and stir again for another 30 seconds, or until smooth and light. Let marinate for about 15 minutes.

3. Mix the bamboo shoots or water chestnuts with the pork. Mix in the scallions. Stir in the 1 tablespoon of oil. The stuffing is now ready.

4. Drain and squeeze out the excess water from the mushrooms but leave damp. Reserve the soaking liquid.

5. Hold a mushroom cap in one hand with the hollow side up. Using a small knife, fill the hollow generously with stuffing, shaping it into a slightly sloping mound to give an attractive appearance. Repeat until all are done. Put on a heatproof dish, stuffing side up, preferably in one layer.

6. Put the dish in a wok or steamer and steam, tightly covered, for 10 minutes over high heat (see page 44).

7. *Prepare the sauce:* A few minutes before the end of the steaming time, mix together the flour, mushroom water, oyster sauce and soy sauce. Pour into a wok or a saucepan. Bring to a boil, stirring continuously as it thickens. Blend in the oil, which will give a sheen.

8. Remove the mushrooms from the steamer. Arrange them in 2 layers, either in the same heatproof dish or on a warm serving dish. Pour the sauce over them. Serve piping hot.

INGREDIENTS

4 ounces pork shoulder or fresh ham
2 ounces canned bamboo shoots, or 3 or 4 fresh or canned water chestnuts, chopped fine
5 scallions, cut into tiny rounds
1 tablespoon peanut or corn oil
28 thick medium dried Chinese mushrooms, with slightly curled edges, reconstituted (see page 39)

FOR THE MARINADE

2 to 4 thin slices fresh ginger root, peeled and finely minced
½ teaspoon salt
½ teaspoon sugar
2 teaspoons thin soy sauce
6 turns white pepper mill
1 teaspoon Shaohsing wine or medium-dry sherry
½ teaspoon potato flour
1 tablespoon water
1 tablespoon egg white

FOR THE SAUCE

1½ teaspoons potato flour, dissolved in 1 tablespoon water
6 ounces mushroom water
1 tablespoon oyster sauce
1 tablespoon thick soy sauce
1½ to 2 tablespoons peanut or corn oil

Serves 6 with 3 or 4 other dishes

Illustrated on page 165

Braised Bamboo Shoots

冒
冬
筍

INGREDIENTS

8 medium dried Chinese
   mushrooms, reconstituted (see
   page 39)
1 ounce dried shrimp, rinsed
1 pound canned bamboo shoots
2 tablespoons thin soy sauce
2 teaspoons sugar
5 tablespoons peanut or corn oil
4 ounces lean pork, cut into
   matchstick-sized pieces
¼ pint clear stock, including
   shrimp water
1 teaspoon potato flour, dissolved
   in 1 tablespoon water
2 or 3 teaspoons sesame oil

Serves 6 with 3 other dishes

Illustrated opposite

*In Fukien, this dish is made from fresh winter bamboo shoots, but
in the West we have to be content with the canned product, which,
fortunately, retains much of its characteristic crispness.*

1. Drain and squeeze out excess water from the mushrooms but
leave damp. Slice into thin strips.

2. Soak the shrimp for about 15 minutes in just enough boiling
water to cover them. Drain them, reserving the soaking liquid.

3. Slice the bamboo shoots into strips about 2 inches long, ½ inch
wide and ¼ inch thick. Put into a bowl, mix in the soy sauce and
sugar and let stand for 3 to 5 minutes.

4. Heat a wok over high heat until smoke rises. Add the oil and
swirl it around. Lift the bamboo shoots with a perforated spoon,
leaving in the bowl as much soy sauce as possible, and add to the oil.
Immediately put the pork into the bowl to soak up the soy sauce.
Sliding the wok scoop or metal spatula to the bottom of the wok,
turn and toss the bamboo shoots so that each piece is coated with the
oil. Remove with a perforated spoon.

5. Add the shrimp to the wok, stir a few times and add the
mushrooms. Stir, then add the pork. Continue to turn and toss for
about 1 minute, or until the pork is almost cooked.

6. Return the bamboo shoots to the wok, stir to mix and add the
stock. As soon as the stock comes to a boil, cover, reduce the heat
and simmer for about 10 minutes, or until all but 5 or 6 tablespoons
of stock has been absorbed.

7. Add the well-stirred dissolved potato flour to the wok and stir to
thicken the sauce.

8. Transfer to a warm plate. Sprinkle the sesame oil on top and
serve.

Facing page, clockwise from the top: Stir-fried bean sprouts with shredded
pork (see page 166); Braised bamboo shoots (see above); Stuffed Chinese
mushrooms (see page 163); Stir-fried Chinese celery cabbage with dried
shrimp (see page 167)

Stir-fried Bean Sprouts with Shredded Pork

肉
絲
芽
菜

INGREDIENTS
6 ounces lean pork
1 small green pepper, halved
    lengthwise and seeded
6 tablespoons peanut or corn oil
3 thin slices fresh ginger root,
    peeled and cut into silken
    threads (see page 35)
1 pound bean sprouts
½ teaspoon salt
2 or 3 cloves garlic, peeled and
    chopped fine
3 scallions, halved lengthwise, cut
    into 2-inch sections, white and
    green parts separated
2 teaspoons Shaohsing wine or
    medium-dry sherry

FOR THE MARINADE
¼ teaspoon salt
¼ teaspoon sugar
2 teaspoons thin soy sauce
4 turns white pepper mill
1 teaspoon Shaohsing wine or
    medium-dry sherry
½ teaspoon potato flour
1 tablespoon water

FOR THE SAUCE
½ teaspoon potato flour
3 tablespoons water
2 tablespoons oyster sauce

Serves 4 with 2 other dishes

Illustrated on page 165

The combination of meat and vegetables is a regular occurrence in Chinese cooking. Even though a small amount of meat is used, it nevertheless adds so much taste and interest to the vegetables that it is worth the effort.

1. Cut the pork into matchstick-sized pieces. Put into a bowl.

2. *Prepare the marinade:* Add the salt, sugar, soy sauce, pepper, wine or sherry, potato flour and water to the pork. Stir in the same direction to coat. Let marinate for about 20 minutes.

3. Slice the green pepper lengthwise into thin strips.

4. *Prepare the sauce:* Mix together the potato flour, water and oyster sauce.

5. Heat a wok over high heat until smoke rises. Add 3 tablespoons of the oil and swirl it around. Add the ginger, and as it sizzles, add the bean sprouts and green pepper. Season with the salt. Sliding the wok scoop or spatula to the bottom of the wok, turn and toss continuously over high heat for about 2½ to 3 minutes. The bean sprouts and green pepper will be cooked but still crunchy. Transfer to a warm serving plate and keep warm.

6. Wash and dry the wok. Reheat over high heat until smoke rises. Add the remaining oil and swirl it around. Add the garlic, and as it sizzles and takes on color, add the white scallions. Stir a few times, then put in the pork. Turn and toss for about 30 seconds, or until the pork begins to turn opaque. Splash in the wine or sherry around the side of the wok. As it sizzles, continue to stir and turn for another 30 to 60 seconds, or until the pork is cooked. Lower the heat. Pour the well-stirred sauce on the pork, stirring as it thickens. Add the green scallions and stir a few more times. Scoop the pork mixture cover bean sprouts. Serve immediately.

Stir-fried Chinese Celery Cabbage with Dried Shrimp

This economical and healthy everyday dish is easy to make. It is as popular in Canton as in Shanghai, but the Cantonese use scallions, ginger and shrimp to heighten the flavor; in Shanghai they prefer just dried shrimp.

INGREDIENTS

1 ounce dried shrimp, rinsed

1 Chinese celery cabbage, about 2 pounds

3 or 4 tablespoons peanut or corn oil

4 scallions, cut into 1-inch sections, white and green parts separated

4 thin slices fresh ginger root, peeled

¼ to ½ teaspoon salt

Serves 4 to 6 with 2 or 3 other dishes

Illustrated on page 165

紹菜炒蝦米

1. Soak the shrimp (a), in just enough boiling water to cover them, for 30 minutes or longer (b). Drain reserving the soaking liquid.

a

b

2. Discard any wilted or hard outer leaves of the cabbage. Then put together similar-sized leaves (c). Chop crosswise into thin strips (d). Remove and discard the hard core.

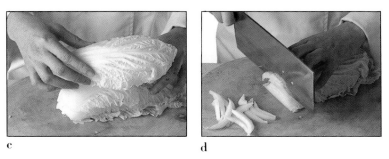

c

d

3. Heat a wok over high heat until smoke rises. Add the oil and swirl it around. Add the white scallions, stir a couple of times, then add the ginger. As they sizzle, add the shrimp, which will "explode" when they touch the oil, releasing a mouth-watering fragrance. Stir the shrimp for a few seconds.

4. Add the cabbage and, sliding the wok scoop or metal spatula to the bottom of the wok, turn and toss for about 1 minute so that the cabbage will absorb the fragrance of the other ingredients. Adjust the heat if the cabbage begins to burn. Pour in the shrimp water, season with the salt, cover and continue cooking for 1 or 2 minutes, or until the cabbage is tender yet still crunchy. Add the green scallions. Transfer to a warm serving plate and serve immediately.

素菜

A Vegetarian Menu

Vegetarian food need not be dull and tasteless and this menu for eight is a fine example of the point. For non-vegetarians, as well as the less strict *vegetarians, the addition of oyster sauce to vegetables does wonders, so be sure to follow the suggestion.*

冬菇芥蘭花 **Stir-fried broccoli and Chinese mushrooms**
Stir-fried floral mushrooms served with broccoli in a light soy and oyster sauce (see page 220).

七彩沙律 **Rainbow salad**
Lightly stir-fried vegetables with a delicate dressing of sesame paste and vinegar (see page 217).

清炒芽菜 **Stir-fried bean sprouts**
Lightly stir-fried bean sprouts served with soy or oyster sauce (see page 219).

腐乳椒絲炒菠菜

Stir-fried spinach in bean curd "cheese" sauce
Spinach stir-fried with garlic and chili, made all
the more special by the addition of bean curd
"cheese" (see page 220).

羅漢齋

Lohan's delight
Buddhist dish, therefore
none of the usual Chinese
condiments – ginger, garlic
and scallions – are used
(see page 218).

醬油豆腐

Bean curd in a simple sauce
Cubed bean curd, briefly
stir-fried and served with soy
sauce and scallions
(see page 219).

RICE, NOODLES AND DUMPLINGS

Boiled Rice

INGREDIENTS
1 cup or 6½ ounces long-grain
    white rice
2 teaspoons peanut or corn oil
1½ cups or 12 ounces water

Serves 4 or 5 with other dishes

Illustrated opposite

Cooked rice, served with other dishes, is the Chinese staple. The general Chinese yardstick for measuring the water required to cook the rice is to put the rice in a pan, then stand an index finger on the surface of the rice and let the water come up to the first joint. However, for those who are less experienced, or who are cooking a smaller amount of rice, the chart below is recommended as a guideline. The rice should be cooked thoroughly, and be tender but not mushy.

Rice	Water	Oil	Cooked rice
1 cup or 6½ ounces	1½ cups or 12 ounces	2 teaspoons	3 cups
2 cups or 13 ounces	2½ cups or 20 ounces	4 teaspoons	6 cups
3 cups or 19½ ounces	3¼ cups or 26 ounces	6 teaspoons	9 cups

1. Wash the rice in 3 or 4 changes of cold or tepid water, rubbing the grains gently with the fingers to get rid of excess starch. Drain.

2. Put the rice into a saucepan, preferably with a copper bottom. Add the oil and water. (The oil prevents the rice from boiling over and from sticking to the bottom of the saucepan; it also enhances the natural flavor of the rice.)

3. Cover and bring to a boil. Stir thoroughly with a wooden spoon and continue to boil, either covered or uncovered, until most of the water is absorbed, leaving only tiny droplets around the rice. Reduce the heat to a minimum.

4. Place a flame tamer under the saucepan. Let the rice simmer with the lid on for 12 to 15 minutes.

5. Before serving, fluff up the rice with a spoon. Either scoop all the rice into a large communal bowl, from which everyone takes a portion, or scoop some rice into individual rice bowls.

Note: To reheat boiled rice in a saucepan, add a little water, about 1 tablespoon per cup of rice; loosen the grains with a spoon and let it simmer over low heat for 10 to 15 minutes.

Facing page, clockwise from the top: Beef-fried rice (see page 173); plain fried rice (see page 172); Boiled rice (see above); Stir-fried glutinous rice (see page 172)

Plain Fried Rice

净炒飯

INGREDIENTS

3 cups or 14 ounces boiled rice,
    cooked at least 3 or 4 hours in
    advance (see page 171)
2 tablespoons peanut or corn oil
2 scallions, cut into small rounds,
    white and green parts
    separated
1 large egg, lightly beaten with 2
    teaspoons oil and ¼ teaspoon
    salt
¼ teaspoon salt or to taste
2 teaspoons thick soy sauce
2 tablespoons clear stock
    (optional)

Serves 2 with 1 other dish

Illustrated on page 171

When cooked rice is stir-fried with egg but without meat or seafood, it is called "plain fried rice", and it often has greater appeal than boiled rice to those who are not used to eating rice as a staple. The stir-frying process adds much taste and fragrance. The Chinese sometimes serve it in place of boiled rice as a measure of economy when there are few dishes to go with it. Since the best result is obtained from cooked rice that has been left for a few hours or overnight, it is also a way to turn any leftover rice into an appetizing dish.

1. Loosen the rice grains as much as possible.

2. Heat a wok over high heat until smoke rises. Add the oil and swirl it around. Add the white scallions, stir a few times, then pour in the egg. Let stand for 5 to 10 seconds, so that the egg sets at the bottom but remains runny on the surface.

3. Add the rice. Sliding the wok scoop or metal spatula to the bottom of the wok, turn and toss continuously for 3 or 4 minutes or until thoroughly hot. Season with the salt and soy sauce. If the rice is very hard, add the stock and stir for a few more seconds. Add the green scallions. Put in a warm serving bowl and serve immediately.

Stir-fried Glutinous Rice

生炒糯米飯

INGREDIENTS

1 pound white glutinous rice
1 ounce dried shrimp, rinsed
10 medium dried Chinese
    mushrooms, reconstituted in
    ½ pint water (see page 39)
1 large wind-dried Chinese pork
    sausage
1 large wind-dried Chinese
    duck-liver sausage
2 tablespoons peanut or corn oil
1 teaspoon salt
4 to 6 scallions, cut into small
    rounds, white and green parts
    separated
6 ounces fatty roast pork belly,
    diced (see page 146)
1 tablespoon thick soy sauce
small bunch coriander leaves,
    torn up

Serves 4 or 5 as a main course

Illustrated on page 171

Glutinous rice is usually steamed or boiled, but because it is very starchy, these methods of cooking can make it into a rather stodgy food. Stir-frying glutinous rice from its raw state until cooked through, however, makes the rice much lighter and more fragrant in taste.

1. Wash the glutinous rice 3 or 4 times, rubbing with the fingers. Drain, then soak in plenty of cold water for 5 or 6 hours. Drain just before ready to use.

2. Soak the shrimp, in just enough boiling water to cover them, for about 20 minutes. Drain them, reserving the soaking liquid.

3. Drain and squeeze out excess water from the mushrooms but leave damp. Reserve the soaking liquid. Dice the mushrooms.

4. Rinse the wind-dried sausages and dice.

5. Heat a wok over high heat until smoke rises. Add the oil and swirl it around. Add the wind-dried sausages and shrimp, and turn and toss for about 1 minute. Then add the mushrooms, continuing to stir-fry for a few seconds.

6. Add the glutinous rice and, sliding the wok scoop or metal spatula to the bottom of the wok, turn and toss about 12 times, adjusting the heat if the rice begins to burn. Sprinkle on 2 or 3 ounces of shrimp/mushroom water, cover and continue to cook over medium to low heat for 2 minutes. Sprinkle on the same amount of liquid again, fold and turn the rice 5 or 6 times, then cover once more. Repeat this procedure 4 times, using ordinary water when the shrimp/mushroom water is used up.

7. Add the salt, white scallions and roast pork belly. Flip and turn to mix and repeat the sprinkling of water and simmering another 3 or 4 times, each time for about 4 or 5 minutes. The rice should be cooked through by this time but, if not, continue to simmer and add more water if necessary.

8. Remove from the heat. Add the soy sauce, green scallions and coriander leaves. Fold and turn to mix, then transfer to a warm serving plate. Serve hot.

Beef Fried Rice

Much of the attraction of this dish lies in the fact that the flavor of the beef and spices permeates the rice while it is being stir-fried.

1. Chop or mince the beef. Put into a bowl.

2. *Prepare the marinade:* Add the salt, sugar, soy sauces, pepper, wine or sherry and potato flour to the beef. Add the water, one spoonful at a time, stirring vigorously in the same direction between additions until too difficult to continue. This makes the beef fluffy and velvety. Let marinate for 15 minutes. Blend in the oil.

3. Loosen the rice grains as much as possible.

4. Heat a wok over high heat until smoke rises. Add 3 tablespoons of the oil and swirl it around. Add the garlic, and when it sizzles, add the ginger and the white scallions. Stir a few times. Add the beef and, sliding the wok scoop or metal spatula to the bottom of the wok, flip and toss, breaking up any lumps at the same time. When partially cooked, splash in the wine or sherry around the side of the wok, continuing to stir as it sizzles. Pour in the beaten egg, tip in the rice, turn and toss for about 2 minutes or until all the ingredients are very hot and well mixed. Slowly pour in the remaining oil around the side of the wok, turning the rice to incorporate it. Remove from the heat.

5. Add half of the lettuce and the green scallions. Scoop to a warm serving dish. Top with the remaining lettuce and serve hot.

INGREDIENTS

8 ounces beef, rump or skirt
    steak
14 ounces or 3 cups boiled rice,
    cooked at least 3 or 4 hours in
    advance (see page 170)
4 or 5 tablespoons peanut or corn
    oil
4 cloves garlic, peeled and
    chopped fine
1/4 inch fresh ginger root, peeled
    and chopped fine
4 scallions, cut into small rounds,
    white and green parts
    separated
2 teaspoons Shaohsing wine or
    medium-dry sherry
1 egg, lightly beaten
2 to 4 leaves iceberg lettuce,
    thinly shredded

FOR THE MARINADE

1/2 teaspoon salt
1/2 teaspoon sugar
2 teaspoons thin soy sauce
2 teaspoons thick soy sauce
6 turns black pepper mill
1 teaspoon Shaohsing wine or
    medium-dry sherry
1/2 teaspoon potato flour
3 or 4 tablespoons water
1 tablespoon peanut or corn oil

Serves 2 as main course

Illustrated on page 171

Yin-Yang Rice

INGREDIENTS
1 pound lean pork
2 pounds tomatoes
12 tablespoons peanut or corn oil
1 clove garlic, peeled and
    chopped fine
½ teaspoon salt
½ teaspoon sugar
about 1¼ pounds or 4½ cups
    boiled rice, freshly cooked (see
    page 170)
3 or 4 cloves garlic, peeled and
    cut into silken threads (see
    page 35)
1 tablespoon Shaohsing wine or
    medium-dry sherry
6 large egg whites, beaten with ½
    teaspoon salt
2 cooked green peas (optional)

FOR THE MARINADE
½ teaspoon salt
¼ teaspoon sugar
1 tablespoon thin soy sauce
1 teaspoon Shaohsing wine or
    medium-dry sherry
10 turns white pepper mill
1 teaspoon potato flour
1 or 2 tablespoons water
1 or 2 tablespoons peanut or corn
    oil

FOR THE SAUCE
juice from the tomatoes
2 teaspoons potato flour
1 tablespoon thin soy sauce
1 tablespoon oyster sauce

*Serves 3 or 4 as lunch or, as last
course, 8 to 10*

Illustrated opposite

Yin and Yang are the all-pervading opposing principles of Chinese philosophy, symbolizing the sun and the moon, man and woman, good and evil, light and darkness. In this dish, the egg white and the red tomato are used decoratively to form the Yin-Yang symbol.

1. Cut the pork into matchstick-sized strips. Put into a bowl.

2. *Prepare the marinade:* Add the salt, sugar, soy sauce, wine or sherry, pepper and potato flour to the pork. Stir to coat, adding the water to make the pork lighter. Let marinate for 20 to 30 minutes. Stir in the oil.

3. Submerge the tomatoes in boiling water for a few minutes, then peel. Seed and cut into chunks. Put into a wire sieve over a bowl to drain, saving the juice for the sauce.

4. Heat a wok over high heat until smoke rises. Add 2 tablespoons of the oil and swirl it around. Add the chopped garlic, and when it sizzles, add the tomato and stir a few times. Season with the salt and sugar. Cook over medium heat, covered, for about 5 minutes. Remove to the sieve and drain, saving the juice for the sauce. Transfer to a bowl and keep warm in the oven.

5. *Prepare the sauce:* Mix together the tomato juice, potato flour, soy sauce and oyster sauce.

6. Spread the rice on a round serving dish. Keep warm.

7. Wash and dry the wok. Reheat over high heat until smoke rises. Add 4 tablespoons of the oil and swirl it around. Add the cut garlic, and when it sizzles and takes on color, add the pork. Sliding the wok scoop or metal spatula to the bottom of the wok, turn and toss for about 1 minute, or until the pork, turns whitish and is partially cooked. Splash in the wine or sherry around the side of the wok, continuing to turn and fold until the sizzling dies down. Add the well-stirred sauce to the pork, stirring as it thickens. Scoop over the rice.

8. Wash and dry the wok. Reheat until hot, add the remaining 6 tablespoons oil and swirl it around. Pour in the egg white and fold continuously with the wok scoop or spatula so that the runny egg white goes to the bottom while the set layers are turned to the surface; lower the heat if necessary. Scoop up the tender flakes of egg white and spread on the right, or Yin, half of the rice, to make the curvy Yin-Yang motif.

9. Spread the tomato on the Yang, or left, side. Garnish with the 2 garden peas, if desired. Serve hot.

Facing page, clockwise from the top: Scallion cakes (see page 178); Yin-Yang rice (see above); Boiled Northern dumplings (see page 176); Sautéed Northern dumplings (see page 177)

Boiled Northern Dumplings

INGREDIENTS

FOR THE DOUGH
1¼ pounds all-purpose flour
¾ pint cold water

FOR THE FILLING
1 ounce dried shrimp, rinsed
1 teaspoon Shaohsing wine or
   medium-dry sherry
2 pounds Chinese celery cabbage,
   trimmed
2 teaspoons salt
1 pound pork with a little fat,
   chopped fine
12 scallions, cut into small
   rounds

FOR THE MARINADE
1½ teaspoons salt
8 turns pepper mill
2 teaspoons Shaohsing wine or
   medium-dry sherry
3 tablespoons sesame oil
3 tablespoons peanut or corn oil

FOR THE DIPS
soy sauce, thin or thick, vinegar,
   Chinkiang wine or hot chili oil
   (see page 225)

Serves 10 as first course
Yields about 100 dumplings

Illustrated on page 175

Northern Chinese people adore these dumplings, chiao-tzu,
*especially during the Chinese New Year. They sometimes eat them
as the only course of a meal, and a man may consume more than 50
at a sitting. To wrap them is an exciting family activity in which
everyone lends a hand. The filling can be a variety of different
vegetables, such as Chinese chives and winter melon, with either
pork or beef or sometimes fish. The size can also vary, but*
chiao-tzu, *when cooked, should always contain a small amount of
liquid (soup) inside the wrapper.*

1. *Prepare the dough:* Sift the flour into a mixing bowl. Gradually
stir in the water and start kneading. Knead for 1 or 2 minutes, or
until smooth. The dough should be firm but pliable and not dry.
Cover the bowl with a towel and leave for about 30 minutes at room
temperature.

2 *Prepare the filling:* Soak the shrimp in enough boiling water to
just cover them, for 15 to 20 minutes. Drain them, reserving the
soaking liquid. Chop the shrimp into the size of matchstick heads
(see page 38) and add the wine or sherry.

3. Shred the cabbage crosswise as thinly as possible and then chop
roughly, cutting out the hard core. Put into a bowl. Mix in the salt
and let stand about 30 minutes, so some of its water can ooze out.

4. *Prepare the marinade:* Add the salt, pepper, wine or sherry and
oils to the pork. Also add 3 tablespoons of the shrimp water (if
insufficient, make up with cold water), and stir vigorously for about
1 minute. Mix in the shrimp and scallions and let marinate until the
dough is ready.

5. Squeeze out the excess water from the cabbage but leave damp.
Add to the pork mixture. Mix thoroughly.

6. Divide the dough into 4 pieces. On a lightly floured board, roll
out one piece with both hands into a long cylinder about ¾ inch in
diameter, and then cut into pieces about ⅗ inch long. Cover spare
dough with a towel.

7. One by one, stand each piece upright on the heel of your hand;
slightly round off the dough then flatten with the other hand. Flour
them lightly. Using a narrow rolling pin, roll out each piece into a
circular wrapper about 3 inches in diameter. Make the center
slightly thicker than the edge by rotating the dough anti-clockwise as
you roll.

8. Place a wrapper in the palm of one hand and put about 1½
teaspoons of the filling in the middle. Pinch tightly to seal the 2 edges
(a). Now hold the dumpling between the thumbs and index fingers of
both hands, seal the right edges by squeezing the thumbs and index

fingers together (b), pinching and pleating to make one or two tucks simultaneously. Seal the left edges in the same way. Put the dumpling in a floured pan. Repeat until all are made.

a
b

9. To boil the dumplings in a wok, bring about 3 pints of water to a fast boil. Put in 5 or 6 dumplings and stir so that they do not stick to the bottom. Add another 14 or 15 and stir again. Cover the wok and return to a boil. Stir, then cover again, lower the heat and continue to simmer gently for another 8 to 10 minutes, or until the dumplings have floated to the surface. (If the cooking is done on an electric burner, where the temperature cannot be controlled instantly, about 8 ounces cold water should be added twice during cooking to prevent the dumplings from bursting.)

10. Serve hot. To eat, dip them in soy sauce, vinegar and hot chili oil, mixing them to individual taste.

Sautéed Northern Dumplings

A combination of cooking methods is used to produce these delicious dumplings, which are crisply sautéed on the bottom and lightly steamed on top. Steps 2 to 7 are the same as for Boiled Northern dumplings.

8. Turn the floured side of a wrapper toward you, make 6 straight pleats, each about ½ inch deep, along the top edge of just under half the circle, forming a little pouch (a). Add about 2 teaspoons of the filling to the pouch. Fold up the unpleated edge (b) and pinch together the 2 edges of the dumpling, making it into a crescent. Repeat until all are made.

INGREDIENTS
same as for Boiled Northern
    dumplings

FOR THE DOUGH
follow step 1 of Scallion cakes
    dough (see page 178)

**FOR SAUTÉEING EACH
    PANFUL**
2 tablespoons peanut or corn oil
4 ounces hot water mixed with 2
    teaspoons oil and 1 teaspoon
    rice or white wine vinegar
1 teaspoon all-purpose flour,
    dissolved in 2 tablespoons
    water

Serves 10 as first course
Yields about 100 dumplings

Illustrated on page 175

a
b

9. To cook the dumplings, heat a heavy 8 to 10-inch frying pan, with a lid, for about 30 seconds, or until hot. Add the oil and swirl to cover the entire surface. Lower the heat and put in about 12 dumplings, in 2 parallel rows, with the dumplings just touching each other. Cover and cook for 3 minutes. Pour in the hot-water mixture carefully, cover and continue to cook over a higher heat for about 7 minutes, or until the water is almost absorbed and the bottoms of the dumplings are turning golden. Pour the dissolved flour along the sides of the dumplings. Cover and cook for 1 or 2 more minutes; the flour forms a crisp film linking the dumplings.

10. With a spatula, remove as many dumplings in a row as possible and turn them, brown side up, on a warm serving plate. Serve right away, while you continue to cook the other dumplings, or keep warm and serve all together.

Scallion Cakes

When the biting wind howls in Peking, people tuck into these hearty, oily cakes, made all the more appetizing by the scallions trapped within their layers. They are often served alone, with tea or Chinese wine, as a meal. Traditionally, lard or rendered duck's fat is used, but margarine is a very satisfactory and healthier substitute.

INGREDIENTS
1¼ pounds all-purpose flour
¾ pint boiling water
1 or 2 tablespoons cold water
1 or 2 teaspoons sesame oil
1½ teaspoons salt
about 4 ounces margarine
35 scallions, about 12 ounces, chopped
peanut or corn oil for frying

Serves 6 for lunch; 10 to 12 as a first course; more as an hors d'oeuvre

Illustrated on page 175

1. Sift the flour into a large bowl. Pour in the boiling water gradually and mix with a pair of chopsticks or a fork as you do so. Rub together with the fingers while the flour is still warm. Add the cold water and knead to form a dough that should be firm but not hard. Continue to knead for 2 or 3 more minutes and then let stand, covered, for at least 30 minutes.

2. Oil a flat surface with 1 teaspoon sesame oil. Also oil a rolling pin with a little sesame oil.

3. Place the dough on the surface. Knead a few times and shape into a roll. Divide into 6 pieces.

4. With the oiled rolling pin, roll out 1 piece into a circular shape about 6½ to 7 inches in diameter, with the edges slightly thinner than the center.

5. Sprinkle with a good ¼ teaspoon of salt, all over, and press it in with your fingers.

6. Generously spread about ½ ounce margarine all over, stopping just short of the edges.

7. Spread about 5 tablespoons of chopped scallions, adding slightly more at the center.

8. With both hands, pick up the sides nearest you and roll the cake up away from you, taking care not to let the scallions fall out.

9. Pinch in both ends (a). Then, holding one end in each hand, roll in toward the middle until the ends meet (b). Lift one end and put on top of the other. Twist the two ends, in opposite directions (c), and press down to make into a ball (d).

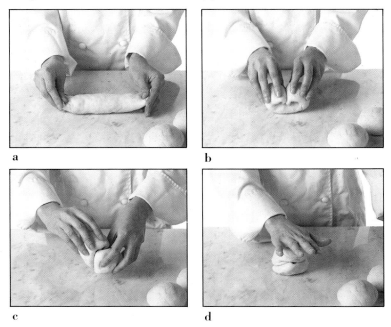

a

b

c

d

10. Gently roll out the ball, turn over and roll out the other side. Repeat this process until it forms a circular shape about 6 inches in diameter. If the surface of the cake should burst during rolling, do not worry, it does not make much difference when cooked.

11. Heat a heavy flat frying pan until hot. Add 2 tablespoons of oil. Put in the cakes, lower the heat and fry, covered, for 4 or 5 minutes, or until spotted golden brown. Turn over and fry the other side, covered, for about the same length of time, checking to make sure it does not burn. Remove, drain on paper towels and keep warm on a warm serving plate.

12. Repeat steps 4 to 10 to prepare another cake while the first cake is being fried. Replenish the oil in the frying pan before frying the second cake. Repeat until all 6 cakes are cooked.

13. Cut each cake into 6 or 8 pieces and serve hot. If served as an hors d'oeuvre, cut into bite-sized pieces.

Note: Scallion cakes can be made ahead of time. They can be reheated either in a frying pan with a little oil or, with margarine spread over them, on a rack in a preheated oven at 350°F for 15 minutes, or until hot and crisp again. They also freeze well.

Dry-braised Yi Noodles

干
燒
尹
麵

INGREDIENTS

2 Yi noodle cakes, 8 ounces (each cake is usually 10 inches in diameter)

1 ounce dried shrimp, rinsed

3½ tablespoons peanut or corn oil

3 cloves garlic, peeled and chopped fine

¼ inch fresh ginger root, peeled and chopped fine

8 ounces cooked white crabmeat

¼ teaspoon salt

¾ to 1 pint prime or clear stock (see page 225)

6 scallions, sliced into 2-inch sections and cut into silken threads (see page 34)

½ tablespoon thin soy sauce

3 tablespoons oyster sauce

Serves 8 as the last dish to end a dinner of 5 or 6 dishes

Illustrated opposite

Called in China "Noodles of the Yi mansion," this dish is believed to have been invented by the scholar-official Yi Ping-shou, in the 18th century. Yi, who had a gourmet's palate for noodles, wanted them kneaded only with egg, no water, then deep-fried before being braised in the best stock. The Yi noodle cakes sold in Chinese stores are already deep-fried.

1. Put 3½ to 4 pints of water in a large saucepan and bring to a boil. Break each noodle cake into 3 or 4 pieces and submerge them in the water. Return to a boil and continue to boil for about 1 minute, or until the noodles are tender but not soggy. Drain in a colander and set aside. (If prepared several hours in advance, rinse under cold running water.)

2. Soak the shrimp for about 15 minutes in just enough boiling water to cover them. Drain them, reserving the soaking liquid. Chop the shrimp into pieces the size of matchstick heads.

3. Heat a wok over high heat until smoke rises. Add ½ tablespoon of the oil and swirl it around. Add the shrimp, toss and stir for 1 or 2 minutes, or until dry. Transfer to a small dish.

4. Rinse and dry the wok and reheat over high heat until smoke rises. Add the remaining oil and swirl it around. Add the garlic, and when it takes on color, add the ginger and stir a few times. Add the crab meat and stir with the wok scoop or metal spatula. Season with the salt.

5. Pour in the stock and bring to a boil. Add the noodles, mix with the crab meat and continue to cook over moderate heat until most of the stock has been absorbed. Add the scallions, season with the soy sauce and oyster sauce, and check for taste.

6. Transfer to a warm serving dish. Sprinkle the shrimp on top and serve.

Note: Leftover noodles reheat well when a little stock is added to them.

Facing page, clockwise from the top: Deep-fried bean paste sauce with noodles (see page 185); Tossed noodles with ginger and scallions (see page 183); Double-faced brown noodles with pork (see page 182); Dry-braised Yi noodles (see above); Singapore fried rice sticks (see page 184)

Double-faced Brown Noodles with Pork

兩面黃炒麵

INGREDIENTS

8 ounces dried or 12 ounces fresh Chinese egg noodles

8 ounces lean pork, boneless pork chop, shoulder, tenderloin, or fresh ham

6 dried medium Chinese mushrooms, reconstituted (see page 39)

12 tablespoons peanut or corn oil

2 or 3 cloves garlic, peeled and chopped fine

6 scallions cut into 1-inch sections, white and green parts separated

1 tablespoon Shaohsing wine or medium-dry sherry

8 ounces bean sprouts

Chinese red vinegar (optional)

FOR THE MARINADE

½ teaspoon salt

½ teaspoon sugar

1 teaspoon thin soy sauce

1 teaspoon thick soy sauce

4 turns black pepper mill

1 teaspoon Shaohsing wine or medium-dry sherry

¾ teaspoon potato flour

1 tablespoon water

FOR THE SAUCE

2½ teaspoons potato flour

½ pint stock and mushroom water

¼ teaspoon salt

1 tablespoon thick soy sauce

2 teaspoons thin soy sauce

1½ tablespoons oyster sauce

Serves 3 for lunch; 8 with 4 other dishes

Illustrated on page 181

A toasted noodle dish, crisp and golden brown on both sides – hence the name – but moist and soft in the middle. The contrast of texture in the noodles themselves is enhanced by the topping of stir-fried ingredients and a sauce that permeates the noodles; a delight to the palate! You can also make up your own toppings; for example, chicken, prawns, fish or vegetables.

1. Plunge the noodles into 2½ pints boiling water in a large saucepan, bring back to a boil and continue to boil, uncovered, until they are *al dente* (generally 4 minutes for dried noodles, 1 to 1½ minutes for fresh noodles, but use your discretion or follow instructions on the package). Separate them with a pair of chopsticks or a fork while boiling.

2. Drain in a colander and immediately rinse thoroughly under cold running water. Let dry for 1 hour, turning them over once to ensure even drying.

3. Cut the pork into matchstick-sized pieces. Put into a bowl.

4. *Prepare the marinade:* Add the salt, sugar, soy sauces, pepper, wine or sherry and potato flour to the pork. Stir in the water and coat the meat thoroughly. Let marinate for 15 to 30 minutes.

5. Drain and squeeze out excess water from the mushrooms but leave damp. Slice into the thinnest possible strips. Reserve the soaking liquid.

6. *Prepare the sauce:* Dissolve the potato flour with a little stock in a bowl. Add the salt, soy sauces and oyster sauce and the remaining stock and mushroom water. Set aside.

7. Heat a large flat frying pan over high heat until hot. Add 7 tablespoons of the oil to cover the surface and heat until smoke rises. Add the noodles and arrange them evenly to the edges like a pancake. Shallow fry for about 1 minute, or until golden brown but not burned. Slip the wok scoop or a metal spatula underneath to check the color and loosen edges. Adjust the heat if necessary. Either turn the cake over with the spatula or toss. Fry the other side until golden brown. Transfer to a warm serving plate and keep warm in the oven, with the door open.

8. Heat a wok over high heat until smoke rises. Add 3 tablespoons of oil and swirl it around. Add the garlic, which will take on color instantly, then add two-thirds of the white scallion, and stir a couple of times. Put in the pork and flip and toss until it turns whitish. Pour in the wine or sherry and continue to stir while it sizzles. Add

the mushrooms and two-thirds of the green scallions; flip and toss some more and transfer to a warm plate.

9. Wash and dry the wok. Reheat over high heat until smoke rises. Add 2 tablespoons of oil and swirl it around; add the remaining white scallions and then the bean sprouts. Flip and toss vigorously and constantly for about 2 minutes, or until just cooked and yet still crunchy and firm. Add the remaining green scallions. Transfer to a warm plate.

10. Lower the heat and pour in the well-stirred sauce. Slowly bring to a boil, stirring to prevent lumps. Pour in the cooked pork and scallions and bean sprouts, stirring to blend with the sauce. When hot, scoop evenly on the noodle cake.

11. To facilitate serving, cut up the noodles with a pair of scissors or a knife and fork. Traditionally, red Chinese vinegar is served at the table to make digestion easier.

Tossed Noodles with Ginger and Scallions

If you wish to have a quick and simple, yet appetizing, bowl of noodles, here is the answer for you. They make an ideal lunch dish.

1. Plunge the noodles into 2½ pints of boiling water in a large saucepan, bring back to a boil and continue to boil uncovered until *al dente*. Generally, allow 1 to 1½ minutes for fresh noodles and 4 minutes for dried noodles. Separate the noodles with a pair of chopsticks or a fork while boiling.

2. Drain in a colander and then remove to a warm dish.

3. Heat a wok over high heat until smoke rises. Add the oil and swirl it around. Add the ginger, stir for a few seconds, then add the scallions and stir until thoroughly hot. Season with the salt. Remove the wok from the heat.

4. Return the noodles to the wok and toss them with a pair of chopsticks or a fork. Add the oyster sauce and toss again. Transfer to a warm serving dish and serve.

Variation: Tossed noodles with cucumber and ham.
Cut up ½ of a long cucumber and 4 to 6 ounces ham into matchstick-sized pieces. Cook the noodles as above. To 3 tablespoons of oil add the cucumber and ham. Toss with the noodles and serve.

INGREDIENTS
8 ounces fresh or 5 ounces dried Chinese egg noodles
3 tablespoons peanut or corn oil
2 inches fresh ginger root, cut into silken threads (see page 35)
8 scallions, cut into 2-inch sections and then into silken threads (see page 34)
½ teaspoon salt
2 tablespoons oyster sauce

Serves 2

Illustrated on page 181

Singapore Fried Rice Sticks

INGREDIENTS
4 ounces fresh or frozen raw
  shrimp or prawns, shelled
6 ounces dried rice sticks
¼ pint peanut or corn oil
1 egg, lightly beaten
1 small onion, skinned and
  shredded lengthwise
1 small green pepper, seeded and
  cut into matchstick-sized
  pieces
4 ounces char-siu (Cantonese
  roast pork, see page 134), cut
  into matchstick pieces
1 teaspoon curry powder

FOR THE MARINADE
⅕ teaspoon salt
½ teaspoon cornstarch
1 tablespoon egg white

FOR THE SAUCE
2 ounces clear stock or water
¾ teaspoon salt
½ teaspoon sugar
1 tablespoon thin soy sauce

Serves 3 or 4 as a snack

Illustrated on page 181

It is always interesting to note how cuisines influence each other. Fried rice sticks were a favorite with the Fukienese, and when they emigrated to Singapore during the 19th century they took this dish with them. As time went by, curry spices were added, to suit local taste, and they remain a distinctive element now that the dish has been readopted by the Southern Chinese.

1. If frozen shrimp are used, defrost thoroughly, then pat dry. Put into a bowl. If prawns are used, devein and quarter.

2. *Prepare the marinade:* Add the salt and cornstarch to the shrimp and stir to mix. Add the egg white and stir vigorously in the same direction until the shrimp are well coated. Let marinate for 2 or 3 hours in the refrigerator.

3. Submerge the rice sticks in sufficiently hot but not boiling water to cover them completely. Soak for about 30 minutes, until soft and pliable. Drain. Make several cuts with scissors to shorten their length so that they can be handled more easily.

4. *Prepare the sauce:* Mix together the stock or water, salt, sugar and soy sauce.

5. Heat a flat frying pan until hot. Add 1 tablespoon of the oil and swirl it to the edges. Turn the heat down, pour in the egg and, tilting the pan, spread it to the edges to make a crêpe. As soon as it is set, turn it over, fry the other side for a few seconds and transfer to a plate. Slice into narrow strips about 2 inches long.

6. Heat a wok over high heat until smoke rises. Add 4 tablespoons of the oil and swirl it around. Add the onion and turn and stir for about 30 seconds. Add the shrimp and toss and turn in rapid succession for about 1 minute, or until cooked and turning pinkish. Scoop onto a dish, leaving as much oil behind as possible.

7. Tip the green pepper into the wok and stir for about 30 seconds. Add the char-siu and stir together for another minute, or until piping hot. Scoop onto a dish.

8. Add another 4 tablespoons of the oil to the wok and swirl it around. Add the curry powder and let it sizzle for a few seconds. Add the rice sticks and sauce. Holding 2 pairs of chopsticks or 2 large wooden spoons, lift and toss the rice sticks until they have absorbed almost all the sauce. Add the remaining oil around the side of the wok to prevent the rice sticks from sticking. Taste, and if they are hard rather than *al dente*, add 2 or 3 tablespoons of stock or water and cook for 1 or 2 minutes over low heat with the wok cover on. Return the onion, shrimp, green pepper, char-siu and egg to the wok, toss and mix with the rice sticks. Remove to a warm serving dish. Serve immediately.

Deep-fried Bean Paste Sauce with Noodles

Because wheat is so widely grown in Northern China, noodles form an important part of the staple diet for the people of that area. On the whole, unlike the Southern Chinese, they do not put their noodles in soup; they prefer them dressed in a sauce. This is a celebrated Peking sauce.

1. *Prepare the bean paste:* Chop the pork by hand or mince coarsely. Heat a wok over high heat until smoke rises. Add the oil and swirl it around. Tip in the scallions, turn and toss for about 20 to 30 seconds to release their fragrance. Add the pork and, sliding the wok scoop or metal spatula to the bottom of the wok, flip and toss for about 1 minute, separating any lumps. Splash in the wine or sherry around the side of the wok, continuing to stir for another 1 or 2 minutes. Transfer to a dish and set aside. If water oozes from the mixture, drain.

2. Add the 12 ounces of oil to a deep heavy saucepan or a wok. Heat until just hot (about 325°F). Gently add the yellow bean sauce and hoisin sauce and lower the heat; there will be fierce sizzling and splashing when the sauces touch the oil. The oil must cover the sauces. Deep-fry for 6 or 7 minutes, or until the sauce becomes thicker, stirring gently with a wooden spoon to prevent it from sticking, turning the heat up again if necessary.

3. Add the pork and continue to deep-fry for another 12 to 15 minutes, or until most of the steam has evaporated. Stir continuously and adjust the heat to prevent the sauce from burning.

4. Remove from the heat and let cool. Scoop the bean paste into glass jars or earthenware pots. Cover it with at least 1 inch of the oil. The bean paste, if stored in the refrigerator, can be kept for several months.

5. *Prepare the bean paste with noodles:* Put about 16 ounces of water with ½ teaspoon of the salt and 1½ teaspoons of oil in a saucepan and bring to a boil. Add the bean sprouts and return to a boil. Pour immediately into a colander and refresh under cold running water. Drain thoroughly.

6. Bring a large pan of water to a boil with the remaining salt added. Add the noodles and boil for about 4 minutes, or until just cooked. Pour into a colander and drain.

7. Transfer to a serving bowl or a platter. Sprinkle with the bean sprouts and cucumber.

8. To eat, each person helps himself to a bowl of noodles and some topping, then mixes some bean paste, starting with no more than 1 tablespoon, into the noodles.

INGREDIENTS

FOR THE BEAN PASTE
1 pound pork, leg or shoulder, with about 2 ounces fat
3 tablespoons peanut or corn oil
12 ounces scallions, cut into small rounds
1 tablespoon Shaohsing wine or medium-dry sherry
¾ pint peanut or corn oil
1½ pounds ground yellow bean sauce
¾ pint hoisin sauce

FOR THE BEAN PASTE WITH NOODLES
1½ teaspoons salt
1½ teaspoons peanut or corn oil
8 ounces bean sprouts
1 pound dried Chinese noodles or thin spaghetti, Korean or Japanese U-Dong
½ long cucumber, about 12 ounces cut into matchstick-sized pieces
deep-fried bean paste (above)

Serves 4 as a light meal

Illustrated on page 181

A Mixed Regional Menu

混
合
菜

In planning your own menus, I urge you to mix the different regional dishes so that you can get the full benefit of the various tastes and flavors

from the four corners of China. This menu for eight should be but a starting point for you.

獅
子
頭 **Lion's head**
Tender pork meatballs
offset by crisp cabbage
and water chestnuts
(see page 222).

八
寶
飯 **Eight-treasure rice pudding**
Decorative dessert
combining boiled rice and
dried fruits served with a
sweet syrup (see page 224).

186

麻辣子雞 **Yu-ling's hot and numbing chicken**
An intriguing dish, deriving its heat from chilies and Szechwan peppercorns (see page 223).

蠔豉髮菜好市發財 **Dried oysters and hair seaweed**
An unusual New Year dish combining stir-fried pork, oysters and mushrooms with seaweed (see page 221).

葱爆羊肉 **Paper-thin lamb with scallions**
Tender pieces of lamb stir-fried with plenty of scallions rightly make this one of Peking's most famous dishes (see page 223).

白灼時菜 **Plain boiled vegetables**
Chinese flowering cabbage, briefly boiled and served with oyster sauce (see page 222).

DESSERTS

Almond Bean Curd

杏仁豆腐

INGREDIENTS
1¾ pints water
about 8 heaped tablespoons or ¼
  ounce cut-up agar
5 tablespoons sugar
6 ounces evaporated milk
1 tablespoon almond essence
1 large can lychees

Serves 6

Illustrated opposite

In cookery, the Chinese often enjoy making up a dish to resemble the looks, if not also the taste, of a particular ingredient and giving the dish the same name. This very light and delightful summer dessert that looks like bean curd is, in fact, not bean curd at all!

1. Put the water in a saucepan and bring to a boil. Add the agar, reduce the heat and simmer, to dissolve, for 20 to 25 minutes, stirring occasionally.

2. Add the sugar and stir until completely dissolved.

3. Remove the saucepan from the heat. Pour in the evaporated milk and stir once.

4. Strain the mixture through a fine sieve into a serving bowl, discarding any dregs from the agar.

5. Stir in the almond essence. Let cool and set, then put into the refrigerator to chill.

6. Cut the "bean curd" into diamond-shaped pieces. Put into a dish and top with lychees. Serve cold.

Note: Other fruits, fresh or canned, such as kiwi, peaches, grapes, pineapple, mangoes, can also be used. Instead of agar, about 6 level teaspoons of powdered gelatin can be used.

Facing page, from the top: Apples or bananas pulling golden threads (see page 190); Almond bean curd (see above); Red bean paste pancakes (see page 191)

Apples or Bananas Pulling Golden Threads

拔絲香蕉蘋果

INGREDIENTS
3 apples, Granny Smith or
    Golden Delicious or 3 fairly
    large bananas, on the unripe
    side
1 tablespoon all-purpose flour
peanut or corn oil for deep-frying
6 tablespoons fresh peanut or
    corn oil
9 tablespoons sugar
1 heaped teaspoon white sesame
    seeds

FOR THE BATTER
4 ounces self-rising flour
1 large egg, lightly beaten
about 8 tablespoons water
1 tablespoon peanut or corn oil

Serves 6 to 8

Illustrated on page 189

In this recipe, an ingenious and foolproof Chinese method of caramelizing sugar in a few tablespoonfuls of hot oil is used in the preparation of this delicious dessert. What's more, the oil is then separated from the caramel and can be reused for other cooking.

1. *Prepare the batter:* Sift the flour into a mixing bowl and stir in the egg. Add the water gradually and stir to blend into a smooth batter, like thick cream in consistency. Let to stand for about 15 minutes, then blend in the oil.

2. Peel and core the apples or peel the bananas and remove any strings. Divide each apple or roll-cut each banana into 8 pieces (see page 34). Sprinkle on the plain flour and toss well to mix.

3. Half fill a wok or deep fryer with oil. Heat to a temperature of 350°F, or until a cube of stale bread browns in 60 seconds. One by one, dip the fruit pieces into the batter. Add to the oil and deep-fry for about 2 or 3 minutes, or until pale golden. Remove with a pair of chopsticks or perforated spoon and drain on paper towels. (This can be done several hours in advance.) Reheat the oil to the same temperature. Deep-fry the fruits for a second time for about 1 minute, or until crisp and golden in color. Remove with a hand strainer or perforated spoon and drain on paper towels.

4. Fill a large bowl with water, add some ice cubes. Set aside.

5. Heat a well-cleaned and salt-free wok or heavy saucepan over high heat. Add the fresh oil, swirl it around and heat until smoke rises. Add the sugar and let it dissolve in the oil over moderately high heat, stirring all the time (a). Almost as soon as the sugar has completely dissolved, it will turn light brown in color. Immediately add all the fruit pieces (b) and sprinkle on the sesame seeds (c). Using two wok scoops or spatulas, toss the pieces around to coat them with the caramelized syrup (d). This must be done with care and speed. Transfer to a large plate (e) and immediately dip them, one by one, into the bowl of ice water, so that the caramel sets. When they are put into the bowl, you will see the golden threads being pulled (f).

a

b

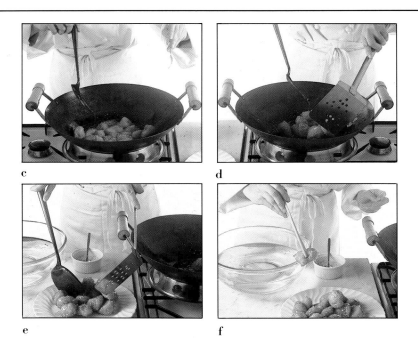

c   d

e   f

6. Quickly lift the pieces from the ice water and put on a serving plate. Serve immediately.

Red Bean Paste Pancakes

This Northern pudding, consisting of two sweet, stuffed pancakes, is both crisp and soft to the bite.

1. In a mixing bowl blend the egg and flour together to a paste. Stir in the water, gradually diluting the paste to a thin, runny consistency. Divide the mixture into 2 equal portions.

2. Put a smear of oil on an 8-inch flat, nonstick frying pan and wipe all over with a paper towel. Pour all but 1 teaspoon of one portion of the mixture into the frying pan and tilt it to let the mixture run evenly to the edges, forming a thin layer.

3. Cook over low heat for about 2 minutes, or until it becomes a thin pancake but without any brown spots. Do not turn the pancake over.

4. Loosen the edges and, using a spatula, lift the pancake to a lightly oiled plate or a flat surface.

5. Make the other pancake the same way.

INGREDIENTS
1 large egg, lightly beaten
5 tablespoons all-purpose flour
4 tablespoons water
a little peanut or corn oil
4 tablespoons canned red bean
    paste
peanut or corn oil for deep-frying

Serves 4 to 6

Illustrated on page 189

6. Spread 2 tablespoons of the red bean paste across the middle third of each pancake, leaving about 1 inch at either end (a). Fold the near flap over the bean paste (b), the side flaps inward (c) and then the far flap over toward the center, (d), sealing with a little of the leftover mixture smeared on the edges.

a   b

c   d

7. Half fill a wok or deep fryer with oil. Heat to a temperature of 350°F, or until a cube of stale bread browns in 60 seconds. Add the pancakes, smooth side up first, and deep-fry for 3 or 4 minutes, or until golden in color, turning over periodically for even browning. The pancakes will puff up, so take care they do not burst. Remove with a perforated spoon.

8. Reheat the oil to 350°F and fry the pancakes for a few seconds to recrisp. Remove and drain on paper towels.

9. Transfer the pancakes to a warm serving plate. Cut each across into 8 strips and serve immediately.

SPECIAL MENUS

DEEP-FRIED APPETIZERS

Deep-fried Wontons

A popular cold starter or a snack that is part and parcel of Cantonese dim sum.

錦
鹵
雲
吞

INGREDIENTS
6 medium raw prawns in the shell, without heads
egg white, lightly beaten
72 wonton wrappers, each 3 inches square
peanut or corn oil for deep-frying

FOR THE SWEET AND SOUR SAUCE
½ pint water
4 tablespoons sugar
3 tablespoons rice or wine vinegar
¾ teaspoon salt
2 tablespoons tomato ketchup
2½ teaspoons potato flour, dissolved in 2 tablespoons water
¼ teaspoons red food coloring (optional)

Serves 8

1. *Prepare the sweet and sour sauce:* Put the water, sugar, vinegar, salt and ketchup in a saucepan and bring to simmering point. Gradually add the dissolved potato flour, stirring as the sauce thickens. Stir in the food coloring. Pour into one or two serving bowls and let cool.

2. If frozen prawns are used, defrost thoroughly. Shell the prawns, devein (see page 39) and pat dry. Cut each one into 6 cubes.

3. *Prepare the wontons:* Pick up 2 wrappers together, one on top of the other, and place them on the fingers of one hand in the shape of a diamond. Place 1 cube of prawn just above the lower triangular point (a). Fold the wrappers over the prawn and roll toward the center, stopping just short of midway (b). Dip the index finger of the other hand into the egg white and smear either the right or left corner of the bottom wrapper. Fold backward toward the center, then put on top of the other corner and pinch the two together to seal (c). Separate the 2 triangular flaps, turn one toward you, and the other away from you (d). Turn it over and you will find the cube of prawn wrapped in the center. Repeat until all are done.

4. Half fill a wok or deep fryer with oil. Heat to a temperature of 350°F, or until a cube of stale bread browns in 60 seconds. Tip in 8 to 10 wontons, or

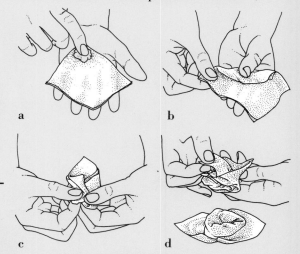

a   b

c   d

however many will float freely, and deep-fry for about 40 to 60 seconds, or until golden in color and crisp in the center. Remove with a hand strainer or perforated spoon and drain on paper towels. Repeat until all are fried.

5. The wontons will stay crisp for several hours and can be served either warm or cold.

6. To eat, spoon sweet and sour sauce on each wonton, then pick up with either chopsticks or fingers.

Note: If left overnight, deep-fried wontons will, of course, lose their crispness. They can, however, be turned into Wonton wrapper crisps soup, which is delicious, if they are put into clear broth and simmered for 1 or 2 minutes, until tender (see page 66).

Deep-fried Five-Spice Rolls

Five-spice powder lends this dish its name as well as its characteristic aroma. In Fukien, where this dish originates, ducks' eggs, both the white and the yolk, are used because of their stronger taste.

INGREDIENTS

1 package dried bean curd sheet (usually 8 ounces, containing 8 sheets, each 13 by 6 inches)

6 ounces water chestnuts, fresh peeled or canned drained

1½ pounds pork with some fat

12 scallions, white parts only, cut into small rounds

3 tablespoons potato flour

2 egg yolks

peanut or corn oil for deep-frying

FOR THE MARINADE

1 teaspoon salt

2 teaspoons thin soy sauce

2½ teaspoons sugar

5 teaspoons Shaohsing wine or medium-dry sherry

2 teaspoons sesame oil

2 teaspoons five-spice powder

1½ egg whites

FOR THE DIPS

tomato ketchup

chili sauce

1 tablespoon thick soy sauce mixed with 1 teaspoon hot prepared mustard

Serves 12

1. Soak the bean curd sheets in cold water for about 4 minutes, or until the sheets are soft and pliable. Lift each sheet carefully with both hands to drain, blot excess water dry and place flat on a large tea towel, one on top of another. Put another tea towel on top to keep them moist. This step can be done 2 or 3 hours ahead.

2. Chop the water chestnuts by hand or mince coarsely.

3. Chop the pork by hand or mince coarsely. Put into a large bowl.

4. *Prepare the marinade:* Add the salt, soy sauce, sugar, wine or sherry, oil, five-spice powder and egg whites to the pork. Stir to coat well. Let marinate for 5 minutes. Add the scallions and water chestnuts. Stir in the potato flour, 1 tablespoon at a time, to ensure smooth mixing.

5. Divide the pork filling into 16 portions.

6. Take one bean curd sheet out of the covered pile and put it on a flat surface with the 13-inch wide side in front of you (a). Halve it.

7. Scoop up one portion of the filling and roll it between your palms into the shape of a sausage. Place the filling near the bottom edge (b) of 1 piece of bean curd sheet and roll as tightly as possible away from you. Using either your fingers or a brush, smear some egg yolk on the opposite edge and seal the roll. Leave the 2 ends open and place the roll in a pan, seam side down. Cover the pan with a damp cloth. Repeat steps 6 and 7 until all are made.

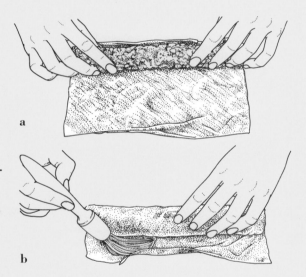

a

b

8. Half fill a wok or deep fryer with oil. Heat to a temperature of 375°F, or until a cube of stale bread browns in 50 seconds. Put in 8 rolls or however many will float freely in the oil and deep-fry for about 8 minutes or until chocolate brown in color. Remove with a hand strainer or perforated spoon and drain on paper towels. Repeat until all the rolls are done.

9. To serve, cut each roll into 5 pieces and put them on a large warm platter. The ketchup, chili sauce and soy sauce with mustard dips can be put either on the table or in the middle of the platter.

炸五香卷

Special Spring Rolls

Spring rolls, also known as egg rolls, are filling wrapped in a thin dough and deep-fried until crispy. The tastier the filling and the thinner the dough wrapper, the more delicious the spring roll.

INGREDIENTS

1 pound carrots, peeled and cut into strips
6 ounces cellophane noodles
10 medium dried Chinese mushrooms, reconstituted (see page 39)
8 ounces lean pork
8 ounces raw shrimp or 10 ounces medium prawns in the shell but without heads
8 ounces sugar peas or French beans, trimmed
5 tablespoons peanut or corn oil
4 cloves garlic, peeled and chopped fine
½ to ¾ inch fresh ginger root, peeled and chopped fine
6 or 8 scallions, cut into small rounds
1 tablespoon Shaohsing wine or medium-dry sherry
6 ounces canned bamboo shoots, cut into matchstick-sized strips

2 tablespoons thin soy sauce
30 to 35 pieces large spring roll wrappers, about 8½ to 9½ inches square
lightly beaten egg white
peanut or corn oil for deep-frying

FOR THE MARINADE

½ teaspoon salt
¼ teaspoon sugar
2 teaspoons thin soy sauce
6 turns pepper mill
1 teaspoon Shaohsing wine or medium-dry sherry
1 teaspoon sesame oil
1 teaspoon potato flour
1½ tablespoons water

FOR THE SHRIMP MARINADE

¼ teaspoon salt
¼ teaspoon sugar
2 teaspoon thin soy sauce
4 turns pepper mill
1 teaspoon sesame oil

Serves 10 to 15

1. Put the carrots in a bowl and add 1 teaspoon of salt to draw out the water. Drain after 30 minutes. Pat dry, if necessary.

2. Put the cellophane noodles into a large bowl and pour 2 pints of boiling water over them. Cover and let soak and expand for at least 30 minutes. Drain well. Cut up roughly.

3. Drain and squeeze out excess water from the mushrooms but leave damp. Shred into thin slivers. (Do not use a food processor.)

4. Cut the pork into matchstick-sized pieces. Put into a bowl.

5. *Prepare the pork marinade:* Add the salt, sugar, soy sauce, pepper, wine or sherry, oil, potato flour and water to the pork. Stir well to coat. Let marinate for 15 to 30 minutes.

6. Shell and devein the prawns, if necessary (see page 39); slice into pieces similar in size to the pork. If shrimp are used, they can be left whole or halved. Put into a bowl.

7. *Prepare the shrimp marinade:* Add the salt, sugar, soy sauce, pepper, and oil to the shrimp or prawns. Let marinate for 15 minutes.

8. Cut the peas or beans diagonally into strips similar to the bamboo shoots.

9. Heat a wok over high heat until smoke rises. Add 3 tablespoons of the oil and swirl it around. Add the garlic, half the ginger and half the scallions. When the garlic sizzles and takes on color, add the pork and turn and toss with the wok scoop for about 30 seconds. Add the shrimp and continue to flip and turn for another minute. Splash in the wine along the edge of the wok and continue to flip and toss. When the sizzling dies down, put in the mushrooms and bamboo shoots. Stir until hot. Remove and cool.

10. Pour the remaining oil into the wok and swirl it around. Add the remaining ginger and scallions. Add the peas and stir-fry for 1 minute. Stir in the carrots and then the cellophane noodles. Continue to stir, over less fierce heat, until hot, letting any excess water evaporate. Season with ¾ teaspoon of salt and the thin soy sauce. Transfer to a large dish and leave to cool.

11. Place a spring roll wrapper on a flat dish or a clear surface, arranging it in a diamond shape. Put about 2 tablespoons of the vegetable filling just off the center and top with about 1 tablespoon of the other filling. Spread it out about 5 inches wide.

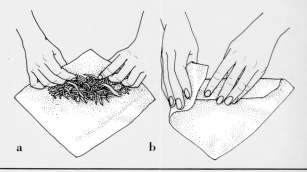

a   b

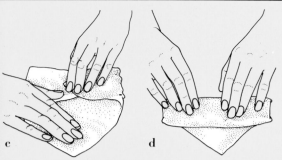

c   d

Tucking in the filling, fold up the bottom flap (a) and start rolling. Midway, fold the 2 side flaps toward the center (b), brush the remaining flap with the egg white (c) and fold it up (d) to seal the spring roll tightly. Repeat until all are done.

12. Half fill a wok or deep fryer with oil. Heat to a temperature of 350°F, or until a cube of stale bread browns in 60 seconds. Carefully add about 6 to 8 spring rolls at a time or however many will float freely and deep-fry for about 4 minutes, or until pale golden, turning over periodically. Remove with a hand strainer or perforated spoon and drain on paper towels. To crisp, reheat the oil to 350°F and deep-fry a second time for 1 or 2 minutes, or until golden. Remove and drain. Serve hot.

Note: Spring rolls can be frozen after the first deep-frying. The second deep-frying can be done just before they are served.

Stuffed Crab Claws

Biting into crab meat and prawn at the same time produces a rich and luxurious feeling. These crisp and juicy crab claws are as good to look at as they are to eat, so they are bound to be a successful starter for a dinner party. You can prepare in advance up to the end of step 6, and then simply recrisp the claws just before serving.

INGREDIENTS	FOR THE MARINADE
1¼ pounds fresh or frozen medium raw prawns in the shell, without heads	1 teaspoon salt
	½ teaspoon sugar
	1 teaspoon cornstarch
	1 egg white, lightly beaten
3 ounces of fatback	1 teaspoon sesame oil
4 tablespoons cornstarch	**FOR THE DIPS**
12 medium fresh or frozen cooked and shelled crab claws	chili sauce
	Worcestershire sauce
peanut or corn oil for deep-frying	*Serves 6*

1. If frozen prawns and crab claws are used, defrost thoroughly. Shell and devein the prawns (see page 39). Pat dry with paper towels.

2. Chop the prawns and fatback by hand or mince coarsely. Put in a bowl.

3. *Prepare the marinade:* Add the salt, sugar and cornstarch to the prawns and fatback. Stir vigorously for about 1 minute, or until the mixture becomes sticky. Add the egg white and stir again for about 1 minute, or until the paste is firm and elastic. Cover and let marinate in the refrigerator for about 30 minutes. Blend in the sesame oil.

4. Put the 4 tablespoons of cornstarch in a bowl. Holding the pincers of one crab claw, dip the meaty part in the cornstarch (a); shake off any excess. Repeat with the rest of the claws.

5. *Stuff the claws:* Divide the paste into 12 portions. Lightly oil a plate. Holding the claw by the pincers, press a portion of the paste on the meat, covering a small area of the shell to seal it (b). Place on the lightly oiled plate. Repeat with the rest of the claws. To prevent your fingers from getting too sticky, wet them with cold water.

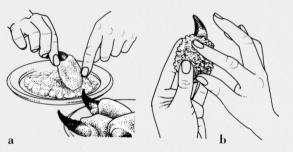

a   b

6. Half fill a wok or deep fryer with oil. Heat to a temperature of 350°F, or until a cube of stale bread browns in 60 seconds. Carefully lower 6 claws into the oil, 1 at a time. Deep-fry for about 4 minutes, or until golden, turning each one occasionally. Remove each claw with a perforated spoon or tongs and drain on paper towels. Repeat with the remaining 6 claws.

7. Deep-fry all 12 claws together for a few seconds to crisp. Remove and drain. Serve the claws immediately. Pass the dips in separate saucers.

百花釀蟹鉗

Deep-fried Milk

This is a very popular dish in Hong Kong: it satisfies the ever-present Chinese craving for a contrast between a crunchy and a tender texture in food. In the same mouthful, one can experience a smooth and creamy filling wrapped in a crispy batter coating. The recipe works equally well without the crab meat.

INGREDIENTS	FOR THE BATTER
4 ounces solid creamed coconut	5 ounces all-purpose flour
4 ounces cooked crab meat (optional)	5 tablespoons cornstarch
1¼ teaspoons salt	1½ teaspoons baking powder
6 turns white pepper mill	½ pint water
5 tablespoons cornstarch	2 tablespoons peanut or corn oil
1 pint milk	
peanut or corn oil for deep frying	*Serves 8*

1. Grate the creamed coconut and put the shavings into a saucepan.

2. Add the crab meat, salt and pepper to the creamed coconut.

3. Stir in the cornstarch and some of the milk and blend to a smooth paste. Over gentle heat, gradually add the remaining milk, stirring continuously until the mixture has become well amalgamated and thickened.

4. Pour into a well-oiled shallow container 8 inches square or 7 to 9 inches rectangular and let set in the refrigerator for 2 hours. It can be left overnight covered with plastic wrap.

5. *Prepare the batter:* Sift the flour and cornstarch into a large bowl; add the baking powder. Gradually stir in the water and blend to a smooth, runny consistency. Let stand at room temperature for a minimum of 30 minutes. Blend in the oil.

6. Loosen the well-set milk mixture with an oiled spatula. Use an oiled knife to cut the mixture into about 32 diamond-shaped pieces.

7. Half fill a wok or deep fryer with oil. Heat to a temperature of 375°F, or until a cube of stale bread browns in 50 seconds. Dip several pieces into the batter and, using either a pair of chopsticks or tongs, put the pieces one by one into the oil. Deep-fry about 12 at a time, or however many will float freely, for about 3 minutes, or until pale golden. Remove with a hand strainer or perforated spoon and drain on paper towels. Repeat until all are done. Remove the "bearded" excess batter with a pair of scissors.

8. To crisp, reheat the oil to 375°F and deep-fry the pieces again briefly in 2 batches, each for about 1 minute. Remove and drain on paper towels. (This step can be postponed until ready to serve.) Serve immediately.

Deep-fried Phoenix-Tail Prawns

This dish derives its name from the Chinese emblem of beauty, the phoenix. Prawns are likened to its long and graceful tail.

INGREDIENTS	FOR THE BATTER
1 pound fresh or frozen medium raw prawns in the shell, without heads	5 ounces all-purpose flour
½ teaspoon salt	5 tablespoons cornstarch
few turns white pepper mill	1½ teaspoons baking powder
1 large green pepper, seeded	½ pint water
peanut or corn oil for deep-frying	½ teaspoon salt
	2 tablespoons peanut or corn oil
	Serves 6

1. *Prepare the batter:* Sift the flour and cornstarch into a large bowl, add the baking powder. Gradually whisk in the water and blend to a smooth consistency. Let stand for a minimum of 30 minutes. Just before using, add the salt and blend in the oil until the batter is smooth and shiny.

2. If frozen prawns are used, defrost thoroughly. Remove the shells but leave the tail intact. Devein (see page 39) and pat dry with paper towels.

3. Turn the prawns upside down, one by one, and make 3 slashes across the abdomen without cutting through completely. This prevents them from curling up when deep-fried. Add the salt and pepper.

4. Cut the green pepper into rectangular pieces.

5. Half fill a wok or deep fryer with oil. Heat to a temperature of 375°F, or until a cube of stale bread browns in 50 seconds.

6 Hold the prawn by its tail and coat the rest of its body in the batter. Lift by the tail and let some of the runny batter drip off. Put into the oil. Add about half of the prawns at a time or as many as will float freely. Deep-fry for about 3 minutes, or until the batter is pale golden in color. Remove with a hand strainer or perforated spoon and drain on paper towels. Snip off any "bearded" excess batter with a pair of scissors.

7. While the prawns are in the oil, put half of the green pepper in the batter and add to the oil to fry with the prawns. Remove them when they look pale golden in color and drain on paper towels.

8. Deep-fry the remaining prawns and green pepper.

9. To serve, pile the green pepper in the middle of a platter and arrange the prawns around it with their tails facing outward.

Note: To reheat, either deep-fry the prawns and green pepper for about 30 seconds, until the batter is crisp again, or put under a preheated grill.

Prawns Wrapped in Rice Paper

This classic dish is one of the Cantonese dim sum *delicacies.*

INGREDIENTS

1 pound fresh or frozen medium raw prawns in the shell, without heads
1 egg white, lightly beaten
1 teaspoon salt
½ teaspoon sugar
2 teaspoons cornstarch
3 ounces fatback, chopped into size of matchstick heads
3 ounces lean ham, chopped into size of matchstick heads
4 ounces canned bamboo shoots, chopped into size of matchstick heads
4 to 6 scallions, cut into tiny rounds
15 sheets rice paper
peanut or corn oil for deep-frying
chili sauce to serve

Makes about 28 rolls

1. If frozen prawns are used, defrost thoroughly. Shell and devein the prawns (see page 39). Pat dry with paper towels.

2. Chop the prawns roughly. Put in a bowl.

3. Add the egg white, salt, sugar and cornstarch to the prawns. Stir until well coated.

4. Add the fatback, ham and bamboo shoots to the prawns and stir well. Mix in the scallions.

5. Cut the rice paper sheets into 30 squares, each 4 inches.

6. Have some cold water in a dish nearby. Put 1 rice paper square on a plate or work surface. Spread on about 1 tablespoon of the filling, almost to the edges. Fold over and roll into a small cigar, leaving both ends open. Seal with a little water smeared on the edge.

7. Half fill a wok or deep fryer with oil. Heat to a temperature of 375°F, or until a cube of stale bread browns in 50 seconds. Using a pair of chopsticks or tongs, lower half of the prawn rolls into the oil. Deep-fry for about 3 minutes, until the filling is cooked and the rice paper crisp. Remove with a hand strainer or perforated spoon and drain on paper towels. Deep-fry the remainder.

8. Reheat the oil to about 350°F. Put in all the prawn rolls and deep-fry a second time for a few seconds. Remove and drain on paper towels. This makes them extra crisp and fragrant.

9. Serve hot with chili sauce.

紙包蝦

SZECHWAN MENU

Fragrant and Crispy Duck

Deep-fried to golden brown, the meat is nevertheless so tender that it comes away from the bones merely with the help of a pair of chopsticks. And therein lies the secret of this Szechwan duck.

INGREDIENTS

1 oven-ready duck, 4 to 5 pounds
2 tablespoons thin soy sauce
2 to 3 tablespoons all-purpose flour
peanut or corn oil for deep-frying
12 lotus leaf buns (see below)
ground roasted Szechwan peppercorns and salt (see page 52, omitting the five-spice powder)

FOR THE MARINADE

2 tablespoons Shaohsing wine or medium-dry sherry
1 tablespoon salt
scant 1 teaspoon five-spice powder
4 slices fresh ginger root, peeled
3 scallions, halved

Serves 6 with 3 other dishes

1. *Prepare the marinade:* Rub the wine or sherry, salt and five-spice powder all over the duck skin and inside the cavity. Put the ginger and scallions inside the cavity. Let marinate for at least 6 hours or overnight.

2. Put the duck in a heatproof bowl or dish with raised sides. Steam in a wok or steamer for 1¾ to 2 hours (see page 45). Quite a lot of fat and juice will collect in the bowl. (The juice, after the fat has been skimmed off, can be used as a tasty stock.)

3. Remove the duck from the bowl and stand it on a rack to let all the juice run out. Place the duck on another dish or stand it up to dry for 30 minutes or longer. Care must be taken to keep the duck whole at this stage.

4. Remove and discard all the ginger and scallions from the cavity.

5. Brush the duck skin with the soy sauce. Dust all over with flour.

6. Half fill a wok or deep fryer with oil. Heat to a temperature of 375°F, or until a cube of stale bread browns in 50 seconds. Place the duck in the oil and deep-fry over low to moderate heat for about 2 minutes. With a wooden spoon or spatula held in one hand and another put inside the cavity, turn the duck over and deep-fry the other side for 2 more minutes. Repeat this process for a total of 8 minutes, after which time the skin should be golden brown. Drain on paper towels.

7. Steam the lotus leaf buns for about 5 minutes or until hot.

8. Place the duck on a warm serving plate and put the buns around it. Serve at the table with either a fork and knife or a pair of chopsticks. The skin of the duck should be so crisp and the meat so tender that they come away easily from the bones with pressure from the chopsticks. Dip in ground peppercorns and salt, and eat with the buns. Silver thread buns also go well with the duck.

Bun Accompaniments

So called because they resemble lotus leaves and silver threads, these buns are the standard accompaniment to the Szechwan Fragrant and crispy duck.

Lotus Leaf Buns

INGREDIENTS

½ teaspoon dried yeast
1 teaspoon sugar
6 ounces tepid water
2½ cups all-purpose flour

2 tablespoons lard
little extra flour
1 tablespoon peanut or corn oil

Makes 24 buns

1. Put the dried yeast and sugar in a small bowl, add the water and stir. Leave in a warm place until the yeast froths on the surface.

2. Sift the flour into a mixing bowl. Rub in the lard. Stir in the yeast liquid and work it into a dough. Knead lightly for 1 or 2 minutes, until the dough is smooth. Either cover the dough with a damp cloth or cover the bowl with plastic wrap. Let stand in a warm place for at least 1 hour, so that the dough will rise to more than double in size.

3. Knead the risen dough on a lightly floured board for a few seconds, until smooth. Divide into 2 equal portions.

4. With both hands, roll each portion into a cylindrical roll 12 inches long. Using a ruler as a guide, divide into 12 equal pieces.

5. One by one, stand each piece upright on the heel of your hand: slightly round off the dough with the other hand, then flatten it.

6. Using a lightly floured rolling pin, roll each into a circle 2 inches in diameter, making the edges slightly thinner than the center.

7. With one finger, smear a little oil on half of the surface of each circle. Fold the other half over to form a semicircle (a).

8. Using an unserrated table knife, make a crisscross pattern on each semicircle. Then, using the blunt side of the knife, make 2 indentations, ½

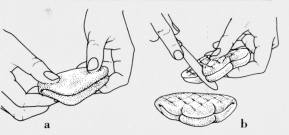

inch deep, along the edge (b).

9. Space the buns out in one layer on a very wet cloth on a steaming rack. Steam in a wok or steamer over high heat for about 12 minutes (see page 45). Remove from the heat.

10. Transfer the buns to a wire rack for a few seconds, then put on a warm plate and serve.

Silver Thread Buns

INGREDIENTS	3½ ounces lard
¾ teaspoon dried yeast	little extra flour
2 teaspoons sugar	2½ tablespoons sugar
½ pint tepid water	*Makes about 18 to 20*
3¾ cups all-purpose flour	*buns*

1. Put the dried yeast and sugar in a small bowl, add the water and stir. Leave in a warm place until the yeast froths on the surface.

2. Sift the flour into a mixing bowl. Rub in 1 tablespoon of the lard with the fingertips. Stir in the yeast liquid and work it into a dough. Knead lightly for 1 or 2 minutes, until the dough is smooth. Either cover the dough with a damp cloth or cover the bowl with plastic wrap. Let stand in a warm place for at least 1 hour, so that the dough will rise to more than double in size.

3. Cream the remaining lard and sugar until well blended.

4. Knead the risen dough on a lightly floured board for a few seconds, until smooth.

5. Roll out the dough with a lightly floured rolling pin into a thin circular or oblong sheet about 20 inches across. Spread evenly with the sugar-and-lard mixture, using a broad knife. Fold the sheet over and over at 3-inch intervals. Slice crosswise into thin "silver" threads about ⅛ inch wide (a).

6. Group 7 or 8 strings of silver threads together and, using both hands, pull them slowly across into a 12-inch-long rope (b).

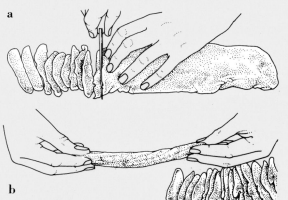

7. Lay the rope on the floured board, turn one end away from you (c), and roll toward the other end to make a spiral tower, the base being about 2 inches in diameter (d). Repeat until all are done.

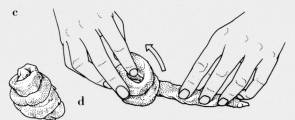

8. Space them out in one layer on a very wet cloth on a steaming rack. Steam in a wok or steamer over high heat for 15 minutes (see page 45). Transfer the buns to a wire rack for a few seconds, then put on a warm plate and serve.

Hot and Sour Soup

酸
辣
湯

Pungent, peppery hot and slightly glutinous in consistency, this Szechwan and Peking peasant soup surprises the palate with its tastes and aftertastes. Now popular with Westerners, it originally called for a special ingredient: fresh chicken's or duck's blood. I must confess, however, that I am quite happy to do without it. Indeed, in restaurants outside China this soup is invariably made without blood.

INGREDIENTS

4 ounces lean pork
6 dried Chinese mushrooms, reconstituted (see page 39)
½ ounce cloud ears, reconstituted (see page 39)
1 ounce golden needles, reconstituted (see page 39)
2 cakes bean curd, drained
2 tablespoons potato flour
4 tablespoons water
2½ pints prime or clear stock (see page 225)
1½ teaspoons salt
¾ teaspoon sugar
1 tablespoon thin soy sauce
1 tablespoon thick soy sauce

2 eggs, lightly beaten with 2 teaspoons oil and pinch salt
1 or 2 ounces fresh coriander leaves, torn into pieces
3 or 4 tablespoons rice or white wine vinegar
1 to 1½ teaspoons ground black pepper
dashes of sesame oil (optional)

FOR THE MARINADE

⅛ teaspoon salt
1 teaspoon thick soy sauce
3 turns black pepper mill
1 teaspoon Shaohsing wine or medium-dry sherry
1 teaspoon potato flour
1 or 2 tablespoons water
1 teaspoon sesame oil

Serves 6 to 8

1. Slice the pork into matchstick-sized strips. Put in a bowl.

2. *Prepare the marinade:* Add the salt, soy sauce, pepper and wine or sherry to the pork. Sprinkle with the potato flour and stir in the water to coat the meat. Let marinate for 15 to 30 minutes or

longer. Blend in the sesame oil.

3. Drain and squeeze out excess water from the mushrooms, cloud ears and golden needles but leave damp. Slice the mushrooms into the thinnest possible slivers. Break up or cut the cloud ears into similar-sized pieces. Cut the golden needles into 2-inch sections.

4. Slice the bean curd cakes into ¼-inch thick pieces and then carefully slice again into strips 1 by ¼ inch.

5. In a small bowl, dissolve the potato flour in the water.

6. In a large saucepan add the mushrooms, cloud ears and golden needles to the stock and season with the salt, sugar and soy sauces. Bring to a boil and add the pork, separating with a pair of chopsticks or a fork. Then add the bean curd, and as soon as the soup returns to a boil, slowly stir in the well-stirred dissolved potato flour. Slowly bring to a boil again.

7. Slowly pour in the beaten egg through the gap of a pair of chopsticks or along the back of a fork, moving the chopsticks or fork in a circular motion at the same time. Remove from the heat and cover for 45 seconds, to allow the egg to set in tender flakes.

8. Add the coriander and stir to mix.

9. Stir in the vinegar and then the black pepper for seasoning.

10. Serve piping hot. Stir in dashes of sesame oil, if desired, just before serving. Put extra vinegar and black pepper on the table for those who like it really hot and pungent.

Note: Leftover soup can be reheated, but a little more vinegar and pepper may have to be added to renew the sharp taste.

Fish Fragrant Shredded Pork

Another Szechwan dish, which uses the special fish fragrant sauce (see page 150).

INGREDIENTS

1 pound lean loin pork or fresh ham

½ ounce cloud ears, reconstituted (see page 39)

6 water chestnuts, peeled fresh or drained canned

2 or 3 ounces canned bamboo shoots

4 or 5 scallions, cut into small rounds, white and green parts separated

5 or 6 tablespoons peanut or corn oil

5 or 6 cloves garlic, peeled and chopped fine

¼ inch fresh ginger root, peeled and chopped fine

1 or 2 tablespoons Szechwan chili paste

(see page 226)

1 tablespoon Shaohsing wine or medium-dry sherry

2 or 3 teaspoons rice or white wine vinegar

FOR THE MARINADE

¼ teaspoon salt

1 teaspoon potato flour

1 tablespoon water

1 teaspoon peanut or corn oil

1 teaspoon sesame oil

FOR THE SAUCE

¾ teaspoon potato flour dissolved in 4 tablespoons clear stock or water

1½ teaspoons thin soy sauce

1½ teaspoons sugar

Serves 4 with 2 other dishes

1. Slice the pork into threadlike strips about 2-to-2½ inches long and ¹⁄₁₆ inch thick. Put in a bowl.

2. *Prepare the marinade:* Add the salt, potato flour and water to the meat. Stir to coat. Let marinate for 20 to 30 minutes. Blend in the oils.

3. Cut the drained cloud ears, water chestnuts and bamboo shoots into narrow strips.

4. *Prepare the sauce:* Mix together the dissolved potato flour, soy sauce and sugar. When ready to cook, add the green scallions.

5. Heat a wok over high heat until smoke rises. Add the oil and swirl it around. Add the garlic, which will sizzle and take on color instantly. Add the ginger and white scallions; stir a few times. Stir in the chili paste and then add the pork, cloud ears, water chestnuts and bamboo shoots. Sliding the wok scoop or metal spatula to the bottom of the wok, flip and toss for 1 minute, separating the pork strips. Splash in the wine or sherry around the side of the wok, stirring as it sizzles. Continue to stir for about 1½ to 2 minutes, or until the pork, having turned white, is cooked. Add the well-stirred sauce, stirring as it thickens.

6. Remove from the heat, add the vinegar and blend well. Put on a warm plate and serve immediately.

Dry-fried Four-Season Beans

A typical Szechwan dish in that it contains a variety of tastes to surprise the palate. Traditionally stir-fried, first, the beans here are deep-fried for speed.

INGREDIENTS

2 tablespoons dried shrimp, rinsed

1 ounce Szechwan preserved vegetable, rinsed

peanut or corn oil for deep-frying

1 to 1¼ pounds green beans, topped and tailed

3 or 4 cloves garlic, peeled and chopped fine

½ inch fresh ginger root,

peeled and chopped fine

½ teaspoon salt

1 tablespoon thin soy sauce

2 teaspoons sugar

2 tablespoons shrimp water

2 teaspoons rice or white wine vinegar

1 teaspoons sesame oil

2 scallions, cut into small rounds

Serves 4 to 6 with 2 or 3 other dishes

1. Soak the shrimp for 15 minutes in just enough boiling water to cover them. Drain them, reserving the soaking liquid. Chop into the size of matchstick heads (see page 38).

2. Chop the preserved vegetable by hand (it does not work with a food processor) into pieces the same size as the shrimp.

3. Half fill a wok or deep fryer with oil. Heat to a temperature of 375°F, or until a cube of stale bread browns in 50 seconds. Add the beans and deep-fry for about 4 or 5 minutes, or until they wrinkle. Remove with a large hand strainer and drain on paper towels. Pour all but 2 or 3 tablespoons of oil into a container and save it for future use.

4. Reheat the oil until smoke rises. Add the garlic, let it sizzle, then add the ginger and stir a couple of times. Add the shrimp and stir continuously. As the aroma rises, add the preserved vegetable and

continue to stir, lowering the heat if they jump about too much.

5. Add the salt, soy sauce, sugar and shrimp water. Return the beans to the wok. Turn up the heat again and, sliding the wok scoop or metal spatula to the bottom of the wok, turn and toss the beans until the water has been absorbed.

6. Sprinkle in the vinegar and sesame oil. Add the scallions and transfer to a warm serving plate.

Note: Since the taste of this dish actually improves if left standing, it can be cooked several hours or even a day in advance and then heated up just before serving. If there is any left over, the beans are also delicious eaten cold.

Pang Pang Chicken

Interestingly, this dish derives its name, not from the peppery-hot and intriguing dressing, as might be expected, but from the wooden stick (pang in Mandarin) that is used to beat the chicken in order to loosen the fibers. To many people, this Szechwan dish is also known as Bon bon chicken.

INGREDIENTS

10 ounces cucumber, peeled
1 teaspoon salt
1 pint clear stock or water
2 chicken breasts, 1 pound to 1 pound 2 ounces boned, but with skin left on
8 scallions, white parts only, cut into silken threads (see page 34)

FOR THE DRESSING
4 teaspoons sesame paste

2 tablespoons thin soy sauce
1 teaspoon rice or white wine vinegar
1½ teaspoons sugar
4 teaspoons hot chili oil with flakes (see page 225)
½ teaspoon ground roasted Szechwan peppercorns (see page 21)
1 teaspoon sesame oil

Serves 4 or 5 as first course

1. Halve the cucumber lengthwise and scoop out the seedy pulp in the center. Cut the cucumber into thin pieces.

2. Sprinkle the salt over the cucumber and mix well. Set aside so that water can ooze out.

3. Put the stock in a saucepan and bring to a boil. Add the chicken and poach for about 15 minutes, or until cooked. Remove the chicken breasts and leave to cool.

4. *Prepare the dressing:* Stir the sesame paste, in the jar, then put in a bowl and stir in the soy sauce, vinegar, sugar, hot chilli oil, peppercorns and sesame oil.

5. Rinse the cucumber in cold water to rid it of the salt, then squeeze out excess water. Arrange attractively on a serving plate.

6. When the chicken breasts are cool enough to handle, beat lightly on the skin side with a wooden rolling pin to loosen the fibers. Peel off the skin and tear the meat into long strips with your fingers. If you like the skin, cut it up into longish strips as well. Arrange them in the center of the plate.

7. Place the scallions on top of the chicken.

8. When ready to eat, pour the well-stirred dressing over the ingredients and mix to coat. Serve cold.

Note: This dish can be prepared hours in advance and refrigerated, covered, until ready to serve. It keeps quite well until the following day, though the dressing inevitably becomes a little watery.

CANTONESE MENU

Clear-steamed Sea Bass

The sea bass and the striped bass are arguably the most popular fish for Chinese living in Europe and America. Not surprisingly, they serve them steamed.

INGREDIENTS

1 sea bass, 1½ to 2½ pounds, cleaned with head left on
¼ teaspoon salt
¼ teaspoon sugar
½ to ¾ inch fresh ginger root, peeled and cut into silken threads (see page 35)
5 to 7 scallions, cut into 2-inch sections and then silken threads (see page 34), green and white parts separated
4 or 5 tablespoons peanut or corn oil
2 or 3 tablespoons thin soy sauce

Serves 2 as a main course; 4 to 6 with 2 or 3 other dishes

1. Pat the fish dry. Make 2 or 3 diagonal slashes on both sides of the fish. Lay it on a heatproof serving dish with slightly raised sides. If your wok or steamer is rather small, the fish can be halved.

2. Steam in a wok or steamer over high heat for about 8 minutes, until the fish is cooked and the flesh flakes easily (see page 45). Remove the cover, reduce the heat or turn it off. If too much water from the steam has collected on the dish, use paper towels to absorb some of it.

3. Sprinkle with the salt and sugar. Spread the ginger, then the green, and finally the white scallions on the fish.

4. Heat the oil in a small saucepan over high heat until smoke rises. Pour it, little by little, over the scallions and ginger. The sizzling oil partially cooks them, enhancing the flavor.

5. Remove the dish from the wok or steamer. Add the soy sauce and serve immediately.

Asparagus with Crab Meat

Crab meat adds rather than detracts from the natural sweetness of asparagus, and the sight of the red-and-white meat on a bed of green makes this dish especially appealing.

INGREDIENTS

1½ pounds asparagus, cleaned and trimmed
5 tablespoons peanut or corn oil
4 thin slices fresh ginger root, peeled
1 tablespoon Shaohsing wine or medium-dry sherry
½ teaspoon salt
3 ounces prime stock (see page 225)
1 or 2 cloves garlic, peeled and chopped fine
¼ inch fresh ginger root, peeled and cut into silken threads (see page 35)
2 or 3 scallions, white parts only, cut into small rounds
8 ounces cooked crab meat

FOR THE SAUCE
¾ teaspoon potato flour
5 tablespoons clear stock or water
2 tablespoons oyster sauce
salt to taste

Serves 6 with 3 or 4 other dishes

1. Cut the asparagus into sections, the tips about 2¼ inches long, the remainder about 1¼ inches long.

2. *Prepare the sauce:* Mix together the potato flour, stock or water, oyster sauce and salt.

3. Heat a wok over high heat until smoke rises. Add 3 tablespoons of oil and swirl it around. Add the ginger and let it sizzle for a few seconds. Add the asparagus and turn and toss with the wok scoop or metal spatula. When hot, splash in ½ tablespoon of the wine or sherry around the side of the wok. When the sizzling dies down, reduce the heat, add the salt and stock. Bring to a boil, cover and simmer fast for 4 or 5 minutes if the asparagus is thin, 6 or 7 minutes if medium-sized, longer if extra thick. The asparagus should be tender but crisp. Remove and keep warm.

4. Wash and dry the wok. Reheat over high heat until smoke rises. Add the remaining oil and swirl it around. Add the garlic, ginger and scallions, stir and let sizzle, releasing their aroma. Add the crab meat and stir to mix. As soon as it is very hot, splash in the remaining wine or sherry. Pour in the well-stirred sauce and continue to stir as it thickens. Remove and spoon over the asparagus. Serve immediately.

Golden Prawn Balls

雪
山
蝦
球

Crunchy to the bite, the prawn paste inside these deep-fried balls is firm but tender in texture. To achieve this, salt and egg white are essential ingredients.

INGREDIENTS

6 to 8 slices white bread, crusts removed
6 water chestnuts, fresh peeled or canned, drained
2 ounces fatback
1 pound medium raw prawns without heads about 12 ounces, shelled

peanut or corn oil for deep-frying

FOR THE MARINADE

1 teaspoon salt
½ teaspoon sugar
1 teaspoon cornstarch
1 egg white, lightly beaten

Serves 6 as a starter; makes about 24 balls

1. The bread is best if left out for 2 or 3 hours. Dice into small cubes, about ¼ inch square.

2. Chop fine or mince the water chestnuts.

3. Chop fine or mince the fatback. Put into a large, deep bowl.

4. Shell and devein the prawns (see page 39).

5. Crush the prawns with the flat side of a cleaver and then chop about 100 times. Alternatively, coarsely mince. Transfer to the bowl with the pork.

6. *Prepare the marinade:* Add the salt and sugar to the prawns. Sprinkle with the cornstarch and stir vigorously for 1 minute.

7. Stir in the water chestnuts.

8. Add the egg white and stir again vigorously for 1 or 2 more minutes. This gives the paste a firm, elastic texture.

9. Refrigerate for about 30 minutes. The paste can be prepared well ahead of time and left, covered, in the refrigerator until ready for use.

10. Spread the bread cubes on a clean pan.

11. Roll about 1 tablespoon of the paste between your palms into a ball. Then roll it on the bread cubes until more or less covered. Set aside. Repeat until the paste is used up.

12. Half fill a wok or a deep fryer with oil. Heat to a temperature of 350°F, or until a cube of stale bread browns in 60 seconds. Add the balls, 8 or 10 at a time or as many as can float freely, and deep-fry for 2 or 3 minutes, or until the bread cubes are golden in color. The paste should be cooked by now. Remove with a hand strainer or perforated spoon and drain on paper towels. Transfer to a warm serving plate and serve immediately.

Dry-fried Prawns

干
烧
明
蝦

This dish traditionally calls for large prawns, but I have adapted it to medium-sized ones.

INGREDIENTS

1½ pounds fresh or frozen medium raw prawns in the shell, without heads
¾ teaspoon sea salt
peanut or corn oil
4 cloves garlic, peeled and chopped fine
½ to ¾ inch fresh ginger root, peeled and chopped fine
2 fresh green chilies, seeded and chopped
4 large scallions, cut into small rounds, white

and green parts separated

FOR THE SAUCE

⅛ teaspoon potato flour
2 tablespoons thin soy sauce
2 teaspoons sugar
1 tablespoon Shaohsing wine or medium-dry sherry
1 tablespoon ketchup

Serves 6 to 8 with 3 or 4 other dishes

1. If frozen prawns are used, defrost thoroughly. Wash the shells well and remove the legs. Devein, if preferred, although there is no harm in not doing so (see page 90). Pat dry with paper towels. Put into a large bowl.

2. Sprinkle with the salt and mix well. Let stand for about 20 minutes.

3. *Prepare the sauce:* Mix together the potato flour, soy sauce, sugar, wine or sherry and ketchup.

4. Half fill a wok or deep fryer with oil. Heat to a temperature of 350°F, or until a cube of stale bread browns in 60 seconds. Tip in all the prawns, "to go through the oil" for about 30 seconds, moving them gently with either long bamboo chopsticks or a wooden spoon. Turn off the heat, remove immediately with a large hand strainer and drain

on paper towels. The prawns, now pinkish, will be almost cooked.

5. Empty all but 2 or 3 tablespoons of oil into another container and keep for future use.

6. Reheat the oil in a wok until smoke rises. Add the garlic, stir a couple of times, then the ginger, stir, then the chili, stir, and then the white scallions and stir a few more times. Return the prawns to the wok and spread them out into a single layer, if possible. Lower the heat and sauté the prawns for about 30 seconds, letting them absorb the aroma of the garlic and ginger. Turn them over and sauté for

another 30 seconds, taking care not to burn them.

7. Pour the well-stirred sauce over the prawns. As you do so, turn and toss the prawns with a wok scoop or metal spatula until most of the sauce has been absorbed. Add the green scallions, transfer to a warm serving platter and serve immediately.

8. To eat, pick up one prawn with a pair of chopsticks, bite into it and shell it with your front teeth while savoring the sauce on the shell. Neatly spit the shell onto a side plate and eat the prawn meat in the normal way. If you want an easier way of eating the prawns, I suggest you use your fingers.

Stir-fried Fillet of Beef with Mango

This sophisticated modern dish is especially popular in the South of China where mangoes are greatly enjoyed. The combination of the sharpness of the ginger, the natural sweetness of the mango and the savory sauce makes the beef an intriguing proposition to the palate.

香芒牛肉

INGREDIENTS
1 pound beef fillet, trimmed
1 large mango, not too ripe
peanut or corn oil for deep-frying
4 cloves garlic, peeled and chopped fine
4 scallions, cut into 1-inch sections, white and green parts separated
¾ inch fresh ginger root, cut into silken threads (see page 35)
1 tablespoon Shaohsing wine or medium-dry sherry.

FOR THE MARINADE
¼ teaspoon salt
½ teaspoon sugar
1 teaspoon thin soy sauce
1 teaspoon thick soy sauce
1 teaspoon Shaohsing wine or medium-dry sherry
4 turns black pepper mill
1½ teaspoons potato flour
2 tablespoons water

FOR THE SAUCE
½ teaspoon potato flour
2 teaspoons oyster sauce
1 teaspoon thin soy sauce
3 tablespoons water

Serves 4 with 2 other dishes

1. Cut the fillet across the grain into chunky strips, about 2 inches long and ½ inch thick. Beat the beef strips with the broad side of a cleaver to loosen the fibers. Put into a bowl.

2. *Prepare the marinade:* Add the salt, sugar, soy sauces, wine or sherry and pepper to the beef. Sprinkle with the potato flour, add the water, 1 tablespoon at a time, and stir vigorously to coat the pieces well. Let marinate in the refrigerator for 20

to 30 minutes.

3. Peel the mango, slice the flesh from the stone and then cut into strips.

4. *Prepare the sauce:* Mix together the potato flour, oyster sauce, soy sauce and water in a cup and put aside.

5. Half fill a wok or deep fryer with oil. Heat to a temperature of 350°F, or until a cube of stale bread browns in 60 seconds. Tip the beef into the oil and, using a long pair of chopsticks or a wooden spoon, stir gently to make sure that all the pieces "go through the oil" for about 30 seconds, to have their juices sealed in. Transfer them at once to a warm plate with a large hand strainer.

6. Empty all but 3 tablespoons of the oil into a container and reserve for other use.

7. Reheat the oil over high heat until smoke rises. Add the garlic, which will sizzle and take on color. Add the white scallions, stirring, and then add the ginger. Now return the beef to the wok and turn and toss with the wok scoop or metal spatula for about 30 seconds. Splash in the wine or sherry around the side of the wok. If you like your beef underdone, remove once the sizzling has died down. If you prefer your beef well done, leave to cook a little longer, stirring until done. Keep warm.

8. Add up to 1 tablespoon of oil to the wok, swirl it around and add the mango. Cover and fry over a gentle heat for about 1 minute.

9. Add the well-stirred sauce to the wok. When it thickens and bubbles, add the green scallions. Attractively arrange the mango, green scallions and sauce with the beef. Serve immediately.

Red Bean Fool

It is not the Chinese custom to serve a dessert after each meal; fruit is served instead. However, this inexpensive pudding is very popular with the Cantonese; it has a thickish consistency and is not overly sweet. They serve it hot, without cream.

INGREDIENTS

8 ounces red beans
   (azuki beans), washed
   and drained
4 teaspoons glutinous
   rice, washed and
   drained
3 pints cold water

1 piece dried tangerine
   peel, washed
3 teaspoons peanut or
   corn oil
1 cup sugar
heavy cream to serve
   (optional)
Serves 6

1. Soak the beans and rice for half a day or overnight in 5 cups of cold water. Do not drain. (This step may be omitted.)

2. Put the beans, rice and peel into a large saucepan, add the oil and the remaining cold water. If step 1 has been omitted, add all the cold water. Bring to a boil. (If boiling water is poured on the tangerine peel, it will taste bitter.) Lower the heat, cover and simmer for 2 hours, stirring occasionally and checking the water level. The volume should be reduced to 4 to 4½ cups for the right consistency – gluey – with water just covering the beans.

3. Add the sugar and simmer until completely dissolved. Remove and discard the tangerine peel. Leave uncovered to cool.

4. Liquidize the bean mixture. Chill the fool in the refrigerator. Serve, with cream, at the table.

Note: For those who like a more pronounced flavor of the tangerine peel, it can be liquidized with the cooked red beans. Also try the fool served hot with cream.

PEKING MENU

Peking Duck

This famous dish was introduced to Europe and America during the latter half of the 19th century: one source gives a definite date of 1875. In the well-established restaurants in Peking, the ducks used are raised for the express purpose of being roasted in a specially constructed oven. Paradoxically, this duck can be made, as in this recipe, in a simple way, with remarkably good results. The duck will be very crisp, with a rich dark red skin, the meat perfectly cooked and juicy. Traditionally, only the skin was eaten with the pancakes. The meat, cut up in the kitchen and stir-fried with bean sprouts, was served as a second course. These days, in both Peking and the West, the meat is carved to be served with the skin.

INGREDIENTS

2 tablespoons honey
½ pint hot water
1 plump oven-ready duck
    4½ to 5 pounds
3 pints boiling water
12 scallions, white parts
    only
1 large cucumber, cut
    into matchstick-sized
pieces
hoisin sauce or sweet
    bean sauce
25 to 30 Mandarin
    pancakes (see page
    210)

Serves 4 as main course, 6 to 7 with 3 or 4 other dishes

1. Melt the honey in the hot water in a cup or jug. Keep warm.

2. Put the duck in a colander. Scald it with the boiling water from a kettle, turning over several times to ensure even scalding. The skin shrinks at once, becoming shiny. Wipe off excess water but leave damp. Put into a large bowl.

3. Pour the honey mixture all over the skin, including the wings, neck and tail. Return the liquid to the cup and repeat the process once more. To ensure even distribution, dip a brush into the liquid and smear over less accessible spots as well.

4. Hang the duck on either a special Chinese 3-pronged duck hook or on 2 butcher's "S" meat hooks, 1 each securing the shoulder joint and wing. Hang in a windy place for 10 to 24 hours, until the skin is parchment dry. Do *not* prick the skin.

5. Place the duck breast side up on a wire rack in the middle of the oven with a pan of hot water underneath to catch the cooking juices. Roast in a preheated oven at 350°F for 20 minutes, at the end of which the skin will have turned golden brown. With a wooden spoon or spatula held in one hand and another spoon put inside the cavity, turn the duck over and roast the other side for 25 to 30 minutes. Turn over once more, breast side up again, and roast for another 20 minutes. If the skin is becoming too dark a red, lower the heat to 325°F; if too pale, raise to 375°F for part of the rest of the roasting time. Do *not* prick the skin during the roasting; the oil that would ooze would spoil both the color and the crispness of the skin. Remove from the oven and put on a wire rack to cool for a few minutes before carving.

6. While the duck is being roasted, cut the scallions into 2-inch sections. Slice each section lengthwise into strips. Arrange on 1 or 2 dishes. Arrange the cucumber on 1 or 2 dishes.

7. Put 1 or 2 tablespoons of hoisin or sweet bean sauce into individual saucers for each person. One saucer can be shared by 2 people, if preferred.

8. Steam the Mandarin pancakes for 10 minutes and transfer to warm serving plates. Bring to the table when the duck is being carved.

9. Just before carving, pour all the juice in the cavity into a container. Carve the skin into pieces about 2 inches square or into irregular shapes of approximate size. Carve the meat in a similar manner. Place the skin and meat on warm serving plates.

10. To eat, put a pancake on a plate (rather than in a bowl), smear on some sauce and top with 1 or 2 pieces of skin, either alone or with meat. Add 1 or 2 pieces of cucumber and scallions before rolling it up and eating.

Variation: Cantonese roast duck
Follow steps 1 to 4, above (the hanging time can be shortened to 6 to 10 hours). Smear a marinade of 4 teaspoons salt, 4 teaspoons sugar, 1½ teaspoons five-spice powder and 2 teaspoons Mei-kuei-lu wine or gin all over and in the cavity of the duck. Roast as in step 5. Serve with a thick soy sauce dip.

北京填鴨

Mandarin Pancakes

Mandarin pancakes are a must with Peking duck, but they are also traditionally served with dishes such as Mu-shu pork (see page 139). The Northern Chinese like these pancakes to be slightly on the firm side; the little bit of cold water added to the dough does the trick.

INGREDIENTS	little extra flour
1 pound all-purpose flour	2 teaspoons sesame oil
¾ pint boiling water	
1 tablespoon cold water	*Serves 6 with Peking duck*

1. Sift the flour into a mixing bowl. Pour in the boiling water gradually, stirring vigorously with a wooden spoon or a pair of chopsticks until well mixed. Then stir in the cold water. As soon as your hands can withstand the heat, form the mixture into a dough and knead lightly either in the bowl or on a lightly floured board, or work surface for 3 or 4 minutes or until soft and smooth. Allow to stand in the bowl for 20 to 30 minutes covered with a cloth.

2. Transfer the dough to a lightly floured board or work surface. Divide into 2 equal portions and knead a few more times, until smooth again. Use as little extra flour on the board as possible or the pancakes will taste floury.

3. Using both hands, roll each portion of dough into a 16-inch-long roll. Then, using a ruler as a guide, divide each roll into 1-inch pieces (a), making a total of 32.

4. One by one, stand each piece upright on the heel of your hand, slightly round off the dough, then flatten with the other hand (b), into a circle of about 2 to 2½ inches diameter.

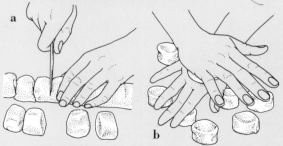

5. Using a brush, paint the surface of half of the pieces (16) with sesame oil (c). Place the remaining pieces on the oiled surfaces (d), making 16 pairs. Shape each pair of circles as evenly as possible.

6. Using a lightly floured rolling pin, roll out each pair into thin pancakes about 6 to 6½ inches in diameter (e). To ensure even thickness and roundness, rotate the circles quite frequently, turning them over as well.

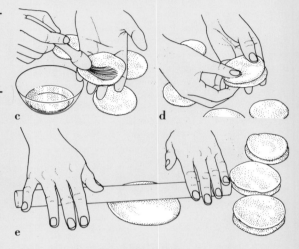

7. Heat an unoiled, flat heavy frying pan or griddle over medium-to-low heat. Put in 1 pair of cakes at a time and fry for 1 or 2 minutes, or until light brown spots appear (f). Turn over to fry the other side. In less than 1 minute part of the surface will puff up, indicating that they are done.

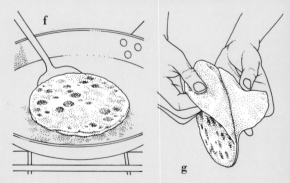

8. Remove from the frying pan, and while they are still hot separate the 2 thin pancakes with the fingers (g). Put on a plate and cover with a cloth to prevent drying. Repeat until all are done.

9. Steam all the pancakes (in 2 batches, if necessary) in a wok or steamer for 5 to 10 minutes before serving (see page 45).

Fish in Wine Sauce

This is a Peking-style fish dish that is very delicate in taste and appearance. It is traditional to use cloud ears to complement the fish.

INGREDIENTS

1 to 1½ pounds lemon sole, Dover sole or flounder fillet, skinned

2 tablespoons cloud ears, reconstituted (see page 39)

peanut or corn oil for deep-frying

4 cloves garlic, peeled and chopped fine

½ inch fresh ginger root, peeled and chopped fine

FOR THE MARINADE

½ teaspoon salt

¼ teaspoon sugar

6 turns white pepper mill

1 egg white, beaten with 1 tablespoon cornstarch until well blended

FOR THE SAUCE

¾ to 1 teaspoon salt

1 tablespoon cornstarch

¼ pint Shaohsing wine or semisweet white wine

¼ pint clear stock

Serves 4 with 2 other dishes

1. Pat the fish dry. Halve each side lengthwise and then slice each half crosswise into about 2-inch pieces. Put into a bowl.

2. *Prepare the marinade:* Add the salt, sugar, pepper and the egg and cornstarch mixture to the fish. Coat the fish well. Cover and let marinate in the refrigerator for about 1 hour.

3. *Prepare the sauce:* Mix together the salt, cornstarch, wine and stock.

4. Drain the excess water from the cloud ears but leave damp.

5. Fill a wok or deep fryer with oil. Heat to a temperature of about 200 to 225°F, or barely hot. Put the fish in very gently and let it "go through the oil" for 1 or 2 minutes, stirring 2 or 3 times to separate the pieces. When the fish turns opaque, turn off the heat and remove with a perforated spoon, handling gently so that the pieces do not crumble. Pour the oil into a container, leaving 2 or 3 tablespoons in the wok.

6. Reheat the oil until smoke rises. Add the garlic, stir, then the ginger, stir, and the cloud ears. Stir a few more times, then add the well-stirred sauce. Slowly bring to a boil, then return the fish to the wok and cook gently in the sauce until thoroughly hot. Transfer to a warm serving dish. Serve immediately.

"Seaweed"

This Northern dish uses a special kind of seaweed, which is not available elsewhere. However, the adapted ingredients used below do produce the desired delicious result.

INGREDIENTS

1 pound cabbage greens, washed and dried

peanut or corn oil for deep-frying

¼ teaspoon salt

2 teaspoons caster sugar

1 ounce blanched, flaked almonds

Serves 6

1. Remove and discard the tough stalks from the greens. Lay them out in a large pan to dry thoroughly.

2. Fold 6 or 7 leaves, or however many you can handle at a time, into a neat roll and, using a sharp knife, slice crosswise into the thinnest threadlike strips possible. Lay out in the pan again to air, for the drier the greens at this stage, the easier it is to achieve the desired crispness, without their losing their vivid color when deep-fried. (They can be prepared up to this point 6 to 8 hours ahead.)

3. Half fill a wok or deep fryer with oil. Heat the oil to a temperature of 400°F, or until a cube of stale bread browns in 40 seconds. Add half the spring greens gently and deep-fry for about 2 minutes or until crisp; they will turn a slightly deeper green color. Remove with a large hand strainer or perforated spoon and drain on paper towels. Deep-fry the remainder.

4. Let cool, then transfer to a serving dish. Sprinkle with the salt and mix thoroughly. Sprinkle with the sugar and again mix thoroughly. Garnish with the almonds.

5. Serve at room temperature. The "seaweed" will stay crisp overnight. Do not refrigerate.

酒溜魚片

賽干貝鬆

Chinese Celery Cabbage in Cream Sauce

奶油津白

It is a well-known fact that, traditionally, the Chinese do not use dairy products in their cooking. However, in this classic modern dish from the Northern and Eastern areas, a small amount of either evaporated milk or cream is used. In Peking and Shanghai, evaporated milk would be used, but light cream is just as good.

INGREDIENTS
1½ to 1¾ pounds
  Chinese celery
  cabbage
1¾ teaspoons salt
4 tablespoons peanut or
  corn oil
1 ounce cooked ham,
  Chin-hua or Virginia,
  chopped

FOR THE SAUCE
1 tablespoon potato flour
3 ounces clear stock
¼ pint evaporated milk
  or single cream

Serves 6

1. Discard the tough outer leaves of the cabbage. Wash the remaining leaves, cut each one lengthways, then slice them across into strips about 2½ inches long.

2. Bring 2½ pints of water to a boil in a large saucepan. Add 1 teaspoon of the salt and 1 tablespoon of the oil. (This will make the cabbage glisten.) Add the cabbage. Boil for about 1 minute, then pour the cabbage into a colander. Refresh under cold running water and let drain until all the excess water has run out.

3. *Prepare the sauce:* Dissolve the potato flour in 2 tablespoons of the stock, then stir in the rest. Stir in the milk or cream and add the remaining salt.

4. Heat a wok over moderate heat until moderately hot. Add the remaining oil and swirl it around. Add the cabbage and stir and turn with a wok scoop or metal spatula until thoroughly hot, taking care not to burn it. Push the cabbage to the sides of the wok, making a well in the center.

5. Pour the well-stirred sauce into the center of the wok. Stir the sauce continually until it thickens, then fold in the cabbage. Transfer to a warm serving plate.

6. Arrange the cabbage attractively, sprinkle the chopped ham on top and serve.

Variation: Cauliflower in cream sauce. Use 2 cauliflowers; cut the florets into bite-sized pieces and cook in the same way as the Chinese celery cabbage.

Pickled Cabbage Peking Style

北京泡菜

Served cold as an hors d'oeuvre, salad or side dish, this dish keeps well in the refrigerator for at least two weeks. Avoid eating the Szechwan peppercorns.

INGREDIENTS
2 pounds white cabbage,
  quartered and cored
2 tablespoons salt
½ to ¾ inch fresh ginger
  root, peeled and cut
  into silken threads (see
  page 35)
5 tablespoons sugar
2½ tablespoons peanut

or corn oil
2½ tablespoons sesame oil
3 dried red chilies,
  seeded and chopped
1 teaspoon Szechwan
  peppercorns
5 tablespoons rice
  vinegar

Serves 6 to 8

1. Shred the cabbage as fine as possible either in a food processor or with a knife. Put into a very large mixing bowl.

2. Sprinkle with the salt and mix. Let stand at room temperature for 2 or 3 hours; the cabbage will decrease in bulk, having released some of its water content. Take a handful at a time and, using both hands, squeeze out the excess water but leave damp. Transfer to a clean bowl.

3. Place the ginger in a bunch on top of the cabbage in the center of the bowl.

4. Sprinkle on the sugar, taking care not to put it over the ginger.

5. Heat the oil and sesame oil in a small saucepan over high heat until smoke rises. Remove from the heat and add the chili and peppercorns. Pour the mixture over the ginger first and then the surrounding cabbage in the bowl. The sizzling oil partially cooks the ginger, enhancing the flavor.

6. Add the vinegar and mix well. Let stand at room temperature for 2 or 3 hours before serving.

SHANGHAI MENU

Red-in-Snow Soup with Pork

Crisp, pickled red-in-snow (labeled pickled cabbage on the can), although quite salty by itself, lends a delicious flavor to the other ingredients of this dish, making a really tasty soup.

INGREDIENTS	FOR THE MARINADE
2 ounces cellophane noodles	2 teaspoons thin soy sauce
4 ounces lean pork	½ teaspoon sugar
3 tablespoons peanut or corn oil	1 teaspoon Shaohsing wine or medium-dry sherry
4 to 6 scallions, cut into 1-inch sections, white and green parts separated	4 to 6 turns white pepper mill
	1½ teaspoons potato flour
	1 tablespoon water
1 small can red-in-snow or 7 ounces, chopped	1 or 2 teaspoons sesame oil
	Serves 5 or 6

1. With a pair of scissors, cut the cellophane noodles into shorter lengths, about 3 inches, for easier handling when cooked. Soak in about 1½ pints boiling water for about 30 minutes. Drain.

2. Cut the pork into matchstick-sized pieces (see page 38). Put into a bowl.

3. *Prepare the marinade:* Add the soy sauce, sugar, wine or sherry, pepper, potato flour and water to the pork. Let marinate for about 15 minutes. Blend in the sesame oil.

4. Put 2 pints of water in a large saucepan and bring to a boil. Add the oil, white scallions and cellophane noodles. Pour in the red-in-snow and return to a gentle simmer.

5. Add the pork to the saucepan and, using a pair of chopsticks or a fork, separate the strips. Simmer until the pork has cooked and turned opaque; this should not take more than 1 minute. Add the green scallions. Transfer to a warm soup tureen and serve.

Fu-yung Egg Slices

Fu-yung is Chinese for lotus. In poetry it is used to describe the pretty face of a young woman, and it is indeed a fitting adjective for this Eastern dish.

INGREDIENTS	
⅓ cup frozen small peas	1½ tablespoon potato flour
1 or 2 medium red tomatoes	2½ cups clear stock
6 large egg whites	1 ounce ham, Chinhua, or Virginia is best, chopped fine
¾ teaspoon salt	
2 teaspoons cornstarch	
peanut or corn oil for deep-frying	*Serves 4 with 3 other dishes*

1. Blanch the peas in boiling water for 2 or 3 minutes. Drain.

2. Plunge the tomatoes in a bowl of boiling water for 1 or 2 minutes, then peel the skin. Halve lengthwise and seed. Slice each half lengthwise into 4 to 6 pieces.

3. Beat the egg whites lightly, add ½ teaspoon of the salt and the cornstarch and beat until homogenized. If there are too many bubbles, skim them off.

4. Half fill a wok or deep fryer with oil. Heat until barely hot, about 210-225°F. Pour in the egg-white mixture, about 2 tablespoons at a time, and let it come slowly to the surface. Lift at once with a perforated spoon and put into a bowl. Repeat until all the mixture is used, always adjusting the heat to make sure the oil is not too hot, so that the velvety tenderness of the egg is maintained.

5. Dissolve the potato flour in 1 or 2 tablespoons of the stock, then blend well into the remaining stock. Add the remaining salt.

6. Place the stock in a saucepan and bring slowly to a boil, stirring as it thickens. Add the peas, cook for a few seconds, until hot, then add the tomato. Now add the *fu-yung* egg slices and cook for a few more seconds, until piping hot. Remove from the heat and gently scoop all the ingredients to a warm deep serving plate.

7. Arrange the peas and tomatoes attractively to give the best visual effect. Sprinkle on the ham and serve immediately.

雪菜肉絲湯

芙蓉蛋片

"Smoked" Fish Shanghai Style

上
海
燻
魚

A favorite cold beginner in Shanghai and Northern restaurants. "Smoked" fish has always been known by this mock title, although the fish is not smoked, but marinated, then deep-fried and steeped in a spiced sauce with a special vinegar.

INGREDIENTS
2 pounds hake or haddock, ideally from the tail of the fish, cut ¾ inch thick
peanut or corn oil for deep-frying

FOR THE MARINADE
1½ inches fresh ginger root, peeled and chopped
3 tablespoons thin soy sauce
1 tablespoons Shaohsing wine or medium-dry sherry

FOR THE SAUCE
1¼ pints cold water
1 whole star anise or 8 segments
1 inch cinnamon stick
1 piece preserved tangerine peel, quarter of whole
1 teaspoon black peppercorns
2 large scallions
4 slices fresh ginger root, ⅛ inch thick
3 tablespoons Chinkiang or red wine vinegar
4 or 5 tablespoons sugar

Serves 8

1. Pat the fish dry with paper towels, pierce the flesh in several places with a fork for better absorption of the marinade, and place on a large plate.

2. *Prepare the marinade:* Using a garlic press, squeeze the juice from the chopped ginger onto the fish and discard the pulp. Add the soy sauce and wine or sherry. Turn the fish over several times so the pieces are coated with the marinade. Let marinate for 2 hours, turning the fish over from time to time.

3. *Prepare the sauce:* Put the water, star anise, cinnamon stick, tangerine peel, peppercorns, scallions and ginger into a large saucepan. Bring to a boil, then lower the heat and simmer, uncovered, for 25 to 30 minutes, to reduce the liquid to about ¾ pint. Strain the liquid into a bowl and discard the solids. Return the liquid to the saucepan and add the vinegar and sugar. Leave to one side while deep-frying the fish.

4. Put the fish on a wire rack to drain for several minutes before deep-frying.

5. Half fill a wok or deep fryer with oil. Heat to a temperature of 400°F, or until a cube of stale bread browns in 40 seconds. Carefully add half the fish and deep-fry for about 15 minutes, until brown and firm but not hard. Remove with a hand strainer or perforated spoon and drain on paper towels. Repeat with the rest of the fish.

6. Bring the sauce to the boil, stirring to dissolve the sugar. Add the fish and ladle the boiling liquid over it for 3 or 4 minutes, using a large spoon. Transfer the fish to a large dish.

7. Continue to boil the sauce until it thickens and is reduced to a syrupy glaze. Pour over the fish. Cool, cover and refrigerate for a few hours, or overnight, before serving cold.

Crystal Sugar Pig's Hock

冰
糖
元
蹄

Eastern Chinese cooks specialize in dishes such as this, where the rind as well as the meat is so tender that only a pair of chopsticks (or a fork and spoon) is necessary to break it up.

INGREDIENTS
1 pig's hock, about 3 to 3½ pounds
4 thickish slices fresh ginger root, peeled
2 or 3 scallions, halved
6 tablespoons thick soy sauce

3 tablespoons Shaohsing wine or medium-dry sherry
1 ounce Demerara or granulated sugar

1. Pluck any hair off the skin of the hock. On the side where the skin is most tender, cut through to, and along the length of, the bone. This helps to keep the hock in shape and to absorb the sauce better as it cooks.

2. Put the hock in a heavy saucepan or flameproof casserole and cover with cold water. Bring the water to a boil and cook, uncovered, for 4 or 5 minutes, so that the scum collects on the surface. Pour off the water and, if necessary, rinse the skin free of scum.

3. Return the hock to the saucepan or casserole. (If possible, place on a thin latticed bamboo mat,

which will prevent the rind from sticking to the pot.)

4. Add the ginger, scallions, soy sauce, wine or sherry and sugar to the pot. Pour in 1¾ pints water, bring to a boil, reduce the heat and simmer, tightly covered, for 1 hour, loosening the skin from the bottom of the pot once during cooking.

5. Turn the pork over, checking the water level to make sure it is about one-third of the way up the pork. Replace the lid and continue to cook for

another 1¼ to 1½ hours, moving the pork 2 or 3 times to make sure the skin is not sticking to the pot. The juice should by now be reduced to about 8 ounces or a little less.

6. Increase the heat and boil to reduce the sauce for a few minutes, or until it is thick and glossy, continually spooning it over the pork with a long spoon.

7. Transfer the hock to a warm serving dish. Discard the ginger and scallions and pour the sauce over the pork.

Eight-Treasure Bean Curd

The 18th-century poet and official Yüan Mei, wrote a cookery book called Sui-yüan Recipes, *a unique legacy of his times from a Chinese man of letters. In the recipe called "Prefect Wang's Eight-Treasure Bean Curd", Yüan Mei briefly outlined how the dish traced its origin to the Imperial kitchen. This dish consists of many hidden ingredients, which, while they melt in the mouth, give just the hint of a nutty bite.*

INGREDIENTS

4 medium dried Chinese mushrooms, reconstituted (see page 39)
2 cakes bean curd, drained
3 egg whites
¾ to 1 teaspoon salt
1 tablespoon solid lard
1½ tablespoons potato flour
2 tablespoons heavy cream
6 ounces prime stock (see page 225)
2 tablespoons melted lard

or 3 tablespoons peanut or corn oil
½ cup cooked chicken breast, chopped fine
¼ cup blanched walnuts, chopped fine
¼ cup blanched almonds, chopped fine
⅓ cup ham, chopped fine, Chinhua or Virginia is best
2 teaspoons melted chicken fat or sesame oil

Serves 6 with 3 or 4 other dishes

1. Drain and squeeze out excess water from the mushrooms but leave damp. Chop fine.

2. Blend or mash the bean curd. The smoother the purée, the smoother the texture of the cooked dish. Put into a large bowl.

3. Add half the egg whites and the salt to the bean curd and beat until well amalgamated. Add the remaining egg whites, the solid lard, potato flour and heavy cream. Beat the mixture until stiff; the volume will have increased. Stir in half the stock.

4. Heat a wok over high heat until smoke rises. Add the melted lard or oil and swirl it around. Pour the bean curd mixture and the remaining stock simultaneously into the wok. Stir with the wok scoop or a large wooden spoon for about 1 minute, or until the mixture turns ivory in color. Lower the heat if the mixture begins to brown. Stir in the mushrooms, chicken, walnuts, almonds and half the ham. When well mixed, bring to simmering point and pour the mixture into a warm deep serving bowl.

5. Add the chicken fat or sesame oil and garnish with the remaining ham sprinkled on top before serving.

王太守八寶豆腐

Yangchow Fried Rice

揚
州
炒
飯

This dish originated in Yangchow, in Eastern China, but has become a favorite with the Cantonese, too. In fact, it is one of the most well-known and popular rice dishes both inside and outside China. Prawns or small shrimp are always used; in the South, char-siu or Cantonese roast pork (see page 134) is used instead of ham.

INGREDIENTS

8 ounces fresh or frozen raw peeled prawns
8 tablespoons peanut or corn oil
2 cloves garlic, peeled and chopped fine
1 tablespoon Shaohsing wine or medium-dry sherry
2 large eggs
salt
about 1¾ pounds or 5 to 6 cups boiled rice, cooked at least 3 or 4 hours in advance (see page 170)

8 ounces frozen green peas
4 scallions, cut into thin rounds, white and green parts separated
8 ounces cooked ham, diced
1½ tablespoons thick soy sauce
2 or 3 tablespoons clear stock

FOR THE MARINADE
scant ½ teaspoon salt
1½ teaspoons cornstarch
½ egg white
Serves 4 as a main course

1. If frozen prawns are used, defrost thoroughly. Devein the prawns (see page 39) and cut into ¾-inch pieces. Pat dry with paper towels. Put into a bowl.

2. *Prepare the marinade:* Mix together the salt, cornstarch and egg white. Stir into the prawns, making sure they are evenly coated. Refrigerate, covered, for a minimum of 3 hours or overnight.

3. Heat a wok over high heat until smoke rises. Add 2 tablespoons of the oil and swirl it around.

Add the garlic and, as soon as it takes on color, tip in the prawns. Separate them, stirring and tossing with a wok scoop or metal spatula for 30 to 45 seconds, or until almost cooked and turning pinkish. Splash in the wine or sherry around the side of the wok; as soon as the sizzling dies down, remove the prawns and put aside. Wash and dry the wok.

4. Beat the eggs lightly with 1 tablespoon of the oil and a little salt. Heat a large frying pan until moderately hot, add 1 tablespoon of the oil and swirl it around to cover the whole surface.

5. Pour in half of the beaten egg and tip the pan to spread the egg evenly to the edges. When firm, turn the crêpe over and fry the other side for a few seconds. Transfer the crêpe to a plate and slice into thin strips.

6. Separate the rice grains as much as possible. Blanch the peas in boiling salted water for 3 minutes and drain well.

7. Reheat the wok over high heat until smoke rises. Add the remaining oil and swirl it around. Stir in the white scallions. Pour in the remaining beaten egg, then immediately tip in all the rice. Sliding the wok scoop or spatula to the bottom of the wok where the runny egg is, turn and toss the rice, separating any lumps.

8. When thoroughly hot, add the ham, stir, then the peas, stir, and then the prawns. Still stirring, add the soy sauce and stock.

9. Finally, put in half of the egg strips and the green scallions. Transfer to a warm serving platter and arrange the remaining egg strips on top for garnish.

VEGETARIAN MENU

Rainbow Salad

This multicolored plate of lightly stir-fried vegetables is made all the more delectable by the subtle dressing of sesame paste and vinegar. This dish can be prepared ahead of time and, if refrigerated, will keep overnight without losing much of its crunchiness.

INGREDIENTS

6 large dried Chinese mushrooms, reconstituted (see page 39)
12 ounces cucumber, halved lengthwise and seeded
1½ teaspoons salt
8 ounces carrots, peeled
1 medium red pepper, halved lengthwise and seeded
5 tablespoons peanut or corn oil
7 scallions, halved lengthwise, cut into 2-inch sections, white and green parts separated
8 ounces bean sprouts
1 large egg, lightly beaten

FOR THE DRESSING

2 tablespoons sesame paste
2 teaspoons water
4 or 5 teaspoons rice or white wine vinegar
½ teaspoon salt
10 turns pepper mill

Serves 4 to 6 with 2 or 3 other dishes

1. Drain and squeeze out excess water from the mushrooms but leave damp. Slice into the thinnest possible slivers.

2. Cut the cucumber into very thin slices. Put in a bowl, sprinkle with ½ teaspoon of the salt to draw out excess water. Let stand for 15 to 30 minutes, then drain thoroughly.

3. Cut the carrots into very thin slices. Put in a bowl, sprinkle with 1 teaspoon of salt to draw out excess water. Let stand for 15 to 30 minutes, then drain thoroughly.

4. Slice the red pepper into thin strips.

5. *Prepare the dressing:* Mix the sesame paste with half of the water first and stir in the same direction; the paste will thicken. Add the rest of the water and continue to stir; the paste will become thinner. Now add the vinegar, little by little, stirring to blend. Stir in the salt and pepper.

6. Heat a wok over high heat until smoke rises. Add 4 tablespoons of the oil and swirl it around. Add the white scallions and stir a couple of times. Stir in the mushrooms, then the red pepper and stir some more. Now add the carrots and bean sprouts. Sliding the wok scoop or metal spatula to the bottom of the wok, flip and turn vigorously over high heat for about 2 minutes, or until the vegetables are barely cooked and still very crunchy. Add the green scallions, stir a few more times and remove to a serving plate to cool. If water starts to ooze, drain.

7. Heat a large frying pan over moderate heat. Add 1 tablespoon of oil, tipping the pan to ensure even spreading. When the oil is moderately hot, pour in the lightly beaten egg and quickly tip the pan to let the egg reach evenly to the edges. When cooked on one side, loosen the edges with a spatula and flip the crêpe over to cook the other side quickly, until firm but not hard. Transfer to a plate and cut into strips about 1½ inches long and ⅓ inch wide.

8. When the stir-fried vegetables are cool, mix in the cucumber. Stir in the dressing and toss well. Arrange the egg strips on top.

9. Chill, covered, in the refrigerator before serving. It can, however, be served at room temperature.

七彩沙律

Lohan's Delight: Buddhist Vegetarian Dish

Lohan (monks or saints), following general Buddhist principles, were also known as "destroyers of the passions." Fittingly, this dish does not use any of the usual condiments – ginger, garlic and scallions – in Buddhist belief they arouse human passions, which, in turn, impede one's hopes of achieving Nirvana, the state of absolute peace and blessedness.

INGREDIENTS

⅓ ounce cloud ears, reconstituted (see page 39)

½ ounce golden needles, reconstituted (see page 39)

12 medium dried Chinese mushrooms, reconstituted in ¾ pint boiling water (see page 39)

½ ounce hair seaweed

3 tablespoons peanut or corn oil

4 ounces canned bamboo shoots, sliced thin

3 to 4 ounces canned ginkgo nuts

20 pieces deep-fried gluten (see page 156)

½ teaspoon salt

1 to 1½ teaspoons sugar

3 tablespoons thin soy sauce

2 teaspoons sesame oil

FOR CURING HAIR SEAWEED

1 pint water

2 thickish slices fresh ginger root, peeled

2 teaspoons Shaohsing wine or medium-dry sherry

2 teaspoons peanut or corn oil

Serves 4 with 2 other dishes

1. Drain the cloud ears and golden needles and squeeze out excess water from the mushrooms, but leave damp. Reserve the mushroom soaking liquid.

2. Soak the hair seaweed in plenty of cold or tepid water for about 10 minutes, so that it will become pliable. Then rinse in many changes of water, picking it over, removing impurities and discarding the fine sand that settles at the bottom of the bowl.

3. *To cure:* Put the water, ginger, wine or sherry and oil in a wok or saucepan and bring to a boil. Submerge the seaweed and boil for about 5 minutes. Drain through a fine sieve and discard the ginger.

4. Heat a wok over high heat until smoke rises. Add 1 tablespoon of the oil and swirl it around. Add the cloud ears and golden needles and toss and turn for about 30 seconds, adjusting the heat if the cloud ears make a loud explosive noise. Transfer to a warm dish nearby.

5. Add the remaining oil and swirl it around. Add the mushrooms and bamboo shoots and turn and stir for about 30 seconds, or until very hot.

6. Return the cloud ears and golden needles to the wok, and add the hair seaweed, ginkgo nuts and gluten pieces. Pour in the mushroom water, add the salt, sugar and soy sauce and bring to a boil. Cover, lower the heat and simmer fast for 10 to 15 minutes, or until most of the water has been absorbed.

7. Transfer to a warm serving plate. Sprinkle on the sesame oil and serve.

Stir-fried Bean Sprouts

Rich in protein, these ubiquitous sprouts, which come from Mung beans, can be eaten cooked or in a salad. The Chinese always cook them, but only slightly, to preserve their crunchiness.

INGREDIENTS

8 ounces to 1 pound bean sprouts

2 or 3 tablespoons peanut or corn oil

2 to 4 scallions, cut into 1-inch sections, white and green parts separated

2 or 3 very thin slices fresh ginger root, peeled

salt to taste or about ½ to ¾ teaspoon

2 or 3 teaspoons thin soy sauce or optional 1 or 2 tablespoons oyster sauce

Serves 2 or 3 with 2 other dishes

1. Do not wash the bean sprouts. Instead, refrigerate them until they are to be cooked. If they have to be washed, make sure to drain them well and shake off any remaining water before refrigerating them.

2. Heat a wok over high heat until smoke rises.

Add the oil and swirl it around. Add the white scallions, and as soon as they sizzle, add the ginger. Tip in the bean sprouts and, leaving the heat on high all the time, slide the wok scoop or metal spatula to the bottom of the wok and then turn and vigorously toss the bean sprouts right and left and all over for 2 or 3 minutes. Sprinkle with the salt and green scallions toward the end. The bean sprouts will be cooked but still firm and crisp, having exuded only the minimum of water.

3. Transfer to a warm serving plate and pour over them the soy or oyster sauce. Serve immediately.

Note: Take care not to overcook this dish. Since frozen bean sprouts are inevitably soggy, never freeze them. When reheated, they will have lost much of their crunchiness.

Variation: Stir-fried lettuce
Use 1¼ to 1½ pounds of iceberg lettuce, tearing large leaves into smaller pieces. Cook as above. Serves 4 with 2 other dishes.

Bean Curd in a Simple Sauce

Reddish bean curd cubes dotted with white and green. The first step of this dish is essential for a perfect result.

INGREDIENTS

4 cakes bean curd

2 or 3 tablespoons peanut or corn oil

5 or 6 scallions, cut into small rounds, white and green parts separated

FOR THE SAUCE

¼ teaspoon salt

¼ teaspoon sugar

1 tablespoon thick soy sauce or optional oyster sauce

1 tablespoon thin soy sauce

1 teaspoon Shaohsing wine or medium-dry sherry

Serves 4 with 2 other dishes

1. Cover the bean curd cakes with hot water and steep for 15 minutes, in order to firm them, making handling easier.

2. Lift them from the water and slice each cake into 32 cubes: divide one cake lengthwise into 4,

then crosswise into 4, and then halve the thickness of each piece, making 32 in all. Handling gently, put them in a sieve to drain excess water.

3. *Prepare the sauce:* Mix together the salt, sugar, soy sauces and wine or sherry.

4. Heat a wok over high heat until smoke rises. Add the oil and swirl it around. Add the white scallions, stir and let sizzle. Then add the bean curd. Sliding the wok scoop or metal spatula to the bottom of the wok, gently turn and fold the cubes to blend with the oil and scallions for about 1 minute.

5. Add the sauce to the wok, continuing to fold and turn gently a few more times, to let the cubes take on color. Lower the heat, cover and cook for another minute.

6. Add the green scallions. Carefully remove the bean curd mixture to a warm serving plate. Serve immediately.

清炒芽菜

醬油豆腐

Stir-fried Spinach in Bean Curd "Cheese" Sauce

腐乳椒絲炒菠菜

If you do not use white bean curd "cheese," which gives the dish an exotic taste, you will still find that the spinach is delicious simply stir-fried in garlic and seasoned with salt.

INGREDIENTS

1 pound fresh spinach, washed

2½ pints water

1 teaspoon salt

5 tablespoons peanut or corn oil

2½ to 3 cakes white bean curd "cheese" with chili

½ teaspoon sugar

4 or 5 cloves garlic, peeled and chopped fine

½ fresh green or red chili, seeded and sliced (optional)

2 teaspoons Shaohsing wine or medium-dry sherry

Serves 3 or 4 with 2 other dishes

1. Remove any stringy roots and hard stalks from the spinach.

2. Place the water in a saucepan, bring to a boil and add the salt and 1 tablespoon of the oil. Blanch the spinach for 1 minute. Drain and rinse with cold water immediately. Drain well and put aside. This can be done a few hours beforehand without the spinach losing its vivid color and texture.

3. Mash the bean curd "cheese" in a small bowl with a small amount of its juice. Stir in the sugar.

4. Heat a wok over high heat until smoke rises. Add 4 tablespoons of oil and swirl it around. Add the garlic, bean curd "cheese" and chili and stir. Splash in the wine or sherry around the side of the wok. Add the spinach and stir and turn continuously with the wok scoop or metal spatula for 1 or 2 minutes, to incorporate the sauce. Lower the heat if the sauce is being absorbed too quickly. Transfer to a warm serving plate. Serve immediately.

Stir-fried Broccoli and Chinese Mushroom

冬菇芥蘭花

For nonvegetarians, this dish is excellent if 2 heaping tablespoons of oyster sauce are used instead of the soy sauce.

INGREDIENTS

12 dried Chinese mushrooms (the thick floral ones are best), reconstituted (see page 39)

12 ounces broccoli, preferably spears

3 tablespoons peanut or corn oil

4 very thin slices fresh ginger root, peeled

4 scallions cut into 1-inch sections, white and green parts separated

½ teaspoon salt

¼ teaspoon sugar

FOR THE SAUCE

1 teaspoon potato flour

6 tablespoons mushroom water

1 tablespoon thick soy sauce or 2 tablespoons oyster sauce

Serves 4 with 2 other dishes

1. Wash the mushrooms and simmer in about ¾ pint of water for about 30 minutes. When cool, clip off the stems and discard. Squeeze out excess water but leave damp. Reserve the soaking liquid.

2. Peel off the hard outer layer of the broccoli stalks. Leave whole or cut into large bite-sized pieces.

3. *Prepare the sauce:* Dissolve the potato flour in the mushroom water. Stir in the soy or oyster sauce.

4. Heat a wok until hot. Add the oil and swirl it around. Add the ginger and white scallions. Stir a few times and then tip in the mushrooms. Stir a few more times and add the broccoli. Sliding the wok scoop or metal spatula to the bottom of the wok, flip and toss for about 30 seconds. Add about 7 tablespoons of mushroom water and sprinkle with the salt and sugar. Cover and cook over moderate heat for about 6 minutes.

5. Remove the cover. Taste to see if the broccoli is ready, it should be tender yet still firm and crisp.

6. Pour the well-stirred sauce over the broccoli and mushrooms, stirring continuously as it thickens. Add the green scallions, stir to mix, then transfer to a warm serving plate.

7. Attractively arrange the mushrooms, cap side up, on top of the broccoli. Serve immediately.

MIXED MENU

Dried Oysters and Hair Seaweed

The Chinese are very fond of puns, and the Chinese language lends itself particularly to play on words, for it is very rich in tones. Mandarin, the official language, has four tones to each sound; Cantonese, the lingua franca in the South, has at least seven. This often allows two, or even three, meanings to a term, each with a slightly different pronunciation. This dish, beloved of the Cantonese, is a classic example of this point. Dried oyster and hair seaweed sounds similar to the Chinese New Year greeting: "Good deeds and prosperity" or "Good business and prosperity." For this reason, Southern Chinese make sure they eat this dish during the first fortnight of the Chinese New Year, when much food and many different dishes are consumed.

INGREDIENTS

24 dried oysters
½ ounce hair seaweed
16 medium dried Chinese mushrooms, reconsistuted in ¾ pint boiling water (see page 39)
12 ounces roast pork belly (see page 146)
2 or 3 tablespoons peanut or corn oil
1 or 2 cloves garlic, peeled and cut diagonally into thin slices
4 to 6 thin slices fresh ginger root, peeled
6 scallions, white parts only, cut into 1-inch sections
1 tablespoon Shaohsing wine or medium-dry sherry
1 pint liquid, made up of oyster water, mushroom water and clear stock
2 tablespoons oyster sauce
1 tablespoon thin soy sauce
½ teaspoon sugar
2 tablespoons potato flour, dissolved in 4 ounces water

FOR CURING HAIR SEAWEED

16 ounces water
2 thickish slices fresh ginger root, peeled
2 teaspoons Shaohsing wine or medium-dry sherry
2 teaspoons peanut or corn oil

Serves 8 with 4 or 5 other dishes

1. Rinse the dried oysters thoroughly, rubbing gently with the fingers to get rid of any impurities. Put into a bowl and pour over them sufficient boiling water to just cover. Soak for 3 or 4 hours or overnight, until quite soft. Remove and discard the hard muscles. Reserve soaking liquid.

2. Soak the hair seaweed in plenty of cold or tepid water for about 10 minutes, so that it will become pliable. Then squeeze and rinse in many changes of water, picking it over, removing impurities and discarding the fine sand that settles at the bottom of the bowl.

3. *Cure the hair seaweed:* Put the water, ginger slices, wine or sherry and oil in a wok and bring to a boil. Submerge the seaweed and boil for about 5 minutes. Drain through a fine sieve and discard the ginger.

4. Drain and squeeze out excess water from the mushrooms, but leave damp. Reserve the soaking liquid.

5. Cut the pork belly into rectangular pieces of more or less the same size as the dried oysters.

6. Heat a wok over high heat until smoke rises. Add the oil and swirl it around. Add the garlic, stir, then the ginger, stir, and the white scallions and stir. Add the pork, oysters and mushrooms and, sliding the wok scoop or metal spatula to the bottom of the wok, turn and toss gently for about 1 minute, or until very hot. Splash in the wine or sherry around the side of the wok. When the sizzling dies down, add the liquid, oyster sauce, soy sauce and sugar. Bring to a boil, reduce the heat and simmer fast, covered, for about 30 to 45 minutes.

7. Make a well in the middle of the wok contents, add the seaweed and continue to simmer fast for another 15 minutes. Add more liquid if necessary – at the end of the cooking time there should be about 6 to 8 ounces of liquid still unabsorbed.

8. Leaving the liquid in the wok, remove the pork, oysters and mushrooms and arrange them attractively on a warm serving plate or in a bowl. Place the whole bunch of seaweed on top in the center so that your family or guests recognize the symbolic greeting of prosperity immediately.

9. Return the liquid in the wok to simmering point. Mix in sufficient well-stirred dissolved potato flour to thicken the sauce enough to coat the back of a spoon. Pour over the ingredients and serve hot.

蠔豉髮菜.好市發財

Lion's Head

This dish originated in Yangchow, in Kiangsu province. It is so called because each pork meat cake is supposed to resemble a lion's head, and the cabbage its mane.

INGREDIENTS

1 pound Chinese celery
   cabbage
8 water chestnuts, fresh
   peeled or canned
   drained
1 pound pork, 2 or 3
   ounces of which is fat
scant 3 tablespoons water
½ teaspoon salt
2 tablespoons thick soy
   sauce
1 tablespoon Shaohsing
   wine or medium-dry
   sherry

1 teaspoon brown sugar
2½ tablespoons
   cornstarch
2 to 2½ tablespoons
   water
3 tablespoons peanut or
   corn oil
½ pint clear stock
2 or 3 teaspoons potato
   flour

Serves 6 with 3 other dishes

1. Cut each cabbage leaf crosswise into 2-inch pieces, separating the stalk from the leafy top pieces.

2. Chop the water chestnuts by hand or mince coarsely.

3. Chop the pork by hand or mince coarsely. Put into a large bowl. Stir in the water, 1 tablespoon at a time, and continue to stir in the same direction for 1 or 2 minutes, or until smooth and almost gelatinous. Pick up the pork mixture and throw it back into the bowl about 20 to 30 times. This stirring and throwing action makes the pork light and tender, producing the desired effect when cooked.

4. Add the salt, soy sauce, wine or sherry and sugar and mix well. Stir in the water chestnuts. Divide the mixture into 4 equal portions, shaping them into thick round cakes – each a lion's head.

5. Mix the cornstarch and water into a thin paste in a slope-sided plate. Roll the lions' heads in the paste to coat all over.

6. Heat a wok over moderate heat. Add the oil, and when smoke rises, put in the lions' heads to brown, 2 at a time, for about 2 minutes each side, or until golden in color. Transfer to a plate, leaving the oil in the wok.

7. Add the stalk pieces of the cabbage and stir-fry for about 30 seconds, then add the leafy pieces and continue to stir-fry for another minute to cook partially and reduce their bulk.

8. Transfer half of this cabbage to line the bottom of a large flameproof or ovenproof casserole. Place the lions' heads on top, then cover them with the remaining cabbage, adding the oil from the wok as well. Add the stock.

9. To cook, either:
Bring the casserole to a boil on top of the stove. Lower the heat and simmer, covered, for 2 hours. This traditional way produces the best result. Or cook in a preheated oven at 350°F for 20 minutes, reduce the heat to 325°F and continue to cook for a further 2 hours.

10. To serve, arrange the cabbage underneath and around the meat cakes on a warm plate, to give the illusion of a lion's head and mane. Thicken the sauce with the potato flour mixed with a little water and pour over the meat.

Plain-boiled Vegetables

In the South, where green vegetables grow in abundance, boiling is as popular a method of cooking as stir-frying. Chinese flowering cabbage and broccoli are especially suitable.

INGREDIENTS

1 teaspoon salt
4 tablespoons peanut or
   corn oil
1 pound Chinese flower
   cabbage, trimmed

2 tablespoons oyster
   sauce or 1½
   tablespoons soy sauce

Serves 6 with 3 other dishes

1. Put 2½ pints of water into a saucepan and bring to a boil. Add the salt and 1½ tablespoons of the oil.

2. Place the cabbage in the water and return to a boil. Boil for 30 to 60 seconds. It should be tender but still have a bite. Drain well in a colander.

3. Transfer the cabbage to a warm serving plate. Pour the rest of the oil over it evenly and then the oyster or soy sauce. Serve hot.

Paper-thin Lamb with Scallions

This is one of the famous Peking dishes. The scallions are an indispensable ingredient, because they add so much flavor to the lamb, not to mention increasing the overall fragrance of the dish.

INGREDIENTS

12 ounces lamb loin, trimmed

3 or 4 tablespoons peanut or corn oil

2 cloves garlic, peeled and sliced thin

8 ounces scallions, sliced into long slivers

dashes of sesame oil to taste

FOR THE MARINADE

2 teaspoons thin soy sauce

2 teaspoons Shaohsing wine or medium-dry sherry

FOR THE SAUCE

¼ teaspoon salt

½ teaspoon sugar

2 teaspoons thick soy sauce

2 teaspoons Shaohsing wine or medium-dry sherry

1 teaspoon sesame oil

Serves 4 with 2 other dishes

1. Slice the lamb into paper-thin pieces (chilling the meat in the refrigerator beforehand for 1 or 2 hours to make slicing easier). Pat dry, if necessary. Put into a bowl.

2. *Prepare the marinade:* Add the soy sauce and wine or sherry to the lamb. Let marinate for 15 to 30 minutes.

3. *Prepare the sauce:* Mix together the salt, sugar, soy sauce, wine or sherry and oil in a small bowl and put aside.

4. Heat a wok over high heat until smoke rises. Add the oil and swirl it around. Add the garlic; let it sizzle and take on color. Put in the lamb and, sliding the wok scoop or metal spatula to the bottom of the wok, turn and toss for 20 to 30 seconds, or until partially cooked. Pour in the sauce, stirring to incorporate, and add the scallions. Flip and toss until the lamb is cooked and the mixture has absorbed most of the sauce. The dish should be slightly dry in appearance.

5. Remove to a warm serving plate and sprinkle with sesame oil to enhance the flavor. Serve immediately.

葱爆羊肉

Yu-ling's Hot and Numbing Chicken

Chiang Yu-ling, my Mandarin teacher and friend, herself an excellent cook of Northern cuisine, has contributed much interest and information to this book. She has kindly given me this recipe.

INGREDIENTS

2 chicken breasts, about 1 pound 2 ounces to 1 pound 4 ounces, skinned and boned

peanut or corn oil

1 teaspoon Szechwan peppercorns

2 large cloves garlic, peeled and sliced

4 thin slices fresh ginger

1 large scallion, cut into 1½-inch sections

2 or 3 fresh green chilies, each about 3 inches long, seeded and sliced diagonally into long strips

1 tablespoon Shaohsing wine or medium-dry sherry

¼ teaspoon salt

¼ to ½ teaspoon sugar

½ teaspoon ground roasted Szechwan peppercorns

½ teaspoon cornstarch dissolved in 2 tablespoons water

1 teaspoon sesame oil

FOR THE MARINADE

½ teaspoon salt

6 turns white pepper mill

1 teaspoon cornstarch

½ egg white, lightly beaten

1. Cut the chicken into large cubes. Put into a bowl.

2. *Prepare the marinade:* Add the salt, pepper, cornstarch and egg white to the chicken. Stir in the same direction until well coated. Let marinate for 20 to 30 minutes.

3. Half fill a wok or deep fryer with oil. Heat until it is just hot (about 225°F). Add the chicken to "go through the oil" for about 60 to 75 seconds, separating the pieces with a long pair of chopsticks. Remove with a large hand strainer or perforated spoon and keep nearby. The chicken, having turned whitish, will be almost cooked.

4. Empty all but 2 tablespoons of the oil into a container and save for other uses. Reheat the oil over medium heat. Add the Szechwan peppercorns and fry for about 1 minute, or until they have released their aroma and turned dark brown. Remove and discard.

5. Add the garlic, ginger and scallion and fry over high heat until the edges are brown and their aroma released. Remove and discard.

麻辣子雞

6. Lower the heat and add the chilies. Stir and turn for about 1 minute to release their peppery hot flavor, taking care not to burn them. Transfer to a small dish and keep nearby.

7. Turn up the heat. Return the chicken to the wok and stir and turn in rapid succession for about 30 seconds, or until hot. Splash in the wine or sherry around the side of the wok, stirring continuously as it sizzles. Add the salt and sugar and sprinkle on the ground peppercorns. Trickle in the well-stirred, dissolved cornstarch and continue to stir as it thickens. Return the chilies to the wok and stir to mix for about another 10 seconds. Sprinkle on the sesame oil, then transfer to a warm serving plate. Serve immediately.

Eight-Treasure Rice Pudding

八寶飯

This Northern pudding is served anytime, but especially during Chinese New Year. "Eight-treasure" is a reference to the eight treasures in Buddhism that guard and enrich one's life. For decorating the pudding, nuts or other dried fruits can be substituted.

INGREDIENTS	
12 ounces white glutinous rice	orange peel
1 pint water	18 golden raisins
6 dried Chinese red dates	18 black raisins
2 tablespoons all-purpose flour	**FOR THE SYRUP**
10 ounces canned red bean paste	Either:
2 tablespoons peanut or corn oil	3 tablespoons sugar
¼ cup lard	1 cup water
3 tablespoons sugar	2 teaspoons cornstarch, dissolved in 2 tablespoons water
1 glacé cherry	Or:
18 small cubes candied	4 ounces maple syrup
	Serves 8

1. Wash the glutinous rice 3 or 4 times, or until the water is no longer milky. Drain and put into a baking pan or a heatproof plate. Add the water. Steam in a wok or steamer for about 25 minutes (see page 45).

2. Meanwhile, soak the dates in hot water for 15 minutes, then slit open and remove the pits, leaving the dates whole.

3. *Prepare the red bean paste:* Add the flour to the bean paste and blend well. Heat a wok or frying pan over moderate heat, add the oil and then the bean paste. Cook for about 5 minutes, turning and stirring all the time to prevent it from sticking. This thickens it sufficiently to keep it from leaking through the rice during steaming. Remove and leave to cool.

4. Well grease a 4-cup glass heatproof bowl, with some of the lard.

5. Blend the remaining lard and the sugar into the cooked rice.

6. Form a decorative pattern in the bottom of the bowl with the dried fruits. Put the cherry in the center. Make a ring of 6 triangles around it with the orange peel. Make 6 lines, alternating golden and black raisins, to go up the sides of the bowl between the orange peel. Place 1 red date between the lines of raisins.

7. Gently but *firmly* press one fairly thick layer of rice on the bottom and sides of the bowl to cover the dried fruits without disturbing the pattern. Put the red bean paste in the center. Cover with the remaining rice, pressing down to make the surface flat and even. There should be about 1 inch between the rice level and the rim of the bowl, so that the rice does not overflow when steamed.

8. Put the bowl inside the wok or steamer and steam for about 1¼ hours. Check the water level periodically, adding more if necessary.

9. About 15 minutes before the rice pudding is ready, prepare the syrup. If the traditional syrup is used, put the sugar and water in a saucepan and slowly bring to a boil. When the sugar is completely dissolved, trickle in the dissolved cornstarch, stirring as the mixture thickens. Pour into a warm bowl. Alternatively, bring the maple syrup to a boil and pour into a warm bowl. This syrup complements the pudding well, in both flavor and color.

10. Remove the bowl from the wok or steamer and invert the pudding onto a warm plate, so that the decorative pattern is on top. The best way to do this is to put the bowl in the middle of a long towel. Cover the bowl with the plate. Pick up the towel, bowl and plate with both hands and turn upside down, then gently remove the bowl as the rice pudding slips onto the plate.

11. Pour the syrup over it and serve hot.

SPECIAL RECIPES

Stock

There are many ways of making stock, but the Chinese believe that the most balanced result comes from a long simmering of chicken, pork and ham. Abalone was traditionally included, but because it is now so expensive, most people are content to dispense with it. In the Chinese kitchen, a distinction is made between the first yield of this simmering, called "prime stock", and the second yield, called "clear or secondary stock".

A question often raised is whether or not you should use stock cubes. If you are desperate, by all means use them, but I suggest using them only in an emergency. Stock keeps well in the refrigerator for up to a week but will keep longer if brought to a boil every second day.

PRIME STOCK

INGREDIENTS	
1½ pounds chicken thighs, drumsticks and necks	pork, without rind
	1½ pounds ham or mild gammon, without rind
1½ pounds mostly lean	*Makes 3 pints*

1. Put the chicken, pork and ham or gammon into a deep stockpot or saucepan and add 5 pints of water. Bring to a boil and skim off the scum that surfaces until the water is clear.

2. Partially cover with a lid. Lower the heat to maintain a fast simmer and cook for about 3 hours. The liquid, which should have reduced to about 3 pints, is the prime stock. Pour through a sieve into a storage container. Refrigerate.

Note: The meat in the stockpot is still tasty enough to serve as a meal if clear or secondary stock is not to be made. Dip the chicken or pork in thin soy sauce and eat the ham as it is.

CLEAR STOCK

INGREDIENTS	
leftover ingredients from prime stock	salt to taste.
	Makes about 1¾ pints

1. Refill the stockpot or saucepan with 3 or 4 pints of water. Bring to a boil, reduce the heat to maintain a fast simmer and cook, partially covered, for 1½ to 2 hours, reducing the liquid to 1½ to 2 pints. This is the clear or secondary stock.

2. Pour through a sieve into a storage container. Discard the meat. Season with salt to taste. Keep in the refrigerator.

Variation

Another way of making prime and clear stock is to use about 4½ pounds of pork or ham bones, spare ribs, chicken or duck carcass, giblets and stalks from dried Chinese mushrooms. Simmer them in about 7 pints of water, reducing the liquid to about 4½ pints for prime stock. Add water again to make more or less the same amount for clear or secondary stock.

Hot Chili Oil

This is sometimes sold in a bottle as Chili oil, but I prefer the taste of this homemade version.

INGREDIENTS

12 dried red chilies, each about 3 inches long, or	24 small onces ½ pint peanut or corn oil

1. Slit open the dried chilies. Remove and discard the seeds. Chop into flakes and put into a glass jar.

2. Heat the oil in a saucepan until it smokes. Remove at once from the heat. Let cool for 3 or 4 minutes.

3. Pour into the jar. The chili flakes will rise to the surface but will sink to the bottom gradually. The oil becomes spicy hot almost immediately, but will become more so in a few days time. It keeps for months in a cool place.

Szechwan Chili Paste

INGREDIENTS

dried red chilies   ground yellow bean sauce

1. Grind sufficient red chilies in a food processor or use a mortar and pestle.

2. In a bowl, mix the chilies and the yellow bean sauce, in the proportion of 1 tablespoon ground

chili to 2 tablespoons ground yellow bean sauce. (Natives of Szechwan will no doubt find this proportion too mild, and people unused to spicy foods will find it almost too hot. Use your judgment to suit your own taste.) The chili paste will keep for months in a jar stored in a cool place.

Sweet Bean Sauce

INGREDIENTS

1 tablespoon water

9 tablespoons sugar

9 tablespoons ground
    yellow bean sauce

1 tablespoon peanut or
    corn oil

1. Put the water, sugar, yellow bean sauce and oil in a wok or saucepan. Heat over low heat for 3 or 4 minutes, or until the sugar has completely dissolved, stirring all the time to mix into a smooth sauce.

2. Let cool and serve at room temperature.

Flavor-Potting

Flavor-potting is a cooking technique popular in every Chinese region whereby meat, poultry or offal is cooked and then steeped in a specially prepared sauce. The idea is that the flavor of the sauce will permeate the meat, and the sauce will in turn be enriched by the taste of the meat and its fat. The spices used in the sauce vary from area to area and from cook to cook, but the ones most frequently used are: star anise, Szechwan peppercorns, fennel seeds, cinnamon, ginger and

liquorice. In China, flavor-potting spices are generally bought ready-made from an herbal pharmacy, and these mixtures, labeled "mixed spices", are now exported and sold in Chinese shops. In this recipe I have also added preserved tangerine peel.

The flavor-potting sauce, if properly kept and periodically reheated, should last indefinitely. Indeed, many families pride themselves on keeping the same sauce for months, if not years!

INGREDIENTS

FOR THE SAUCE

4 ounces mixed
    flavor-potting spices or
    12 whole star anise

½ ounce cinnamon

1 cardamom (*t'sao kuo*)

1 teaspoon cloves

3 tablespoon fennel seeds

4 tablespoons Szechwan
    peppercorns

⅕ ounce liquorice

1 ounce dried ginger root

5 to 5½ pints water

2 ounces fresh ginger

root, unpeeled and
    bruised

2 or 3 large pieces
    preserved tangerine
    peel

2 tablespoons sea salt

16 ounces thick soy sauce

2 ounces thin soy sauce

5 ounces Demerara or
    granulated sugar

6 ounces Shaohsing wine
    or medium-dry sherry

2 tablespoons mei-kuei-lu
    wine or gin

1. Put the mixed spices in a bag made from 3 layers of cheesecloth or muslin and tie the opening with cotton or string. Put into a large, deep stockpot.

2. Add the water, fresh ginger and tangerine peel. Bring to a boil, reduce the heat and simmer for about 15 minutes, to release the aromatic flavors.

3. Add the sea salt, soy sauces, sugar and wine or sherry, continuing to simmer until the sugar has completely dissolved. Check the taste of the sauce: it should be quite salty, rich and aromatic. It is now ready for other ingredients to be cooked in it.

GLOSSARY

Beans and Bean Products

Bean curd "cheese," red fermented
Brick red in color, very strong and cheesy in taste, this type of bean curd is fermented with salt, red rice and rice wine. It is used for flavoring meat, poultry and vegetarian dishes and is usually stored in jars or earthenware pots in 1 to 2-inch square cakes. After a jar has been opened, the bean curd "cheese" keeps for months if refrigerated.

Bean curd "cheese," white fermented
Ivory in color, sold in 1-inch cakes, this fermented bean curd sometimes has chili added to it. It is used to flavor certain vegetables, or is served as a side dish with rice or congee. It is sold in jars and keeps for months if refrigerated.

Bean curd, fresh
White, custardlike product made from ground soybeans and used extensively in Chinese cooking. Its role is equivalent to that of dairy products in Western cuisine. Bean curd is made from soybeans that have been finely ground with water, then strained through a cloth. The resulting "milk" is brought to a boil before gypsum is added to set it into a curd. The curd is then put into boxes and weights are applied to squeeze out the remaining whey. Because it is impractical to make at home, bean curd is usually sold in Chinese stores in cakes about 1 inch thick and 2½ inches square. Bean curd keeps for up to 3 days in the refrigerator if the water in which it stands is changed every day.

Bean curd, puffed
Fresh bean curd cubes, deep-fried until golden in color and airy inside. They keep well in the refrigerator for about a week.

Bean curd sheets
Thin, dried bean curd sheets, about 6 by 18 inches, usually sold with about one-third of their length folded in. To make them pliable, either soak them or spray them with water. Store them in a cool, dry place.

Black beans, fermented
Whole soybeans preserved in salt and ginger. Although pungent in taste, when combined with garlic and cooked in oil they lend a delicious flavor to any other ingredients. Some black beans are canned in brine, but the dried ones are by far the best. They keep for months if stored in a cool, dry place.

Crushed (ground) yellow bean sauce
Nut brown purée of fermented yellow soybeans, wheat flour, salt and water. Usually sold in cans labeled "Crushed yellow bean sauce" or "Ground yellow bean sauce," this is a major seasoning in Chinese cooking of all regions. Once opened, store in a covered jar in the refrigerator.

Red beans (*Phaseolus angularis*), **azuki beans**
Native to China, but now also grown in America and Europe, these small red beans are the seeds of the plant *vigna angularis*. In Chinese cuisine they are eaten mostly as a dessert.

Red bean paste
Thick, reddish-brown paste made from puréed, sweetened red beans or azuki beans; a very popular filling for sweet dishes.

Soybean paste, hot
Very hot and spicy paste of soy-beans crushed with chili, sugar and salt; an indispensible ingredient for making Szechwan twice-cooked pork (see p.126). Usually sold in jars, it keeps for a long time.

Sweet bean sauce
Made of crushed yellow bean sauce sweetened with sugar. This is the traditional dipping sauce for the famous Peking duck, although the readily available hoisin sauce is more widely used in the West.

Szechwan chili paste, chili paste
Hot paste of dried red chili peppers and ground yellow bean sauce (below). It forms the basis of the famous Szechwan fish fragrant sauce. When topped with a little oil to prevent it from drying out and stored in a covered jar, it keeps for months in a cool place.

Yellow beans in salted sauce
Whole yellow soybeans fermented with salt, wheat flour and sugar. Although not as widely used as fermented black beans, they too are used as a seasoning when cooking meat or vegetables. Sold in cans, they should be refrigerated in a covered jar once opened.

Cereals, Grains and Noodles

Buckwheat noodles
Very thin, beige-colored noodle strips made of buckwheat flour and wheat flour with water. They are a great favorite of the Northern Chinese and are available as dry noodles in some Chinese and Japanese stores.

Cellophane noodles, transparent vermicelli, bean thread
Made from ground mung beans, these noodles are usually sold in a bundle tied by a thin thread. Wiry and hard in their dry state, they have to be soaked in water and then drained before use. Not so much as a staple, they are eaten as a vegetable, which absorbs tastes from other ingredients and provides a slippery texture. They keep indefinitely in a cool place.

Egg noodles, fresh or dry
Made of wheat flour, egg and water, these are the most common all-purpose Chinese noodles. They are usually sold in two widths: thin thread-like and broad strip. Fresh, soft noodles are sold in plastic bags; dry noodles are sold in compressed rounds (often called noodle cakes) and are sometimes precooked by steaming. Fresh noodle cakes keep well in a sealed bag in the refrigerator for up to a week or they can be frozen if each is wrapped individually. Dried noodles keep for months in a covered jar. Egg noodles, seldom made at home, are bought in Chinese grocery stores. Noodles from other countries can be used as a substitute; the only difference is that Chinese noodles are more elastic in texture.

Long-grain rice *(Oryza sativa, spp.)*
The white grains of this versatile rice are husked and polished. It is known that the Chinese grew and ate this rice as early as the 12th century B.C. in the Chou dynasty, and indeed, it remains the staple food for the Chinese today. Rice keeps for months in a covered container.

Rice noodles, rice sticks
Wiry white noodles made from rice flour. Although slender too, they do not look translucent, like cellophane noodles. They are sold, dried, in tightly folded bundles and keep for months in a covered jar. Only a brief soaking and cooking time are required.

River rice noodles
Made from rice ground with water which has been steamed in thin sheets, then rolled and cut up into strips about ½ inch wide, these noodles are sold both dry and fresh. The dry noodles have to be boiled and drained before use. Despite the fact that the dry variety will last for months in a covered jar, the fresh ones are by far superior, especially for stir-frying. However, they must be used within 1 or 2 days after buying or they will lose their tender quality.

Spring roll wrappers
Two types: Cantonese, which are smooth, like noodle dough, and Shanghai, which are transparent, like rice paper. Sold frozen, they are easily pulled apart when defrosted. The Shanghai type is used in this book.

Tientsin fen pi
Dry, transparent, brittle round sheets, about 9 inches in diameter, made from ground mung beans. When soaked in boiling water, they have a slippery texture and are eaten as a cross between rice noodles and cellophane noodles. They keep for a long time in a cool place.

U-dong noodles
Off-white noodle strips about ⅛ inch wide, made of wheat flour and water. These Japanese and Korean noodles are similar in texture to Northern Chinese noodles and are available as dry noodles in Oriental stores.

White glutinous rice *(Oryza sativa spp.)*
More rounded in shape than long-grain rice, white glutinous rice is sticky when boiled. It is eaten by the Chinese both as a savory (see Stir-fried glutinous rice) and as a pudding (see Eight-treasure rice pudding); it is also used as a stuffing (see Duck stuffed with glutinous rice). It keeps for months in a covered container.

Wonton wrappers
Made of the same dough as egg noodles (wheat flour, egg and water), and sold in 3 inch squares. Like noodles, they are not usually made at home but are bought fresh from Chinese stores. They can be frozen.

Yi noodles, yifu noodles
Egg noodles woven into a round cake, already deep-fried when sold in Chinese stores. They keep well in a cool place for about 2 weeks. If left too long, they may become rancid.

Dried Products

Abalone *(Haliotis tuberculata)*
For many people, this shelled mollusk is available only in canned form, with its ivory-colored flesh already cooked. Even so, it is delicious eaten cold or hot, alone or with other ingredients. If eaten hot, it must be cooked very briefly; overcooking will make it rubbery. The juice in the can is valuable as a basis for sauces or soups.

Agar
Processed gelatin extracted from dried seaweed, it is usually sold in bundles of long, narrow crinkly strips. Used as a thickener, it is extremely heat resistant and can only be dissolved slowly in boiling water. Store in a sealed plastic bag in a cool place, but *not* in the refrigerator.

Bird's nest
Nests made by swallows of the genus Collocalia which live on the cliffs of Southeast Asian islands. What makes these nests unique is that the birds line them with a gelatinous mixture of predigested seaweed, which hardens to form a transparent layer. There are many grades of bird's nest, but since whole nests are extremely expensive and rarely available in the West, it is all right to use the broken ones. The whiter the color and the fewer specks of feathers there are, the better the quality of the nest. Sold in Chinese stores, they are usually preprocessed, so the cleaning job is not too laborious.

Chinese black mushrooms *(Lentinus edodes)*
Edible tree fungi that add both flavor and texture to a dish. They vary in quality, size and price. The best and most expensive are the floral mushrooms (*fa gu* in Cantonese, *hua ku* in Mandarin). These have floral patterns on the surface of the caps, which curl under. Second in quality are the mushrooms whose relatively thick caps also curl slightly inward along the edges. The lowest quality are the mushrooms that have thin flat caps. Usually available in Chinese stores are packages of mixed quality and sizes. They keep for a long time in a covered container.

Chinese sausages
Wind-dried pork, or pork and duck-liver sausages, usually sold in pairs about 6 inches long. The pork sausages should look pinkish with white pork fat showing through the casing; the liver sausages should look dark brown. Both types must be cooked before eating. In a covered jar, they will keep well for months in the refrigerator.

Cloud ears *(Auricularia auricula)*
Edible tree fungi grown in large quantities in the western provinces of Szechwan, Hunan and Yunnan. Thin and brittle when dry, they expand to form thick brown clusters when soaked for about twenty minutes. More delicate and refined than wood ears, they are used in stir-fried dishes to absorb flavors from other seasonings and, above all, to provide a slimy but crunchy texture. They should be well rinsed to remove sand, and the hard knobs should be removed if necessary. Store in a covered container.

Cornstarch
Fine, white starch extracted from corn, it is used to thicken sauces and marinades.

Creamed coconut
Milky white in color and solid in form, like a bar of soap, concentrated coconut milk can be kept in the refrigerator for months.

Dried red dates *(Ziziphus jujuba)*
Dried fruit of the jujube tree. It has a sweet, prunelike taste.

Edible jellyfish *(Rhopilema esculenta)*
Beige in color and rubbery to the touch, this jellyfish is sold in round sheets about 15 to 16 inches in diameter, dried, folded and packaged in a plastic bag with large grains of salt between the folds. The salt must be shaken off and the jellyfish soaked in water for 2 to 3 days before use. Packages of jellyfish already cut up in strips are also available, but it is more economical to buy the former. Jellyfish keep indefinitely in a sealed bag.

Golden needles *Hemerocallis fulva)*, **tiger-lily buds**
Dried buds of the tiger-lily, which grows in abundance in Northern China. Usually about 3 inches long, they are called golden needles because of their color and shape. They absorb the tastes of other ingredients they are cooked with and also provide a subtle lightness of texture. They keep indefinitely if stored in a covered jar or in a sealed plastic bag.

Oysters *(Crassostrea gigas)*
Brown, rectangular and quite firm to the touch, these oysters have been salted and dried in the sun. Considered an epicurean delicacy, they add a "smoky" taste to meat and bland ingredients. Because they are expensive, make sure that they are not moldy when you buy them. If refrigerated they keep for a long time.

Potato flour
Flour ground from cooked potatoes. As a thickening agent, it is more gelatinous than cornstarch and gives a more subtle and glossy finish to a sauce. In thickening the same amount of liquid, use about two-thirds the amount of potato flour as you would cornstarch. Tapioca and arrowroot are also popular thickening agents.

Rock sugar, crystal sugar
This crystallized, pale topaz-colored cane sugar comes in lumps and has a "pure" taste. Demerara sugar comes closest to it in taste but white granulated sugar can also be used as a substitute. It keeps indefinitely in a dry container.

Scallops *(Amusium pleuronectes)*
Golden and round, the large ones weighing⅓ to ½ ounce each, these are white scallops that have been dried in the sun. Inherently sweet, they are used to add a sweet flavor to other ingredients; they are also used as the main ingredient in sophisticated dishes such as Dried scallop soup (see page 59). They keep for a long time in a covered jar in a cool place.

Shark's fin
The cured and sun-dried fin of one of several species of shark. Many countries in Asia, Europe and South America produce shark's fin, but the product from Manila, the "Manila yellow," is the best. Such fins are, however, extremely expensive and take about four days to prepare. The fin used in this book had already been processed, partially cooked and dried again, and it consisted of the cartilage with some "fin needles." Shark's fin has no taste, but when combined with other ingredients in a prime stock, it is without peer. The Chinese regard highly nutritious, shark's fin, whether in a soup or a red-braised dish, as the pinnacle of gastronomy. Store in a covered jar in a cool place.

Shrimp
Small, shelled shrimp of various sizes, salted and dried in the sun. They are used as a seasoning for vegetables and meat and are very often used in stuffings. Choose those with a fresh, pinkish color. To store, put in a covered jar in a cool place.

Straw mushrooms *(Volvariella volvacea)*, **paddy-straw mushrooms**
Small mushrooms with cone-shaped black caps, cultivated on rice straw in paddy fields. The canned product, mostly from Taiwan, is popular but should be drained and rinsed before use.

They add texture more than taste to other ingredients. (Dried straw mushrooms, with their stronger smell, are used to lend taste to bland vegetables or in soups.) Store in the refrigerator.

Tangerine peel
Dark brown, hard and brittle peel of dried tangerines, often used in combination with star anise and Szechwan peppercorns. Sold in packages, it keeps indefinitely in a cool place.

Water chestnut flour
Flour with a grayish tinge ground from water chestnuts, used as a thickener in certain savory and sweet dishes when a light and subtle effect is called for.

Wood ears *(Auricularia polytricha)*
Like cloud ears, these edible fungi are cultivated in large quantities in Western China. They are larger in size than cloud ears, coarser in texture, often black on the surface and white underneath, and need to be cooked for a longer period of time. They are used more in soups than in stir-fried dishes. Store in a covered container.

Oils and Fats

Chicken fat
Rendered by slowly frying the solid fat removed from near the tail and other parts of the chicken, it is used by the Chinese for stir-frying certain vegetables to enhance their flavor.

Corn oil
Light, odorless, polyunsaturated oil processed from corn. Even though it lacks the special nutty flavor of peanut oil, it is a very satisfactory substitute because it is less expensive and often more easily available.

Hot chili oil, chili pepper oil
Easily made by steeping dried red chili flakes in hot oil (see p. 225), this oil is used to add extra spiciness to food. It can be bought in bottles but the homemade product is generally superior.

Lard
Fat rendered from pork, this used to be considered the aristocratic fat for cooking in China because of the flavor and richness it added to food. Even today cookbooks published in China call for the use of lard in stir-frying and deep-frying. However, lard is heavy and high in saturated fats, and most Chinese people do not use it for daily home cooking; they use peanut oil, corn oil or other vegetable oils instead. Lard keeps well in the refrigerator for several months.

Peanut oil, groundnut oil
Before the introduction of peanuts or groundnuts to China from America in the 16th century, vegetable oils, in particular rapeseed oil, were commonly used for cooking. Since the intensive cultivation of peanuts in succeeding centuries, peanut oil, with its rich and nutty flavor, has become the most important cooking oil in China. Corn oil, which is much more easily available and less expensive in other parts of the world, can be used as a satisfactory substitute. (For deep-frying, however, other vegetable oils will do equally well.)

Sesame oil, sesame seed oil
Thick, aromatic, and light brown in color, this oil is pressed from roasted white sesame seeds. As such, it is quite different from the cold-pressed Middle Eastern sesame oil, which should not be used as a substitute. Chinese sesame oil is not used for general cooking; rather, because of its heavenly aroma, it is used for marinating or for sprinkling on food just before it is served. It will keep indefinitely in a cool place.

Sauces

Chili sauce
This tangy, orange-red sauce is made of crushed fresh chili peppers, vinegar, salt and plums. It is used both as a spicy hot seasoning and as a dip for crisp food. Store in a cool place.

Fish sauce
Golden brown, transparent sauce made from fish, salt and water. It adds more fragrance and taste to other ingredients or sauces than a sniff of it alone might suggest. Stored in a cool place, it keeps for a long, long time.

Hoisin sauce
Reddish brown and thick, sweet yet slightly hot, this sauce is made from soybeans, wheat flour, salt, sugar, vinegar, garlic, chili and sesame oil. It is used as a dip as well as in cooking and marinating. It keeps in a covered jar for a long time and, if refrigerated, will keep indefinitely.

Oyster sauce
Nut brown in color, this sauce is made from oyster juice, wheat flour, cornstarch and glutinous rice, salt and sugar. Not as strong as soy sauce, the sweet and "meaty" taste it lends to other ingredients, whether as part of a sauce mixture or as a dip for meat, poultry and vegetables, makes it a special favorite with the Cantonese. Bottled oyster sauce can be kept in a cool place; canned oyster sauce, once opened, should be transferred to a covered jar or bottle.

Sesame sauce, sesame paste
Thick, aromatic paste of pulverised sesame seeds. The paste has to be thoroughly incorporated with the oil covering it and then thinned with oil or water before use. Tahini paste should *not* be used as a substitute; rather, use peanut butter, which has a similar fragrance.

Shrimp paste, shrimp sauce
Made from ground shrimp fermented in brine, this paste is available in two forms: a pinkish purée and a more solid, slightly saltier pâté. The purée form is used in this book. Both kinds have to be diluted with water before being used, very often to enhance the taste of bland seafood, such as squid. Usually sold in a jar, it keeps almost indefinitely in a cool place.

Soy sauce
Made from fermented soybeans with wheat or barley, salt, sugar and yeast, this sauce is one of the most ancient seasonings in Chinese cookery. It is at once the most basic and the most versatile condiment for all Chinese cuisines, whatever the regional differences. There are two main kinds of soy sauce: the thick, also called dark, and the thin, also called light. Both are used in general cooking, for marinating and as dips. Very often they are used together with salt. It is the mark of a good cook to know how much of each to use, thereby achieving the delicious end result.
Thick soy sauce is thicker in consistency than thin soy sauce, darker brown in color and sweeter in taste. Since it gives a reddish brown hue to food, it is the predominant sauce in red-braised dishes and in flavor-potting. Because of its sweetness, it is preferred by many as a dip at the table.
Thin soy sauce is thinner in consistency, lighter brown in color and saltier in taste.

Wines and Vinegars

Chinkiang vinegar
Thick, dark brown product of Chinkiang in Chekiang province, this has a low vinegar content and a special fragrance and flavor. It is used in cooking or as a dip. It comes in bottles and keeps indefinitely in a cool place. If red wine vinegar is used as a substitute, use less of it or add more sugar.

Kao-liang liqueur
A clear spirit made from sorghum (*kao-liang* in Chinese) grown in Northeast China. This very strong liqueur, which the Chinese drink with food, is produced in the distillery founded in Harbin in 1930. Vodka can be used as a substitute.

Mei-kuei-lu wine
Made from Kao-liang spirit and the petals of a special species of rose, this is a very strong liqueur with a unique aroma. It is used in the master sauce for flavor-potting, and is used to add fragrance to marinades. Gin or vodka can be used as a substitute.

Moutai wine
Production of this spirit began in 1704 in a small town called Moutai in Kweichow province, Western China. Made from wheat and sorghum, it is as much these ingredients as the local spring water that give this spirit its distinctive bouquet. It is drunk in small quantities with food.

Red vinegar
Red in color, this vinegar is also low in vinegar content. It is usually used as a dip to go with fried noodles or Shark's fin soup because the Chinese believe that it makes these foods more easily digestable.

Rice vinegar
Clear in color and used in cooking or pickling vegetables, this vinegar is neither as sharp nor as pungent as malt vinegar. It keeps indefinitely. Use cider or white wine vinegar as a substitute.

Shaohsing wine
Named after the town in the Eastern province of Chekiang, this yellow wine, with its golden sheen, is one of the oldest wines produced in China. Fermented from glutinous rice with yeast, this wine owes its fame as much to these ingredients as to the water from Chien Lake. Between 15 and 20 proof, there are numerous brands of Shaohsing wine, differing in age and quality, although the one most commonly available in Chinese stores abroad is labeled simply Shaohsing wine. The Chinese drink it warm, with food, because it tastes much better that way. It is also used in small quantities in marinades and in cooking, to enhance the flavor and the taste of the food. Medium-dry sherry can be used as a substitute.

Herbs and Spices

Cassia (*Cinnamomum cassia*), **Chinese cinnamon**
Dried bark of the cassia tree. It is used in the master sauce for flavor-potting and is one of the ingredients of five-spice powder. Cinnamon sticks can be used as an alternative.

Dried red chilis (*Capsicum frutescens*), **chili peppers**
Crimson red, very often simply called dried chilis, they are sold in two sizes: small, up to 1½ inches long, and large, about 3 inches or longer. They are an indispensable ingredient in Szechwan/Hunan cuisine, because they provide the fiery spiciness. For the uninitiated, it is perhaps advisable to remove the seeds and the white internal walls, since they are the hottest part of a chili. They keep indefinitely in a covered container.

Coriander (*Coriandrum sativum*), **Chinese parsley, cilantro**
Fresh, green herb with a long stalk branching into flat, serrated leaves; usually sold by the bunch. Pungent, acidic and aromatic, it is used both as a garnish and as a seasoning, especially in Northern China. It will remain fresh for up to a week if refrigerated in an open plastic bag.

Five-spice powder
Golden brown powder, consisting of five and sometimes six ground spices, with a liquorice-like flavor. The four basic spices are: star anise, cassia or Chinese cinnamon, cloves and fennel seeds. The remainder are often Szechwan peppercorns and sometimes ginger and cardamom. Five-spice powder is mostly used in marinades for meat, poultry or fish, but it must be used sparingly. It is sold in small packages and can be kept indefinitely in a covered jar.

Flavor-potting mixed spices
Labeled Mixed Spices, these ready-mixed packages are sold in Chinese stores especially for use in flavor-potting. Each package contains the most commonly used spices in flavor-potting: star anise, Szechwan peppercorns (fagara), cinnamon, ginger, fennel seeds, cloves, liquorice and cardamom.

Garlic (*Allium sativum*)
The bulb of a perennial plant. Like ginger root and spring onion, it is indispensable in Chinese cooking.

Ginger powder
Dried ginger root ground into a powder. Used as a seasoning, it cannot be used as a substitute for fresh ginger root.

Ginger root, fresh *(Zingiber officinale)*
The knobbly, yellowish green root stalk of the ginger plant. Spicy hot in taste, it is used to provide flavor and to counter rank odor, especially fishiness. Like garlic and spring onion, it is an essential ingredient in Chinese cooking, dating back to Han times. Choose firm ginger with smooth skin. It keeps well for several weeks if refrigerated in a perforated plastic bag.

Ground roasted Szechwan peppercorns
Szechwan peppercorns roasted in a dry wok and then ground up into a powder. Used to add aroma to other ingredients, they can be made at home.

Scallions *(Allium cepa)*, **spring onions**
Young onion with a long white bulb topped by tubular green leaves. "White" refers to the firm, essentially white, section that makes up most of the onion; "green" refers to the leaves. The roots attached to the white end must be chopped off and discarded before use. Dating back to Han times, spring onions form one of the three basic condiments in Chinese cooking; the other two are garlic and ginger. They keep fresh in the refrigerator for a few days.

Shallots *(Allium ascalonicum)*
Small, firm onions with a milder flavor than Spanish onions.

Star anise *(Illicium verum)*
Shaped like a star, with eight segments, and reddish brown in color, this hard spice is widely used in Chinese cooking to flavor meat and poultry; it has a distinctive liquorice taste and aroma. It keeps indefinitely in a covered jar.

Szechwan peppercorns *(Xanthoxylum piperitum)*
Tiny, reddish brown peppercorns that have a stronger aroma than black peppercorns and produce a numbing rather than a burning effect. Available both whole and seeded. The seeded variety have a better aroma and flavor.

White sesame seeds *(Sesamum indicum)*
Tiny, flat seeds from the sesame plant; they keep for a long time in a covered container. (See also sesame oil and sesame paste.)

Vegetables

Bamboo shoots *(Dendrocalamus latiflorus)*
The young shoots of several species of bamboo cultivated for consumption in China. Those available from November to January are called winter shoots and those available from January to April are called spring shoots. Fresh bamboo shoots are only occasionally available in the West; what are available, however, are canned bamboo shoots in chunks or in slices; they should be rinsed before use. If they are not all used at once, the remainder must be transferred to another container, covered with water and refrigerated. If the water is changed every other day, they keep well for 2 to 3 weeks.

Bean sprouts *(Phaseolus aureus)*
Tender sprouts from small green mung beans, about 2 to 4 inches long. When choosing these sprouts, which are high in protein look for those that are white and plump and avoid any that are limp and yellow. Although bean sprouts can be eaten raw in salads, the Chinese prefer to eat them slightly cooked but retaining their light and crisp qualities. Fresh bean sprouts can be kept refrigerated in a plastic bag for up to 3 days. Do not buy canned bean sprouts; they are just a soggy mass.

Chinese broccoli, *(Brassica alboglabra)* **Chinese kale, gaai-laan**
Chinese broccoli is distinguished by its oval-shaped leaves, which have a bluish green sheen, and the white flowers in the middle of the plant. The stalk is like that of broccoli but the taste is more pronounced, reminiscent of asparagus. It keeps in the regrigerator for about 3 days.

Chinese cabbage *(Brassica chinensis)*, **Chinese white cabbage, bok-choy, bai-tsai**
Thick, white-skinned cabbage with tender dark green leaves. It is similar in appearance to Swiss chard, but it is sweeter and juicier.

Chinese celery cabbage *(Brassica pekinensis)*, **Tientsin cabbage, Peking cabbage, Chinese leaves, wong nga baak**
A tight head of cylindrical white stalks extending into yellowish-white crinkled leaves. This Northern Chinese vegetable is popular among most Chinese because of its sweet, mild flavor and its versatility: it can be stir-fried, braised and put into soups. In recent years, it has become popular in the West and is therefore available in supermarkets. Choose firm heads and see that the leaves are not shriveled. If refrigerated, it keeps for about 2 to 3 weeks.

Chinese chives *(Allium tuberosum)*
Similar to chives in appearance, they are, however, darker green in color, more fibrous in texture,

stronger in taste and have flat, not tubular, leaves. They are available only in Chinese supermarkets, and keep well in a plastic bag in the refrigerator.

Chinese flowering cabbage (Brassica parachinensis) choi-sum
This vegetable is distinguished by its yellow flowers and long stems of about 6 to 8 inches. Because of its subtle taste, it is a great favorite of Southern Chinese, served either stir-fried or simply blanched; the stems need not be peeled. It keeps well in the refrigerator for about 3 days.

Ginkgo nuts (Ginkgo biloba), silver apricot
The ginkgo tree was originally a sacred Chinese tree, but it now grows in Japan and other parts of the world. The nuts, pits of the ginkgo fruit, have to be cracked and peeled. Unfortunately, the flesh inside the beige shell seems to dry up easily, with the result that exported nuts are often rotten and hard inside. It is therefore advisable to use canned ginkgo nuts. Mild and tender, they are a favorite of vegetarians. Any leftover nuts should be transferred to a container, covered with water and put in the refrigerator.

Hair seaweed (Borgia fuscopurpurea), cow hair seaweed, fa-t'sai
Black, hairlike moss, this product of Hopeh and Shensi provinces is sold in a dried form and must be reconstituted by soaking. Totally tasteless alone, it absorbs other flavors and provides a slippery and bouncy texture. Stored in a covered container, it keeps indefinitely.

Mustard green (Brassica juncea), mustard cabbage, gaai-choi
There are many varieties of mustard green and some, with their bitter tangy taste, are more suitable for pickling than cooking. A common variety, whose green stalks extend into single, large oval, ribbed leaves, has a distinctive taste when simply blanched or put into soup. It is sold only in Chinese supermarkets. Choose firm green plants and avoid those with limp yellow leaves. It keeps well for a few days in a plastic bag in the refrigerator.

Red-in-snow (Brassica juncea var. multiceps), pickled cabbage
A red-rooted variety of mustard plant grown in Chekiang province which, being very resistant to cold, can be seen sprouting up through the spring snows, hence the name. This crisp green vegetable is cut and preserved in salt. Available in cans and soaked in brine, it is mostly used as an accompaniment to pork or in soup.

Sugar peas, snow peas, mange tout (Pisum sativum)
Tender green peapods containing flat, barely formed peas. Valued for their crisp texture and sweet, subtle flavor, they are best stir-fried. When choosing, look for the flat, tender green ones. If refrigerated in a plastic bag, they keep for more than 1 week.

Szechwan preserved vegetable (Brassica juncea var. tsatsai), cha-t'sai, ja-choi
Made from the swollen nodules on the stems of a species of mustard plant grown in Szechwan province which have been preserved in salt, pressed to squeeze out much of their liquid content and then pickled with a fine red chili powder. The chili has to be rinsed off before use. Spicy hot and salty, it gives both a crisp texture and a peppery flavor to other ingredients. Sold in cans, it keeps for a long time if stored in a covered jar.

Taro (colocasia antiquorum)
Root vegetable that, whether small, like potatoes, or long and fat like yams, has dark brown skin, often with earth-encrusted root hairs, and a gray or purple flesh. When choosing, press the skin to make sure that it is firm, rather than soft, rotten or dried up. When cooked, it is slimy. It is often cooked with duck or fatty pork. Taro keeps well in a cool place for more than a week.

Water chestnuts (Eleocharis tuberosa)
Fresh water chestnuts are the walnut-sized bulbs of a sedge cultivated in swampy paddy fields or in muddy ponds. As a result, their mahogany-colored skin is often encrusted with mud, but when washed and peeled, the flesh is white, very crisp and subtly sweet; they can be eaten raw. Canned water chestnuts, although less crisp and sweet, will provide a crunchy texture to vegetables and meat dishes. Press fresh water chestnuts to make sure they are not rotten or dried up. They can be kept in the refrigerator for up to a week. Canned ones last up to 1 week if covered with water.

Winter melon (Benincasa hispida)
Wax gourd with a white pulp, which can weigh from a few pounds up to 100 pounds; it is often cut up and sold by weight in wedges. When buying a wedge, make sure that the pulp has not dried up or turned yellow. The flesh, which when cooked is almost transparent, is often used in soup with pork, chicken or duck. A whole winter melon keeps for 2 to 3 months in a cool place; a wedge keeps for up to a week if refrigerated in a plastic bag.

Young corn (Zea mays)
Tender, miniature corn on the cob, usually sold in cans. They are either put into vegetarian dishes or used as an ingredient with meat.

INDEX